THE
MORE
VEG
COOKBOOK

THE MORE VEG COOKBOOK

CAROLYN HUMPHRIES

LONDON, NEW YORK, MELBOURNE, MUNICH, AND DELHI

DK LONDON
Senior Editor Bob Bridle
Project Art Editor Katherine Raj
Cookery Editor Diana Vowles
Managing Editor Dawn Henderson
Managing Art Editor Christine Keilty
Senior Jacket Creative Nicola Powling
Jacket Design Assistant Rosie Levine
Producer, Pre-Production Sarah Isle
Senior Producer Jen Scothern
Art Director Peter Luff
Publisher Peggy Vance

DK INDIA
Project Editor Manasvi Vohra
Senior Editor Dorothy Kikon
Senior Art Editor Balwant Singh
Assistant Art Editor Nikita Sodhi
Managing Editor Glenda Fernandes
Managing Art Editor Navidita Thapa
CTS/DTP Manager Sunil Sharma
DTP Designer Rajdeep Singh

Photography William Reavell

First published in Great Britain in 2013 by
Dorling Kindersley Limited
80 Strand, London, WC2R 0RL
Penguin Group (UK)

Copyright © 2013 Dorling Kindersley Limited

2 4 6 8 10 9 7 5 3 1

001–186071–Apr/2013

A CIP catalogue record for this book is available from the British Library.

ISBN 978-1-4093-1823-1

Colour reproduction by Opus Multimedia Services

Printed and bound by South China (DK)

Discover more at
www.dk.com

Contents

Foreword

We all know that vegetables form a crucial part of our five-a-day – and whether you shop in a farmer's market, an independent green grocer, or a large supermarket, there is certainly no shortage of produce on offer.

With an abundance of sumptuous-looking veg available – from roots, tubers, and stems to flowers, vegetable fruits, and leaves – there is every reason for vegetarians and non-vegetarians alike to make vegetables a central part of their diet. Packed with mouth-watering vegetarian recipes, all carefully balanced to provide the required nutrients for a healthy diet, *The More Veg Cookbook* celebrates this bounty of fresh produce.

Eating the seasons
I grew up in the country, where my father had a large vegetable garden. My brother and I always enjoyed helping him dig the potatoes, pull the lettuces, string the onions, and pick the beans. We were used to eating fresh, seasonal vegetables every day and what we didn't grow ourselves had been produced locally. I now have just a small garden and can only grow fresh herbs and the occasional tomato, bean, or courgette, but it doesn't stop me from continuing to enjoy fresh vegetables every day. In fact, today you can buy just about any vegetable from around the world thanks to – or rather, because of – international transport and refrigeration. It is worth remembering, though, that vegetables have proper seasons when they mature, still attached to their plants, taking nutrients from the soil and ripening in the sun. Many are plucked before they are ripe to be transported half way around the world,

and never achieve their optimum flavour or texture. Large-scale global movement of produce also has a negative impact on the environment, with the fuel used drastically increasing the amount of carbon dioxide released into the atmosphere.

Brave new world

Thanks to new growing techniques, many vegetables that are native to tropical climates are grown in controlled conditions in cooler countries, giving us all a much wider choice. There is an argument that the polytunnels used for growing these vegetables spoil the look of the countryside and that fuel is sometimes needed to heat them to the required temperature – but we can't have it both ways. When progress provides work for local people and allows us to enjoy great, locally grown food, it should, I believe, be embraced.

When selecting fresh produce, remember to consider what season it is, decide whether the vegetables are likely to have been home-grown, and check their source before you buy. When shopping in farmer's markets you can be confident that the food has been produced in the local area, but nowadays supermarkets also tell you where their produce has come from so you can make informed decisions about the food you buy. Not only will this boost the local economy but it will also ensure that you are getting the tastiest and most nutritious vegetables available.

Making the right choice

When home-grown food isn't available, it's worth considering ethical trading. The Fairtrade Foundation is an independent body offering disadvantaged producers in the developing world a better deal for their produce. Many of the goods – not just vegetables – sold through the foundation may not be available to you at home and, therefore, make excellent additions to the shopping basket. By actively seeking them out, even if it means paying a little more, you will be making a much-needed difference to people who really need the help.

Fresh food at your fingertips
If you're not lucky enough to have a vegetable garden or allotment, try growing herbs on a windowsill, lettuces in a window box, or mushrooms from a kit in the airing cupboard instead. Visit local pick-your-own farms where freshness is guaranteed and produce can work out cheaper than in the shops. Another option is to go foraging. Mushrooms are the obvious choice but – and it cannot be stressed enough – only pick fungi if you know exactly what to look for. Other delicious wild plants include garlic, sorrel, and nettles. (Remember never to pull up roots or take too much, though, as wild plants must be allowed to propagate and continue to flourish in an area.)

Fresh isn't always best
It's worth highlighting that pulses – dried peas, beans, and lentils – are vital to many dishes for their protein and carbohydrate content. Also, for the record, frozen vegetables are just as nutritious as fresh and have an important role to play in a busy cook's life, so don't be afraid to keep plenty in the freezer for those meals in a hurry.

A word to the wise
While most cheeses are now suitable for vegetarians, a few of the ones called for in this book, such as Parmesan and Gorgonzola, contain animal rennet. In place of Parmesan, try using a hard Italian cheese called Vegetalia, or hard sheep's cheese. A blue cheese such as Dolcelatte is made with

vegetable rennet and can be used instead of Gorgonzola. Also note that Worcestershire sauce contains anchovies, but vegetarian options, such as Henderson's Relish, are available as well.

More veg, please!

This book has been great fun to put together and I hope I have created some inspiring dishes to get your taste buds tingling. Use the ideas here as a starting point for your own repertoire and keep in mind that it is important to be bold when cooking vegetarian food. Experiment with new flavours, use lots of herbs and spices, and don't be afraid to mix and match – when leaves meet roots or tubers tangle with stems, the colours, textures, and tastes can be simply stunning!

Carolyn Humphries

Store-cupboard essentials

Discover how to select, store, use, and combine a wide range of fresh, seasonal vegetables – and find out about the many different herbs, spices, pulses, nuts, seeds, and oils that can help bring out the best in your recipes.

Introduction

In this chapter are the vegetables featured in the book, as well as information about seasonal availability, what to look for when selecting, and preparation guidelines.

It's important to store vegetables properly, too. Most should be kept in the chiller box at the bottom of the refrigerator and used within a week. The exceptions are whole, uncut onions, roots, tubers, and winter squashes, which should be stored in a cool, dark, frost-free place. On these pages you'll also find the herbs, spices, pulses, nuts, seeds, and oils that can enhance the flavour of vegetables. There's information on perfect flavour pairings, too, so you can make the most of every ingredient in your store cupboard.

Variety is the key to a healthy, balanced diet. Aim to eat at least five portions of vegetables and fruit every day to get the essential vitamins, minerals, and fibre needed for good health and wellbeing. This includes frozen, dried, and canned (preferably in natural juice or water) fruit and vegetables, as well as pure juices. Cereals, grains, and potatoes are also important as they contain the complex carbohydrates needed for energy and warmth.

Pulses, nuts, seeds, soya beans and products such as tofu, and quinoa, a grain-like grass, make an ideal base for many vegetarian dishes and are a good source of protein (for body growth and repair), complex carbohydrates, and fibre. Eat a mixture of these to get the right balance of essential proteins, as

"Calcium is found in dried figs and apricots, green leafy vegetables such as spinach, kale, and spring greens, and in whole grains, nuts, and seeds."

"Eat foods rich in omega 3 and 6 – the essential fatty acids needed for warmth, nerve function, and healthy nails, hair, and skin."

they do not all contain complete, or whole, proteins. Nuts, seeds – especially flaxseed – and their oils, olive oil, leafy green vegetables, grains, and eggs are also an important source of the essential fatty acids omega 3 and 6 (for warmth, nerve function, and healthy nails, hair, and skin).

Dairy products are a good source of calcium (for healthy teeth and bones) and protein. They contain saturated fats, though, so choose reduced-fat options if possible. (Coconut milk is also high in saturated fat, so look for a reduced-fat option unless you want a particularly rich and creamy result.)

Leafy green vegetables, pulses, and bread contain iron (for the production of red blood cells). These foods should be accompanied by produce rich in vitamin C, which aids iron absorption, so be sure to include plenty of red and yellow vegetables, fruit, and pure fruit juice in your diet. Avoid tea and coffee at mealtimes, however, as they impair iron absorption.

Fortified breakfast cereals and bread are a source of vitamin B12 (to help prevent anaemia and keep the brain and nervous system working well). This is the only vitamin not readily available in vegetables. Yeast extract is another good source of B12, which is good news for Marmite and Vegemite lovers.

Everything you need for a healthy, balanced diet is contained in this book, and keeping a well-stocked store cupboard will mean that you can create any of the recipes whenever the mood takes you.

Cabbages and leafy greens

Always choose firm cabbages and fresh-looking leafy greens.

« SAVOY CABBAGE
This crinkly-leaved variety has a sweet heart and tender leaves that are best shredded then lightly steamed, boiled, or stir-fried. The outer leaves are good stuffed. Best in winter.

WHITE CABBAGE ⌃
Popular as coleslaw or fermented as sauerkraut; also good steamed or stir-fried. Try with caraway or fennel seeds, and dried fruits. Best in winter and spring.

⌃ CAVOLO NERO
Also called Tuscan black cabbage, has dark, coarse, leaves that should be crisp and straight. Goes well with tomatoes, garlic, and olives. Available autumn and winter.

⌃ POINTED CABBAGE
Has an excellent, sweet flavour and even the outer leaves can be shredded and cooked. Particularly good stir-fried or lightly steamed. Best in spring.

BRUSSELS SPROUTS »
Steam, briefly boil, or shred in salads, soups, and stir-fries. Good with chestnuts and white beans. Small, firm ones are sweetest. Leafy Brussels tops can be cooked as greens. Best in winter.

SORREL ⌃
Use these lemony-flavoured spear-shaped leaves like spinach; best used fresh. Baby ones are delicious raw in salads. Available spring to autumn.

KALE »

The tight, curly, dark-green leaves have an intense flavour. Cut out any tough fibrous stalks first. Use fresh as it can turn bitter if stored too long. Best in autumn and winter.

GREEN CABBAGE ⌃

Numerous varieties are available and they are great all-rounders. Particularly good with nuts and celery or shredded in soups and stews. Available most of the year.

SWISS CHARD ⌃

Chop and cook in soups, stews, casseroles, and stir-fries, or separate leaves and stalks: wilt the leaves, steam the stalks. Available summer and autumn.

SPRING GREENS ⌃

Shred in soups, stews, stir-fries, and casseroles, or very finely shred and deep-fry for a few seconds as crispy "seaweed". Best in spring.

BABY SPINACH ⌃

Great wilted as a vegetable or added to stir-fries, soups, and stews; baby leaves are delicious in salads. Particularly good flavoured with nutmeg. Different varieties are grown throughout the year.

RED CABBAGE ⌃

Use finely shredded and braised, pickled, or marinated as a salad. It turns a lovely bright red when used with vinegar, lemon juice, or wine. Best in winter and spring.

PAK CHOI (BOK CHOY) »

Asian mustard greens with fleshy stalks and soft leaves. Steam baby ones whole; chop or shred larger ones and stir-fry, or use raw in salads. Best summer to winter.

Store-cupboard essentials
Vegetable flowers

These beautiful vegetables make for sumptuous eating.

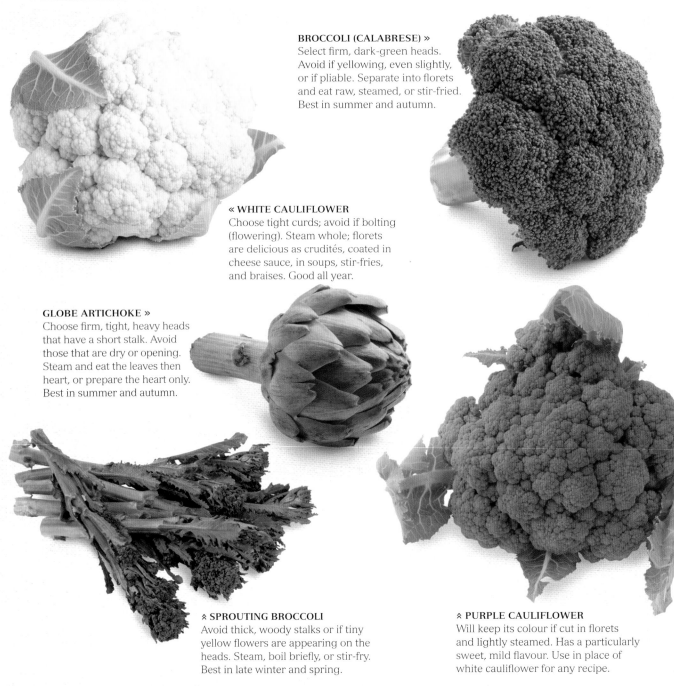

BROCCOLI (CALABRESE) »
Select firm, dark-green heads.
Avoid if yellowing, even slightly,
or if pliable. Separate into florets
and eat raw, steamed, or stir-fried.
Best in summer and autumn.

« WHITE CAULIFLOWER
Choose tight curds; avoid if bolting
(flowering). Steam whole; florets
are delicious as crudités, coated in
cheese sauce, in soups, stir-fries,
and braises. Good all year.

GLOBE ARTICHOKE »
Choose firm, tight, heavy heads
that have a short stalk. Avoid
those that are dry or opening.
Steam and eat the leaves then
heart, or prepare the heart only.
Best in summer and autumn.

⌃ SPROUTING BROCCOLI
Avoid thick, woody stalks or if tiny
yellow flowers are appearing on the
heads. Steam, boil briefly, or stir-fry.
Best in late winter and spring.

⌃ PURPLE CAULIFLOWER
Will keep its colour if cut in florets
and lightly steamed. Has a particularly
sweet, mild flavour. Use in place of
white cauliflower for any recipe.

Shoots and stems

Succulent vegetables that all grow above ground.

« WHITE ASPARAGUS
Grown without light to prevent it from turning green, white asparagus is highly prized for its delicate flavour and creamy texture. Often served cold. Best in spring and summer.

⌃ GREEN ASPARAGUS
The most common variety. Look out for sprue: the cheaper, slim "thinnings" of the crop. Steam, griddle, roast, or use in soup. Best in spring and early summer.

⌃ PURPLE ASPARAGUS
Often less fibrous than green varieties and slightly sweeter, so there is no need to pare even thicker stalks. Cook and serve as per green asparagus.

FLORENCE FENNEL ⌃
Has an aniseed flavour. Shred raw in salads, or quarter and braise or roast. Don't confuse with the herb, wild fennel, which does not form a bulb. Best in summer and autumn.

⌃ KOHLRABI
Tastes like a cross between white cabbage and a mild-flavoured turnip. Eat raw if very fresh, or stew, braise, or add to soups. Best in summer and autumn.

WHITE CELERY »
More delicately flavoured than green, white celery can be either "self-blanching" or green celery that is earthed up while still growing. Use like green celery.

GREEN CELERY ⌃
Has a pronounced flavour that is excellent with cheese, fruit, and nuts. Chop the outer leaves for flavouring soups and stews; use the hearts raw or braised. Best in autumn and winter.

Store-cupboard essentials
Salad leaves

There is a huge variety of tasty leaves available, some grown all year.

⌃ WATERCRESS
Sprigs of round, peppery tasting leaves. Trim off thick feathery stalks before using in salads or as a garnish, or chop to flavour sauces, soups, and egg dishes. Available all year.

⌃ ROUND (BUTTERHEAD) LETTUCE
The large, outer leaves make perfect wraps instead of bread or are good cooked in soup; the heart leaves are excellent dressed (at the last minute) for a salad. Available all year.

« LAMB'S LETTUCE
Clusters of small, soft leaves with a sweet nutty flavour, also known as corn salad. Lovely in a mix of leaves for a salad, and makes a pretty garnish. Best in summer and autumn.

⌃ WHITE CHICORY
Also available red, has a bitter core that should be cut out before separating into leaves, or chopping, for salads. Fill whole spears with soft cheese, dips, or salsas. Good braised whole. Available autumn to spring.

« CHINESE LEAVES
Pale-green, creamy-yellow leaves with thick, fleshy, white stalks, a crunchy texture, and a juicy, sweet flavour. Excellent steamed, used in stir-fries, or eaten raw. Best in autumn.

ROMAINE (COS) ⌃
Crisp, tall leaves with a sweet flavour. Torn in pieces, the classic leaf for Caesar salad; even the outer leaves can be used in salad. Best summer and autumn.

ICEBERG ⌃
Crisp and juicy, with a firm, tight head. Carefully peel off the outer leaves (discard if wilted) to use as a receptacle for cold or hot food; shred or tear up the inner leaves. Best in summer and autumn.

LITTLE GEM »
A small, tight lettuce with juicy round leaves. Use sautéed in halves or quarters, or enjoy raw. The whole leaves make good receptacles for pastes and salsas. Best from spring to autumn.

ROCKET ⌃
Has a pronounced peppery flavour. Usually served raw, but can be wilted on pizzas and in tarts; great for pesto. Keeps best if bought unwashed. Available all year.

⌃ MIZUNA
When young, the dark green serrated leaves with thin, white stalks have a mild, slightly spicy, mustardy taste, similar to rocket. Cook large leaves like pak choi. Best in winter.

« PEA SHOOTS
The tender young tops and tendrils of pea plants, these have a sweet, pea flavour. Perfect for salads and sandwiches (handle carefully as they are delicate). Available late spring and summer.

The onion family

When cooked, alliums take on an irresistible, creamy sweetness.

⌃ ROUND SHALLOTS
With sweet, mild, purple-tinged flesh, use finely chopped in any dish needing a delicate onion flavour. Good for pickling and in dressings, too. Best from autumn to spring.

BROWN ONIONS ⌃
Excellent all-rounders with gold to brown skins and a fairly strong flavour. Baby ones are used for pickling or cooking whole. Best in late summer and autumn.

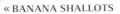

« BANANA SHALLOTS
These torpedo-shaped shallots are highly prized by cooks for their sweet, delicate flavour. Use like round shallots. Best from autumn to spring.

⌃ RED ONION
With a sweet and mild flavour, use thinly sliced in salads; also great roasted, but a good all-rounder. Best in late summer and autumn.

WHITE ONION »
With white flesh and a sweet, mild flavour, this doesn't have to be fried-off before adding to a dish. Popular eaten raw in cheese sandwiches. Best in late summer.

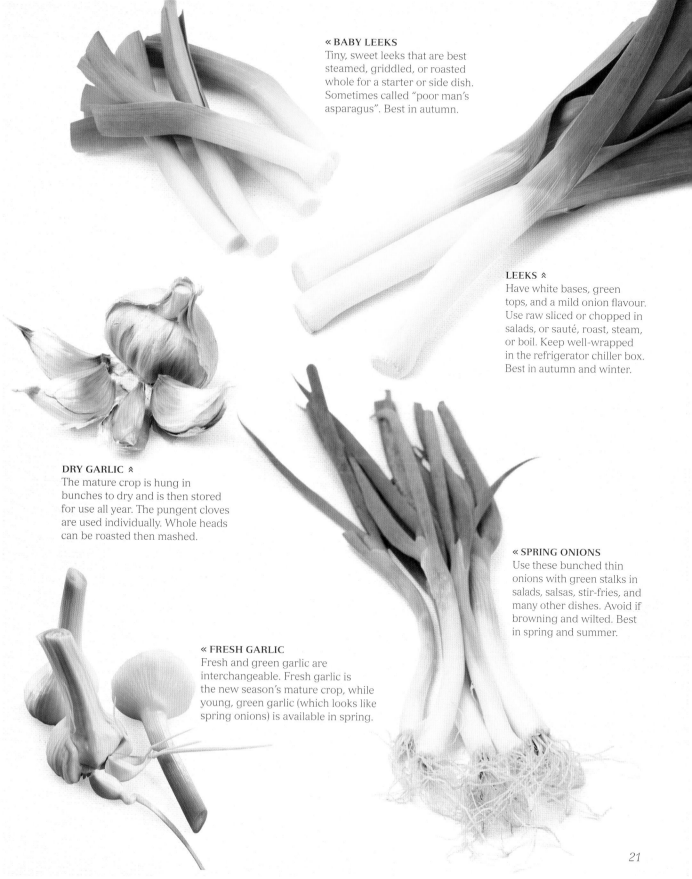

« BABY LEEKS
Tiny, sweet leeks that are best steamed, griddled, or roasted whole for a starter or side dish. Sometimes called "poor man's asparagus". Best in autumn.

LEEKS ☆
Have white bases, green tops, and a mild onion flavour. Use raw sliced or chopped in salads, or sauté, roast, steam, or boil. Keep well-wrapped in the refrigerator chiller box. Best in autumn and winter.

DRY GARLIC ☆
The mature crop is hung in bunches to dry and is then stored for use all year. The pungent cloves are used individually. Whole heads can be roasted then mashed.

« SPRING ONIONS
Use these bunched thin onions with green stalks in salads, salsas, stir-fries, and many other dishes. Avoid if browning and wilted. Best in spring and summer.

« FRESH GARLIC
Fresh and green garlic are interchangeable. Fresh garlic is the new season's mature crop, while young, green garlic (which looks like spring onions) is available in spring.

21

Store-cupboard essentials
Roots and tubers

These staples of the vegetable world are full of nutrients and flavour.

TURNIPS »
Baby turnips are mild; larger ones have a mustard-like kick. Peel thinly and grate raw, or dice, boil, or steam. Baby ones (use whole) are available in summer; larger ones all year.

MARIS BARD POTATOES »
Small, earthy-tasting new potatoes like these are harvested in summer. They have thin skins that should scrape or scrub off easily. Steam or boil.

« PINK FIR POTATOES
Small, waxy, round and fingerling varieties like these are good steamed or boiled, whole or halved, and served warm or cold with salad. Best in summer and autumn.

« DESIREE POTATOES
This Dutch variety is a good all-rounder (much like Maris Piper). With fairly firm flesh, they are neither too floury nor too waxy and good for general potato cooking. Great for chips.

SWEET POTATOES »
Not actually related to the potato, these tubers have sweet creamy-yellow or orange flesh. Can be cooked just like potatoes, with or without skins. Available all year.

DAIKON ⌄
Also known as mooli or white radish. Originally from Japan, it has a strong taste similar to turnip or a hot radish and can be used in the same way as either. Best in summer and autumn.

KING EDWARD POTATOES ⌃
This floury variety has a dry texture, which becomes "fluffy" when cooked. Good for roasting, mashing, baking, and for chips.

⌃ YUKON GOLD POTATOES
This waxy variety has a firm, yellow flesh with a buttery flavour. Best boiled, steamed, baked, or for potato wedges.

BEETROOTS »
These round roots have firm skin and red, golden, or pink and white-striped flesh. They have a rich, sweet, earthy flavour. Serve raw or cooked, grated, sliced, or diced. Best from summer to winter.

BUNCHED CARROTS »
These sweet, fragrant summer carrots can be scrubbed and grated raw, or lightly cooked. The greens should be fresh and bright, but remove before storing or the carrots will go limp.

« PARSNIPS
The sweetness and creaminess of parsnips are most intense in winter. Look out for baby ones to cook whole. Steam, boil, roast, or grate raw.

« JERUSALEM ARTICHOKES
These tubers have a sweet, smoky flavour. Scrub or peel before use and choose ones with fewest knobs. Delicious in soup; also roast, steam, boil, or purée. Best from autumn to spring.

« RADISHES
Small, red, pink, or purple spheres, with a hot, peppery taste, or milder, longer-bodied breakfast varieties. Use raw or cook in place of turnips. Best in spring and autumn.

⌄ MAINCROP CARROTS
These are mature carrots that, once harvested, are stored for use during winter. Purple and yellow or white varieties are also available. Don't buy if over-chilled and damp.

SWEDE »
A large vegetable with thick outer skin and sweet orangey-gold flesh. Delicious roasted or mashed, and in soups, stews, and casseroles. Best during winter.

⌄ CELERIAC
Creamy textured with a strong, sweet, celery-like aroma and flavour. Peel thickly then grate raw, or boil, steam, mash, or roast. Great for low-carb chips. Best in autumn and winter.

CHANTENAY CARROTS »
Originating in France, these very sweet cone-shaped carrots can be just trimmed and cooked whole; larger ones can be quartered lengthways. Best in summer.

Squashes and cucumbers

Winter squashes need cooking, while summer ones can be eaten raw.

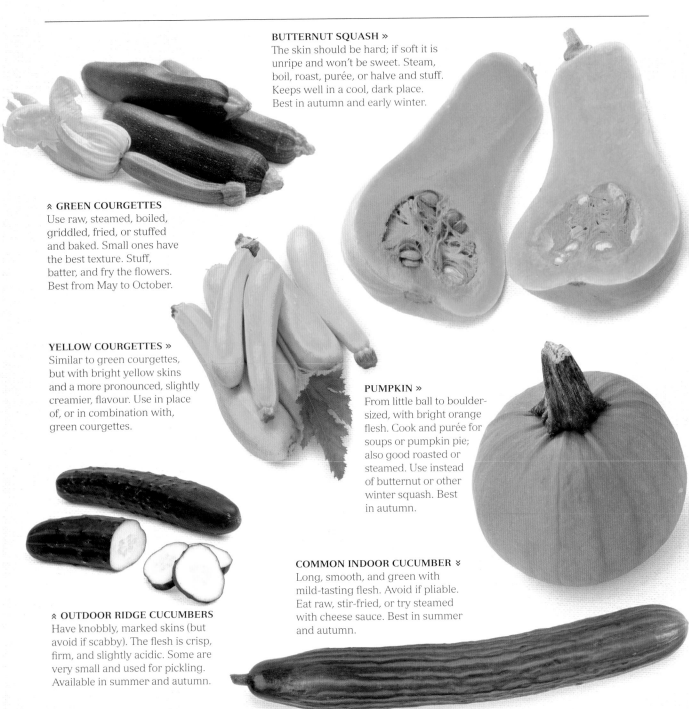

BUTTERNUT SQUASH »
The skin should be hard; if soft it is unripe and won't be sweet. Steam, boil, roast, purée, or halve and stuff. Keeps well in a cool, dark place. Best in autumn and early winter.

⌃ GREEN COURGETTES
Use raw, steamed, boiled, griddled, fried, or stuffed and baked. Small ones have the best texture. Stuff, batter, and fry the flowers. Best from May to October.

YELLOW COURGETTES »
Similar to green courgettes, but with bright yellow skins and a more pronounced, slightly creamier, flavour. Use in place of, or in combination with, green courgettes.

PUMPKIN »
From little ball to boulder-sized, with bright orange flesh. Cook and purée for soups or pumpkin pie; also good roasted or steamed. Use instead of butternut or other winter squash. Best in autumn.

⌃ OUTDOOR RIDGE CUCUMBERS
Have knobbly, marked skins (but avoid if scabby). The flesh is crisp, firm, and slightly acidic. Some are very small and used for pickling. Available in summer and autumn.

COMMON INDOOR CUCUMBER ⌄
Long, smooth, and green with mild-tasting flesh. Avoid if pliable. Eat raw, stir-fried, or try steamed with cheese sauce. Best in summer and autumn.

Beans and pods

Some are eaten pods and all, others are shelled before use.

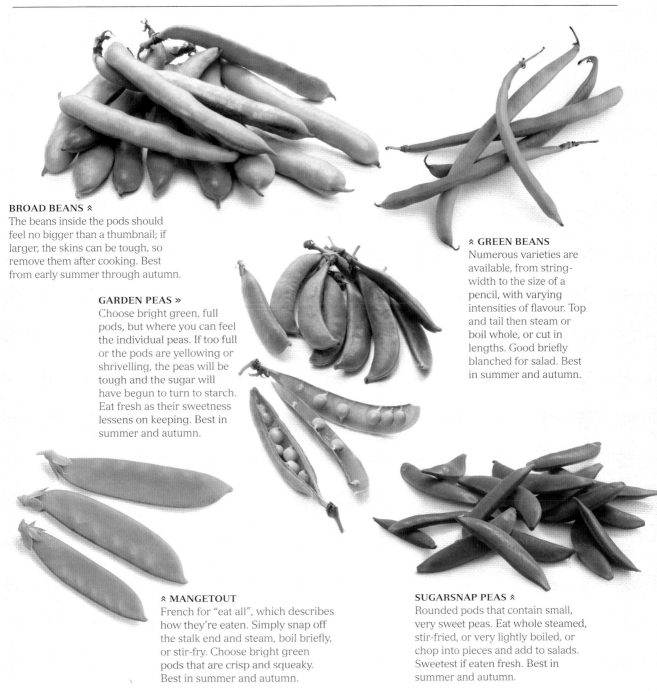

BROAD BEANS ⌃
The beans inside the pods should feel no bigger than a thumbnail; if larger, the skins can be tough, so remove them after cooking. Best from early summer through autumn.

GARDEN PEAS »
Choose bright green, full pods, but where you can feel the individual peas. If too full or the pods are yellowing or shrivelling, the peas will be tough and the sugar will have begun to turn to starch. Eat fresh as their sweetness lessens on keeping. Best in summer and autumn.

⌃ **GREEN BEANS**
Numerous varieties are available, from string-width to the size of a pencil, with varying intensities of flavour. Top and tail then steam or boil whole, or cut in lengths. Good briefly blanched for salad. Best in summer and autumn.

⌃ **MANGETOUT**
French for "eat all", which describes how they're eaten. Simply snap off the stalk end and steam, boil briefly, or stir-fry. Choose bright green pods that are crisp and squeaky. Best in summer and autumn.

SUGARSNAP PEAS ⌃
Rounded pods that contain small, very sweet peas. Eat whole steamed, stir-fried, or very lightly boiled, or chop into pieces and add to salads. Sweetest if eaten fresh. Best in summer and autumn.

Vegetable fruits

Although classed as fruits, the following are all eaten as vegetables.

FUERTE AVOCADOS »
Larger than Hass with smooth, shiny-green skins. They have a mild flavour and pale yellow flesh that slices well. Use like Hass. Ideal for salads and salsas. Best from winter to early summer.

⌃ HASS AVOCADOS
The rough skin turns black when ripe. Halve and fill cavity, purée, mash, slice, or dice. Can be baked. A good choice for dips and spreads. Best from spring to autumn.

« AUBERGINES
Also known as eggplants because of their ovoid shape. Baby ones, stripy pink and white, white, or tiny pea varieties are also available. All have a slightly smoky-sweet flavour. Roast, griddle, fry, or purée. Best in summer and autumn.

BABY CORN »
A specialist vegetable, deliberately grown to be harvested before the kernels develop. Eat whole or chopped in pieces, raw, steamed, boiled, or in stir-fries. Best in late summer and early autumn.

SWEETCORN »
Cobs are harvested when the kernels are just ripening. Pick pale-looking corn and eat fresh; golden, riper corn is not as sweet. Best in late summer and early autumn.

⌃ RED BELL PEPPER
A member of the *Capsicum* genus, the plant also produces green, yellow, and orange fruits according to ripeness (and even purple or white ones). Use in any recipe calling for sweet peppers. Best in summer and autumn.

BIRD'S EYE CHILLIES
Also known as Thai chillies, these are thin and tapering (approx. 3–7.5cm/1¼–3in long). As a rule, long, thin chillies such as these are hotter than long, fat ones, such as jalapeños. Often used in Thai and Indian cooking. Hot.

JALAPEÑO CHILLIES
Shiny green or red, large, and cone-shaped. Also available pickled. Can be stuffed and are particularly good in Mexican cooking. Moderately hot.

SCOTCH BONNETS »
Said to resemble a "Tam o' Shanter" hat, these crinkly, rounded chillies are available in a variety of colours. They are popular in Caribbean cooking and are similar to habanero chillies. Extremely hot.

BEEF TOMATOES ⌄
Large, fat tomatoes that can weigh up to 450g (1lb) each. Excellent stuffed and baked, or sliced for salads and sandwiches. Best in summer and autumn.

ROMANO PEPPERS »
Spear shaped and longer and flatter than bell peppers, these are very sweet. Usually available as red or yellow fruits, they are good stuffed whole, or split first then grilled or roasted. Best in summer and autumn.

« BABY PLUM TOMATOES
A tiny, plum-shaped variety with a very sweet flavour. Particularly good halved or whole tossed in pasta, rice, or other grain-based dishes (add near the end of cooking). Best in summer and autumn.

« PLUM TOMATOES
Oval-shaped, these are excellent for cooking as they have more pulp and less juice than other varieties. Very good for tomato sauce and widely used for canning. Best in summer and autumn.

⌃ CHERRY TOMATOES
Baby versions of standard tomatoes. Best bought on the vine to eat whole or halved in salads, or thrown into dishes towards the end of cooking so they hold their shape. Best in summer and autumn.

⌃ STANDARD TOMATOES
The classic round tomato. An excellent all-rounder for grilling, frying, slicing, or for salads. Buy on the vine for the most flavour. Best in summer and autumn.

Mushrooms

Only forage for wild mushrooms if you know exactly what to look for.

⌃ BUTTON MUSHROOMS

These cultivated white mushrooms are picked at various stages of growth (from tiny button ones, through closed-cup, to large open-cup or flat mushrooms). The flavour develops as they grow. Eat raw or cooked, whole, sliced, or chopped. Also available dried.

⌃ FIELD MUSHROOMS

These wild white mushrooms have gills varying from pink to almost black. They are found in meadows where horses, sheep, or cows graze. Very good flavour. Large, flat ones may be peeled before use. Grow wild in autumn.

« MOREL MUSHROOM

Highly prized and sought after, the morel is found in woodlands (particularly ash and elm). It has a honeycomb hood and a rich flavour. Often sold dried. Grows wild in spring and early summer.

« NAMEKO MUSHROOMS

A cultivated mushroom very popular in Japan. Has an earthy flavour and a silky, almost gelatinous texture when cooked in stir-fries and soups. Trim off the base and separate the mushrooms before use.

« CEP MUSHROOM

Found in woodland clearings, particularly beech, this mushroom is also known as porcini in Italian cuisine. It is meaty and delicious with smooth, creamy flesh. Available dried. Grows wild in autumn and early winter.

⌃ OYSTER MUSHROOMS
Delicately flavoured, pale grey (or sometimes in pastel shades of brown, yellow, or pink), silky mushrooms favoured in Asian cookery. Cut up or cook whole. Often cultivated, but grow wild in autumn and early winter.

ENOKI MUSHROOMS »
Originally from Asia, these cultivated pale clumps have a crisp texture and a mild mushroom flavour. Trim and separate the mushrooms into smaller groupings before use in stir-fries, salads, wraps, and sandwiches.

⌃ PORTOBELLO MUSHROOMS
These cultivated brown mushrooms have a meaty texture and a good flavour. As with white cultivated mushrooms, these are picked at various stages of growth, from crimini (button), through chestnut (cup), to portobello (large and flat). Use like field or white mushrooms.

⌃ CHANTERELLE MUSHROOMS
Have a yellow or orange trumpet shape, a frilly top, and gills running down the stem. Found in many woodlands, but also cultivated and available dried. Have a slight smell of apricots and a delicious flavour. Grow wild from summer to winter.

⌃ SHIITAKE MUSHROOMS
Cultivated mushrooms originally from Asia with a brown cap and white gills. Have an excellent, meaty flavour that is particularly good in Chinese- and Japanese-style dishes. The stalks are often tough so remove and use for stock. Also available dried.

Pulses

These are all rich in proteins, carbohydrate, and fibre.

ADUKI BEANS ⌃
Richly coloured with a good, sweet, nutty flavour, they are excellent all-rounders, that hold their shape well. Great in casseroles, soups, and stews. Also good for burgers.

BORLOTTI BEANS ⌃
Big, brown, rich, meaty, and with a lovely creamy texture, these beans are excellent in pasta dishes, stews, soups, and bakes as they hold their shape, even when cooked for a long time.

« BUTTER BEANS
Large, soft, and floury with a slightly dry texture when cooked, these beans have a distinctive, rich flavour. They are great for soups, stews, dips, and pâtés.

CANNELLINI BEANS »
A member of the haricot family, these classic Tuscan white beans can be mashed to a smooth paste. They have a creamy, slightly nutty flavour.

BROWN LENTILS ⌃
There are several varieties of brown (and green) lentils, which are interchangeable. All have a nutty flavour and a soft, almost meaty texture, making them a great substitute for minced meat in many dishes.

PUY LENTILS ⌃

These small, green lentils from France are often considered an upmarket ingredient. Particularly good braised with vegetables. They have an earthy, rich flavour and hold their shape even after cooking so are also good in salads.

FLAGELOT BEANS ⌃

These pretty green beans have an excellent, creamy texture and a mild, sweet flavour. They are particularly good in salads, but also take on flavours such as garlic and herbs extremely well.

RED KIDNEY BEANS ⌃

Robust, floury-textured beans with a sweet, full-bodied flavour. They taste particularly good with chilli peppers and strong spices.

SOYA BEANS ⌃

Highly nutritious, these silky-textured beans have a mild flavour, which makes them a good base for complex flavour combinations. Also used for making other soya products such as tofu.

CHICKPEAS ⌃

These coarse pulses have a distinctive, nutty flavour and a buttery texture. They hold their shape even after long cooking. Also use puréed for dips (particularly hummus) and sauces.

« HARICOT BEANS

Popular small, white beans, famous for their role in cassoulet, and as baked beans in tomato sauce. Excellent all-rounders for soups, stews, and casseroles with a mild flavour and a soft, creamy, yet slightly floury texture.

YELLOW SPLIT LENTILS »

Unlike yellow split peas, lentils hold their shape when cooked (although, for chana dhal you can substitute split peas; the result is just more pulpy). They have a distinctive, nutty flavour.

RED LENTILS ⌃

Small, split lentils that cook quickly to a pulp. They are ideal for soups and sauces as they thicken the liquid naturally. Also essential for spicy dhals.

Store-cupboard essentials
Nuts, seeds, and oils

These add nutrients, and delicious flavours and textures to many dishes.

PECANS »
Native to North America, these nuts, which have a smooth, ovoid shell, can be used in place of walnuts, but have a milder, sweeter, more buttery flavour.

WALNUTS ☆
The dry, brown, ripe kernels are good with blue cheeses, celery, cabbages, parsnips, sweet potatoes, and leeks. The bright green, unripe fruits, which have soft, milky nuts inside, are picked whole and pickled.

« ALMONDS
Sweet almonds add a delicate yet distinctive flavour. Use them whole, flaked, chopped, or ground in a variety of dishes, including curries, stir-fries, and rice and other grain dishes.

PEANUTS ☆
Technically legumes (they grow underground). Use them raw, roasted, or ground in peanut butter in spicy sauces, rice and noodle dishes, stir-fries, and soup.

« CASHEWS
The creamy texture and sweet flavour of raw or roasted cashews go well with sweetcorn, root vegetables, and smoked paprika. Also use in Asian curries, stir-fries, rice, and noodle dishes.

« HAZELNUTS
These small, round nuts have a wonderful, distinctive flavour. Use them whole, chopped, or ground. They are good in stuffings, with rice and other grain dishes, and with mushrooms.

CHESTNUTS »
Sweet, floury, and perfect for puréeing for soups and pâtés. Roast them in their skins, or shell them, then boil or bake. Also available ready-cooked in cans or vacuum-packs.

PINE NUTS ☆
Soft, with an oily texture and subtle flavour. Often toasted, use in stuffings, with rice and other grain dishes, and as an essential ingredient for pesto and pistou. Also great with spinach.

COCONUT »
Coconut flesh (grated fresh or dried), flakes, cream, and milk all add an amazing flavour to many recipes, particularly curries, soups, rice, and noodle dishes.

BLACK ONION SEEDS »
Also known as Nigella seeds, they have a nutty, earthy flavour and are good with pulses, rice, root and green vegetables. Also add to breads.

FENNEL SEEDS ⌃
Light brownish-green in colour with pale, stripy ridges, these have a strong liquorice flavour. They work well with beetroot, cucumber, cabbage, lentils, rice, potatoes, and beans.

SESAME SEEDS ⌃
Gold, black, or, most commonly, creamy-white, these benefit from being toasted before use to enhance their flavour. Good with all vegetables, pulses, rice, and noodle dishes. Also used to make tahini paste.

CARAWAY SEEDS »
These aniseed-flavoured seeds are brown with pale stripy ridges all round. Add to breads or use with cabbages, onions, potatoes, root vegetables, tomatoes, and noodle dishes.

⌃ PUMPKIN SEEDS
Popular as a snack or garnish, these seeds have a crunchy texture and a nutty flavour that is enhanced by toasting. Good with pasta, cheese, chillies, harissa paste, and in salads.

CHILLI OIL ⌃
There are many different types, but all are pungent with spicy tones. Drizzle over pasta, pizzas, and salads, or add to noodle dishes, soups, and stews for added heat.

OLIVE OIL ⌃
May be a blend of oils or from one type of olive, is an excellent all-purpose oil with a great (and variable) taste. Use as a base for marinades, for grilling, shallow-frying, in sauces, and in breads.

EXTRA VIRGIN OLIVE OIL ⌃
The best, cold-pressed olive oil has an excellent, rich flavour and an intense dark-green or green-gold colour. Use for dressings and for dipping bread.

TRUFFLE OIL ⌃
An expensive oil with the distinctive flavour of woody, earthy truffles. Delicious with eggs and drizzled over pasta or salads. Use with grated fresh or bottled truffles for added effect.

SESAME OIL ⌃
Made using toasted sesame seeds, has a strong, roasted-nut aroma and flavour. Add at the end of cooking for an intense finish or with sunflower oil for stir-fries. Also delicious in dressings.

« WALNUT OIL
Rich and flavoursome with a distinctive walnut flavour. Use in salad dressings, drizzled over pasta, with vegetables, and in stir-fries.

⌃ SUNFLOWER OIL
A good all-purpose oil for cooking and light dressings, has a mild, light, oily taste. Suitable for deep-frying, but don't use more than three times or it will start decomposing into saturated fat.

Store-cupboard essentials
Herbs

Imparting fragrance and flavour, herbs will lift any dish to a new level.

⌃ SPEARMINT
Many varieties are available, but spearmint and garden mint are the most common for flavouring. Dried mint is often used in Middle Eastern and Indian cookery. Good with potatoes, peas, lettuce, cucumber, yogurt, bulgur, rice, and lentils.

⌃ DILL
A delicate and feathery herb with a mild aniseed flavour. Seeds are used for flavouring, too. Good with beetroot and other roots, broad beans, courgettes, potatoes, spinach, rice, and eggs

ROSEMARY ⌃
Has a flowery fragrance. Use sprigs whole then remove after cooking, or chop leaves and add. Good with peppers, aubergines, lentils, mushrooms, onions, parsnips, and tomatoes.

« OREGANO
Interchangeable with marjoram with a strong, sweet flavour. Dried is popular in Greek and Italian cuisine. Add fresh at the end of cooking. Good with most vegetables, rice, pasta, and pulses.

« CORIANDER
Sweet and pungent, loved or hated, with thin, frilly-edged leaves similar to flat-leaf parsley. Its seeds are dried and used as a spice (see p37). A must for curries and spicy dishes; good with avocados, cucumbers, root vegetables, and sweetcorn.

« MARJORAM
Interchangeable with oregano and similar in flavour but slightly spicier. Dried is often used in its own right in Greek and Italian cuisine. Add fresh at the end of cooking. Use with most vegetables, rice, pasta, and pulses.

« CHIVES
These grass-like stalks have an aroma and flavour between onions and leeks. Snip with scissors. Add stalks and flowers as a garnish before serving. Use with avocados, courgettes, potatoes, root vegetables, cream cheese, and eggs.

« DRIED BAY LEAVES
Have a sweet fragrance reminiscent of cloves and basil. The leaves (both dried and fresh) are used to impart their flavour in a dish, but are not eaten. Essential for béchamel sauce and good with tomatoes, pulses, chestnuts, and rice.

⌃ SAGE
Pale, felt-like greenish-grey leaves with a stringent, spicy, sweet yet bitter taste. Use sparingly in cooking. Lovely fried for a garnish. Good with pulses, cheeses, onions, and tomatoes.

« FLAT-LEAF PARSLEY
Italian flat-leaf parsley is favoured by cooks. Use on its own or with other herbs. Perfect chopped, in sprigs, or deep fried as a garnish. Use with most vegetables, eggs, rice, lentils, and bulgur.

« COMMON PARSLEY
Readily available, common parsley is good for basic flavouring and as a garnish. Use a sprig tied with bay leaf and thyme for a simple bouquet garni.

« CHERVIL
Chervil's feathery leaves have an unusual sweet, spicy aroma with a hint of caraway. Don't cook. Particularly good as a garnish with asparagus, peas, beans, beetroot, carrots, tomatoes, cheese, and eggs.

⌃ BASIL
Has a warm, heady, slightly peppery flavour. Look out for Greek, and Thai basil (*horapa*), too. Add at the end of cooking. A must for green pesto and pistou; also good with tomatoes, aubergines, beans, courgettes, eggs, and mozzarella cheese.

GARDEN THYME »
There are many varieties of thyme, but garden thyme is the most common. Has a sweet, spicy, soothing scent. The tiny leaves are stripped off the stem and added whole or chopped during cooking. Good with most vegetables.

TARRAGON »
Long, soft, thin leaves with a distinctive spicy–sweet fragrance and a pungent aniseed flavour. Use sparingly. Good with artichokes, asparagus, courgettes, mushrooms, potatoes, and tomatoes.

Spices

Spices add breadth and depth of flavour to vegetable-based dishes.

« CAPERS
The buds of the caper bush, pickled in vinegar or preserved in salt. Essential in tapenade and tartare sauce, but also good with artichokes and aubergines.

« CINNAMON STICKS
Have a warm, sweet scent and flavour. Used widely in Greek, Middle Eastern, and Indian cuisines. Use with almonds, tomatoes, rice, and other grains.

« DRIED FENUGREEK LEAVES
Crushed, dried leaves with a fragrant smell like sweet hay. Add to green and root vegetables, potatoes, pulses, rice, and tomatoes.

⩘ CLOVES
Warm and powerful with a sweet mouth-numbing taste. One of the Chinese five-spices. Use with cabbage, carrots, beetroot, onions, squashes, and sweet potatoes.

BLACK MUSTARD SEEDS »
Often used in Indian cooking, either ground in spice blends or as whole seeds. Delicious toasted and added to dressings for grated root vegetables.

SWEET PAPRIKA ⩘
Ground, dried red peppers, with a caramel fruitiness. Adds fragrance and colour to tomato- and pulse-based goulashes and is good with cheeses. Smoked or Spanish paprika (pimentón), on the other hand, has a rich smokiness that adds an intense meaty flavour to vegetable dishes. Choose either mild or hot.

FRESH LEMONGRASS »
Refreshing, tart spice with a strong citrus flavour. Crush or finely chop for use with most vegetables. Essential in many noodle dishes and Asian curries.

⩘ GROUND TURMERIC
Has a rich, woody aroma, slightly bitter flavour, and intense yellow colour. Essential in Indian curry powders and pastes. Use with pulses, rice, pasta, eggs, beans, aubergines, spinach, and potatoes.

« WHOLE DRIED CHILLIES
Also available as crushed flakes and powder, adds pungency and heat. Essential in curry powders and pastes, harissa, jerk seasoning, salsas, and pickles.

TAMARIND PASTE ⌃
From the soaked pods of the tamarind tree. An essential ingredient in Worcestershire sauce. Adds a fruity tartness to curries and spice dishes.

« STAR ANISE
Pretty star-shaped spice with a liquorice flavour and aroma and a warm pungency. Use with leeks, squashes, root vegetables, and pulses.

JUNIPER BERRIES ⌃
Bitter-sweet berries of the juniper bush, usually available dried. Use crushed in cabbage dishes (particularly sauerkraut), and with celery, peppers, and root vegetables.

FRESH CURRY LEAVES ⌃
Also available dried, but fresh leaves have a better flavour. Often added towards the end of cooking. Use with most vegetables, lentils, and rice.

GROUND CUMIN ⌃
Also available as seeds, has a strong, heavy scent and a rich, slightly earthy flavour. Use with aubergines, beans, root vegetables, potatoes, and squashes.

KAFFIR LIME LEAVES ⌃
Have a powerful fragrance between lemon and lime. Use with mushrooms, green vegetables, and with coconut milk in Thai-style curries.

⌃ CORIANDER SEEDS
Also available ground, coriander has a sweet, woody fragrance and floral flavour. Particularly good with mushrooms and onions.

« GARAM MASALA
Used a lot in northern Indian cuisine, a pungent spice blend that is often added at the end of cooking to enhance the flavours in the dish.

FRESH GINGER ⌃
Essential for curries and most spicy dishes. The knobbly fresh root should be peeled then sliced or grated. Ground ginger is hotter than fresh.

« SAFFRON
The yellow stigmas of the sativus crocus are the most expensive spice in the world. Rich, pungent, musky, and floral. Infuse in water or stock. Use with rice, pasta, and most vegetables.

WHOLE NUTMEG ⌃
Also available ground, but best grated fresh from the whole nut. Use with spinach, parsnips, potatoes, cabbage, squashes, and sweet potatoes.

GALANGAL ⌃
Much used in Southeast Asia, has a lemony sourness, and a gingery flavour. Use in sauces, curries, soups, and stews. Good with chilli, fennel, shallots, garlic, and lime.

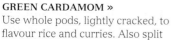

GREEN CARDAMOM »
Use whole pods, lightly cracked, to flavour rice and curries. Also split to remove the seeds, which can then be added to pulses, potatoes, sweet potatoes, and root vegetables.

The recipes

Every recipe in this book puts vegetables at the centre of the plate. You'll find delicious vegetable combinations and flavour pairings, as well as exciting ways to make the most of any vegetable by using a range of herbs, spices, nuts, pulses, and seeds.

Soups and salads

Gazpacho

SERVES 6–8   **PREPARATION 30 MINS**

Wonderfully refreshing, this is a perfect lunch for a hot summer day. It's fantastically quick to make and healthy, too. Serve with garlic-rubbed toast.

INGREDIENTS

1 red pepper, deseeded
  and chopped
10 spring onions, chopped, or
  1 red onion, finely chopped
5 garlic cloves, chopped
1 cucumber, finely chopped
1kg (2¼lb) ripe tomatoes,
  finely chopped
1 tbsp chopped thyme,
  marjoram, parsley, mint,
  or basil
100g (3½oz) stale bread
1 chilli, deseeded and finely
  chopped, or ½ tsp cayenne
  pepper (optional)
2 tbsp red wine vinegar
3 tbsp olive oil, plus extra
  for drizzling
salt and freshly ground
  black pepper

1 Place a serving bowl in the refrigerator. Put the pepper, spring onions or onion, garlic, cucumber, and tomatoes in a mixing bowl, then add the herbs.

2 Whizz the bread in a blender to make breadcrumbs, then add to the mixing bowl along with the chilli or cayenne pepper, if using, vinegar, and oil. Gradually add 100ml (3½fl oz) chilled water to give it a nice thick consistency; use more if preferred.

3 Transfer to the blender and, depending on your preference, either whizz briefly so that the odd chunk of cucumber remains or blend the soup until smooth. Season generously with salt and pepper. Transfer to the serving bowl, add a few ice cubes, and drizzle with oil.

Chicory gazpacho

SERVES 4   PREPARATION **15 MINS, PLUS CHILLING**

A delicious variation on the cool classic, this soup has a zesty twist. Use a **romaine lettuce heart or even a bunch of watercress** instead of chicory, if preferred.

1 Thinly pare the zest of half the orange. Cut in thin strips and boil in water for 1 minute. Drain, rinse with cold water, and drain again. Set aside for the garnish. Finely grate the remaining zest of the orange, squeeze the juice, and set aside.

2 Cut a cone shape out of the base of each head of chicory and discard. Separate the heads into spears. Reserve four of the smallest spears for the garnish. Roughly chop the remainder.

3 Soak the bread in water for 2 minutes. Squeeze out some of the moisture, then put the bread in a blender with the chopped chicory, garlic, spring onions, tomato, stock, oil, white balsamic condiment, basil leaves, and the orange juice and finely grated zest. Purée the soup in a blender or food processor, then season with salt and pepper. Chill until ready to serve.

4 Ladle into 4 shallow soup plates and drizzle with a little oil. Garnish each with a tiny chicory spear and a few strands of blanched orange zest. Serve cold.

INGREDIENTS

1 large orange
2 heads white chicory
2 slices bread,
    crusts removed
1 garlic clove,
    roughly chopped
4 spring onions,
    roughly chopped
1 large beef tomato, skinned,
    quartered, and deseeded
450ml (15fl oz) vegetable stock
2 tbsp olive oil, plus extra
    for drizzling
2 tbsp white balsamic
    condiment
4 large basil leaves
salt and freshly ground
    black pepper

French red onion soup with brandy and Gruyère croûtes

SERVES 4 **PREPARATION 10 MINS** **TO COOK 40 MINS**

Rich and full of flavour, onion soup cannot be beaten on a cold day. Red onions add colour and are sweeter and more intensely flavoured than brown onions.

INGREDIENTS

60g (2oz) butter
4 large red onions, quartered
   and thinly sliced
2 tbsp soft light brown sugar
1 litre (1¾ pints) vegetable
   stock
2 tbsp brandy
salt and freshly ground
   black pepper
8 diagonal slices of baguette
175g (6oz) Gruyère
   cheese, grated

1 Melt the butter in a large saucepan. Add the onions and fry, stirring, for 2 minutes. Cover, reduce the heat to low, and cook gently for 10 minutes until really soft, shaking the pan occasionally.

2 Increase the heat, add the sugar, and fry, stirring continuously, for 5 minutes or until richly browned (but take care not to burn). Add the stock, brandy, and a little salt and pepper. Bring to a boil, reduce the heat, and simmer gently for 15 minutes.

3 Meanwhile, make the croûtes. Preheat the grill and toast the bread on both sides. When ready to serve, add the cheese to the croûtes and grill until just melted and sizzling.

4 Ladle the soup into warmed bowls and float 2 cheese croûtes on each. Add a grinding of pepper and serve immediately.

Fennel soup with Parmesan thins

SERVES 4　　**PREPARATION 20 MINS**　　TO COOK **45 MINS**

Parmesan thins are simplicity itself to make and, along with a garnish of delicate fennel fronds, **elevate this rich, creamy soup** to dinner-party sophistication.

INGREDIENTS

1–2 tbsp olive oil
50g (1¾oz) butter
1 onion, finely chopped
salt and freshly ground
　black pepper
1 celery stick, finely chopped
1 carrot, finely chopped
2 garlic cloves, finely chopped
3–4 fennel bulbs, trimmed
　and finely chopped, fronds
　reserved to garnish
750ml (1¼ pints) hot
　vegetable stock
4 tbsp finely grated
　Parmesan cheese
200ml (7fl oz) double cream
pinch of grated nutmeg

1 Heat 1 tbsp oil and the butter in a large pan. Add the onion and cook over a low heat, stirring, for 5–6 minutes until soft. Season with salt and pepper. Add the celery and carrot and continue to cook, stirring occasionally, for 10 minutes, or until nicely golden. Add the garlic and fennel and cook over a very low heat, stirring occasionally, for 5 minutes until the fennel begins to soften, adding more oil if needed. Pour over a little stock and bring to a boil. Add the remaining stock and bring to a boil again. Reduce to a simmer and cook for 20 minutes until the fennel is tender.

2 For the Parmesan thins, place 4 equal heaps of the grated Parmesan in a large, non-stick frying pan. Set the pan over a low heat and flatten each heap with the back of a spoon. Cook for a few minutes until the Parmesan begins to melt and forms a crust. Once it has begun to crisp on the bottom and tiny bubbles start to appear around the edges, carefully flip each thin using a palette knife. Cook for a further minute or so, then remove the pan from the heat, leaving the thins in the pan to keep warm.

3 Transfer the soup to a food processor and blend until smooth, then return to the pan; alternatively, use a hand blender. Season well, then pour in the cream and heat gently. Serve in wide bowls, sprinkled with a pinch of nutmeg and topped with a Parmesan thin. Garnish with the reserved fennel fronds.

Borscht

SERVES 4   **PREPARATION 15 MINS**   TO COOK **1 HR 30 MINS**

This thickly textured, satisfying soup is a Russian classic that can be enjoyed at any time of year. Try it with grated carrot piled on top and hunks of dark rye bread.

1 Melt the butter in a large saucepan over a medium heat. Add the beetroot, onion, carrot, and celery. Cook, stirring, for 5 minutes, or until just softened. Add the tomatoes and garlic, if using, and cook for 2–3 minutes, stirring frequently, then stir in the stock.

2 Tie the bay leaves and cloves in a small piece of muslin or new disposable kitchen cloth and add to the pan. Bring the soup to a boil, then lower the heat, cover, and simmer for 1 hour 20 minutes. Discard the muslin bag, stir in the lemon juice, and season to taste with salt and pepper. Ladle the soup into warmed bowls and add a swirl of soured cream to each one.

INGREDIENTS

45g (1½oz) butter or goose fat
2 large beetroot, grated
1 onion, roughly grated
1 carrot, roughly grated
1 celery stick, roughly grated
400g can chopped tomatoes
1 garlic clove, crushed
 (optional)
1.7 litres (3 pints) hot
 vegetable stock
2 bay leaves
4 cloves
2 tbsp lemon juice
salt and freshly ground
 black pepper
200ml (7fl oz) soured cream

Cheese, red pepper, and sweetcorn chowder

SERVES 4   **PREPARATION 15 MINS**   **TO COOK 35 MINS**

When time is short, use a large can of sweetcorn with peppers instead of the corn cobs and pepper. Simmering the cobs in the stock is not essential.

INGREDIENTS

2 large corn cobs
1 litre (1¾ pints) vegetable
  stock
knob of butter
1 onion, finely chopped
1 potato, peeled and
  finely diced
1 red pepper, deseeded
  and finely chopped
1 bouquet garni
3 tbsp cornflour
150ml (5fl oz) milk
115g (4oz) strong Cheddar
  cheese, grated
2 tbsp chopped parsley,
  plus extra to garnish
salt and freshly ground
  black pepper

1 Remove the corn kernels from the cobs (see p321). Put the stripped cobs in a saucepan with the stock. Bring to a boil, cover, and simmer gently for 5 minutes to extract the flavour. Strain the stock into a bowl and discard the cobs.

2 In the same saucepan, melt the butter and fry the onion gently, stirring, for 2 minutes until softened, but not browned. Add the reserved stock, all the prepared vegetables, and the bouquet garni. Bring to a boil, then reduce the heat, partially cover, and simmer gently for 15 minutes until the vegetables are soft. Discard the bouquet garni.

3 Blend the cornflour with the milk and stir into the soup. Bring back to a boil and simmer, stirring, for 1 minute until slightly thickened. Stir in the cheese until melted, add the parsley, then season with salt and pepper to taste. Ladle into bowls and sprinkle with a little extra chopped parsley.

Spicy watercress soup

SERVES 4–6   **PREPARATION 20 MINS**   TO COOK **25 MINS**

Peppery watercress, curry leaf oil, and caramelized pear make a **marvellous melange of flavours**. The oil can be made a few days before and kept refrigerated.

INGREDIENTS

3 tbsp curry leaves
150ml (5fl oz) olive oil,
    plus 2 tbsp for the soup
1 onion, chopped
2 potatoes, peeled `
    and chopped
1 litre (1³/₄ pints) hot
    vegetable stock
250g (9oz) watercress
salt and freshly ground
    black pepper
2 tbsp crème fraîche

For the garnish

1 conference pear, peeled
    and finely diced
2 tbsp icing sugar
pinch of coarsely ground
    black peppercorns
1 tbsp crème fraîche

1 First, make the curry leaf oil. Drop the leaves into a pan of boiling water and cook for about 30 seconds. Remove and refresh with cold water, then pat dry with kitchen paper and transfer to a blender. Warm the oil and gradually pour into the blender as the leaves are being processed. Blend to a smooth paste. Line a sieve with kitchen paper and pour the curry leaf mixture into it – the oil will slowly drip through.

2 For the soup, heat 2 tbsp oil in a large pan and add the onion and potato. Cover and fry over a gentle heat for about 5 minutes, stirring frequently, until softened, but not coloured. Pour in the stock and simmer for 10 minutes until the potatoes are cooked. Add the watercress and cook for a further minute. Remove from the heat, season, and stir in 2–3 tsp curry leaf oil. Blend with a hand blender until smooth and sieve to remove any tough fibres.

3 For the garnish, toss the pear in icing sugar seasoned with pepper. Heat a frying pan over a moderate heat and fry the pear until caramelized.

4 Reheat and season the soup again and whisk in 2 tbsp crème fraîche. Ladle into bowls and top with an extra dollop of crème fraîche. Scatter the pear over and finish with an extra drizzle of curry leaf oil.

Lettuce soup with peas

SERVES 4 **PREPARATION 20 MINS, PLUS CHILLING**

Round or butterhead lettuces are ideal for puréeing as their soft leaves are not fibrous. Here they are combined with sweet peas and mint for a fresh summer soup.

1 Bring a small amount of water to a boil in a pan, add the peas, and cook for 3 minutes. Drain (reserving the cooking water), rinse under cold running water, and refrigerate. Cut the garlic in half, removing any green at the centre, and crush with a pinch of coarse salt.

2 Combine the garlic with all the other ingredients (except the peas) in a blender or food processor, adding just enough of the reserved cooking water to get the blades moving or until the desired consistency is achieved – this will vary according to the type of lettuce and the kind of machine being used, but the soup is nice if it is fairly smooth, with a bit of texture.

3 Transfer the soup to a large bowl and place in the refrigerator for 30 minutes. When ready to serve, stir through the cooked peas, leaving a few to use as a garnish.

INGREDIENTS

125g (4½oz) peas
   (shelled weight)
1 small garlic clove
pinch of coarse salt
2 round lettuces (approx.
   500g/1lb 2oz in total),
   torn into pieces and
   solid cores discarded
250g (9oz) plain yogurt
2cm (¾in) piece root
   ginger, finely grated
handful of mint leaves
juice of ½ lemon
salt and freshly ground
   black pepper

Potato soup with broccoli, shallot, and mascarpone cheese

SERVES 4   **PREPARATION 20 MINS**   TO COOK **40 MINS**

Broccoli and shallot add colour and freshness to this **delicate potato and cheese soup.** Try crumbled Caerphilly or Wensleydale instead of mascarpone.

INGREDIENTS

1 tbsp olive oil

10g (¼oz) butter

2 large banana shallots, finely chopped

350g (12oz) floury potatoes, peeled and chopped into 2.5cm (1in) chunks

1.4 litres (2½ pints) vegetable stock

1 large bay leaf

salt and freshly ground black pepper

1 large head broccoli, cut into florets

4 tbsp mascarpone cheese

4 × 1cm (½in) slices baguette

30g (1oz) creamy, strong-flavoured blue cheese, such as Roquefort, Fourme d'Ambert, or Gorgonzola Piccante

1 Heat the oil and butter in a saucepan over a medium heat. Add the shallots and potatoes and cook for 5 minutes, stirring often.

2 Add the stock and bay leaf and stir well. Season lightly with salt and pepper and bring to a simmer. Lower the heat, cover with a lid, and simmer for 10 minutes. Add the broccoli, stir, cover again, and cook for 10–15 minutes, or until the broccoli is tender. Leave to cool for several minutes.

3 Transfer the contents of the pan to a food processor and whizz until smooth. Strain the soup back into the pan through a sieve, using a wooden spoon to push as much of the mixture through as possible.

4 Place the pan over a medium heat and stir in the mascarpone cheese; keep stirring until it has blended in. Season well and discard the bay leaf. Toast the baguette slices until golden, and spread them with the blue cheese. Ladle the soup into bowls and float a piece of the bread in the centre of each one.

Soups and salads
Creamy spinach and rosemary soup

SERVES 6   **PREPARATION 15 MINS**   TO COOK **25 MINS**

With this **fragrant and vividly coloured soup,** the spinach is added at the last moment so that it does not overcook and lose any of its colour or flavour.

1 Melt the butter in a heavy-based pan. When it starts to foam, add the onion and potato, and stir to coat well. Season with salt and pepper, then cover the pan with a lid and sweat the vegetables over a gentle heat for 10 minutes.

2 Add the stock or water and milk, bring to a boil, then cover again and simmer for 5 minutes or until the potato and onion are completely cooked. Add the spinach and boil the soup with the lid removed for 2–3 minutes, or until the spinach is tender, but not overcooked. Remove from the heat. Add the chopped rosemary, then, using a hand blender or transferring to a food processor, whizz the soup until smooth. Reheat gently.

3 Serve in warmed bowls garnished with a swirl of cream and a sprig of rosemary. When in season, sprinkle a few rosemary flowers over the top for extra pizzazz. Serve with crusty bread or cheese scones.

INGREDIENTS

50g (1¾oz) butter
1 onion, finely chopped
1 large potato, peeled
  and diced
salt and freshly ground
  black pepper
450ml (15fl oz) hot vegetable
  stock or water
450ml (15fl oz) creamy milk,
  made from 335ml (11fl oz)
  whole milk mixed with
  120ml (4fl oz) single cream
350g (12oz) spinach, destalked,
  rinsed, and roughly chopped
1 tbsp chopped rosemary
2 tbsp single cream, sprig of
  rosemary, and rosemary
  flowers (optional), to garnish

Leek, barley, and root vegetable broth with basil oil

SERVES 4–6   **PREPARATION 10 MINS**   TO COOK **45 MINS**

Barley adds substance to this delicate soup. For a more filling meal and extra protein, add a 410g can of haricot beans and an extra 200ml (7fl oz) vegetable stock.

INGREDIENTS

200ml (7fl oz) dry white wine
1.5 litres (2¾ pints) vegetable
   stock
75g (2½oz) pearl barley
1 onion, chopped
2 carrots, finely diced
½ small swede, finely diced
1 potato, peeled and
   finely diced
1 turnip, finely diced
1 large bay leaf
2 star anise
salt and freshly ground
   black pepper
crusty bread, to serve

For the basil oil
handful of basil leaves,
   roughly chopped
4 tbsp olive oil

1 Put the white wine in a large saucepan and bring to a boil. Boil rapidly for 2–3 minutes until reduced by half.

2 Add the remaining soup ingredients. Bring to a boil, then reduce the heat, cover, and simmer gently for 40 minutes until the barley is tender. Discard the bay leaf and star anise. Taste and adjust the seasoning.

3 To make the basil oil, blend the basil with the oil in a blender or small food processor.

4 Ladle the soup into warmed bowls. Drizzle the basil oil on top of each and serve with crusty bread.

Celery and celeriac soup

SERVES 4   **PREPARATION 15 MINS**   TO COOK **35–40 MINS**

This earthy soup combines **mildly nutty celeriac and the more assertive flavour of celery** to create a fragrant, satisfying winter warmer.

INGREDIENTS

1 tbsp sunflower or groundnut
  oil, or mild-flavoured
  olive oil

30g (1oz) butter, plus 30g (1oz)
  chilled butter, diced

500g (1lb 2oz) celeriac, peeled
  and chopped

1 large head celery, cored
  and chopped

1 floury potato, peeled
  and chopped

sea salt and freshly ground
  black pepper

1 litre (1¾ pints) light
  vegetable stock

4 slices walnut bread, lightly
  toasted, to serve

1 Put the oil and 30g (1oz) butter in a large sauté pan over a medium heat. Add the celeriac, celery, and potato. Stir well for 2–3 minutes, then reduce the heat a little. Add 3–4 tbsp water and season lightly with salt and pepper. Cover the pan and leave to stew gently for 15–20 minutes until very soft. Stir the vegetables from time to time and keep the heat low.

2 Transfer the cooked vegetables to a food processor and purée. Return to the pan and add the stock. Season and stir briskly to blend. Bring to a simmer over a medium heat, stirring frequently. Reduce the heat a little and leave to simmer gently for 10–15 minutes, still stirring occasionally. Taste and adjust the seasoning.

3 Just before serving, whisk in the chilled, diced butter. Serve hot with toasted walnut bread.

Turnip noodle soup with pimento and chilli

SERVES 4–6   **PREPARATION 10 MINS**   **TO COOK 35 MINS**

Turnips are often overlooked, but this **light, colourful soup with a chilli kick** will not disappoint. Larger turnips have a stronger flavour and are perfect for this recipe.

1 Put the spring onions, turnips, chillies, star anise, tomato purée, and stock in a saucepan and bring to a boil. Lower the heat, partially cover, and simmer gently for 30 minutes, or until the turnips are really tender. Discard the star anise.

2 Meanwhile, put the noodles in a bowl, cover with boiling water, and leave to stand for 5 minutes, stirring to loosen. Drain the noodles and stir into the soup along with the pimento. Season with soy sauce and pepper, then stir in half the coriander. Heat through for 1–2 minutes. Ladle into warmed soup bowls, top with the remaining coriander, and serve.

INGREDIENTS

4 spring onions, chopped
2 large turnips, diced
½ tsp crushed dried chillies
1 green jalapeño chilli, deseeded and cut into thin rings
2 star anise
2 tsp tomato purée
900ml (1½ pints) hot vegetable stock
1 slab dried, thin Chinese egg noodles
1 preserved pimento, drained and diced
soy sauce, to taste
freshly ground black pepper
small handful of coriander leaves, torn

Carrot and orange soup

SERVES 4   PREPARATION **10 MINS**   TO COOK **40 MINS**

A refreshing soup with a hint of spice, this is the perfect start to a summer meal. Try adding a swirl of cream or a spoonful of low-fat plain yogurt before serving.

INGREDIENTS

2 tsp light olive oil
  or sunflower oil
1 leek, sliced
500g (1lb 2oz) carrots, sliced
1 potato (approx. 115g/4oz),
  chopped
½ tsp ground coriander
pinch of ground cumin
300ml (10fl oz) orange juice
500ml (16fl oz) vegetable stock
1 bay leaf
salt and freshly ground
  black pepper
2 tbsp chopped coriander,
  to garnish

1 Place the oil, leek, and carrots in a large saucepan and cook over a low heat for 5 minutes, stirring frequently, or until the leek has softened. Add the potato, coriander, and cumin, then pour in the orange juice and stock. Add the bay leaf, season with salt and pepper, and stir occasionally.

2 Increase the heat, bring the soup to a boil, then lower the heat, cover, and simmer for 40 minutes, or until the vegetables are very tender.

3 Allow the soup to cool slightly, then transfer to a blender or food processor and process until smooth, working in batches if necessary.

4 Return to the saucepan and add a little extra stock or water if the soup is too thick. Bring back to a simmer, then transfer to warmed serving bowls and sprinkle with chopped coriander.

Avocado, cucumber, and sorrel soup

SERVES 4–6 **PREPARATION 5–10 MINS**

This lovely, cool summer soup is just perfect when it's too hot to cook. Track down sorrel at a local farmer's market; its lemony-spinach flavour is unique.

1 Put the avocado in a blender with the sorrel, cucumber, yogurt, and garlic. Add about 120ml (4fl oz) water and blend until smooth. Taste and adjust the seasoning, adding more sorrel, or salt or pepper, or thinning down with a little more water as desired.

2 Divide between 4–6 serving bowls or cups and drizzle a thin thread of avocado oil on the surface. Serve at once, or at least within the next hour while it is fresh and vivid.

INGREDIENTS

1 ripe, buttery avocado, halved, stoned, and peeled (see pp324–5)
generous handful of sorrel leaves (discard any tough stalks)
¼ large cucumber, roughly diced but not peeled
75g (2½oz) Greek-style yogurt
1–2 garlic cloves, chopped
salt and freshly ground black pepper
avocado oil, for drizzling

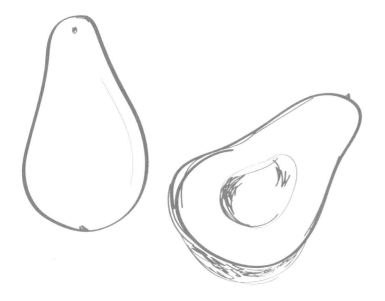

Jerusalem artichoke soup with saffron and thyme

SERVES 4–6   **PREPARATION 15 MINS**   **TO COOK 35–45 MINS**

Use whatever proportion of carrots and Jerusalem artichokes you have, making 700g (1lb 9oz) in total. Carrots enhance the colour and sweetness of the soup.

INGREDIENTS

2 tbsp sunflower oil or olive oil, plus extra to garnish

2 onions, chopped

3 garlic cloves, chopped

350g (12oz) Jerusalem artichokes, scrubbed and roughly chopped

350g (12oz) carrots, scrubbed and roughly chopped

sea salt and freshly ground black pepper

1.2 litres (2 pints) hot vegetable stock

1 tbsp thyme leaves or 1½ tsp dried thyme

large pinch (about 30 strands) of saffron

juice of ½ lemon

1 Heat the oil in a large pan over a medium heat. Add the onions and fry for 5 minutes, or until soft and translucent. Add the garlic and fry for 30 seconds, or until fragrant. Stir in the artichokes, carrots, and a little salt. Cover with a lid and sweat, stirring frequently, for 10–15 minutes, or until the vegetables are softened.

2 Add the stock, thyme, and saffron. Bring to a boil, then lower the heat to a simmer and cook, covered, for 20 minutes or until the vegetables are thoroughly soft. Cool briefly, then whizz until smooth in a blender of food processor. Stir in the lemon juice and season with salt and pepper. Serve in warmed bowls, with a drizzle of oil on top.

Lentil soup

SERVES 4   PREPARATION **20 MINS**   TO COOK **35 MINS**

This hearty soup has just a touch of spice and is quick and easy to prepare. It can be puréed for a smooth finish. Serve with plenty of warm, crusty bread.

1 Heat the oil in a large pan over a medium heat. Add the onions, celery, and carrots. Cook, stirring, for 5 minutes, or until the onions are soft and translucent.

2 Add the garlic and curry powder and cook, stirring, for another minute. Then add the lentils, stock, and tomato juice.

3 Bring to a boil, then lower the heat, cover, and simmer for 25 minutes, or until the vegetables are tender. Season with salt and pepper and serve hot.

INGREDIENTS

1 tbsp olive oil
2 onions, finely chopped
2 celery sticks, finely chopped
2 carrots, finely chopped
2 garlic cloves, crushed
1–2 tsp curry powder
150g (5½oz) red lentils
1.4 litres (2½ pints)
   vegetable stock
120ml (4fl oz) tomato juice
   or vegetable juice
salt and freshly ground
   black pepper

Four ways with
Mushrooms

Mushroom soup ▶

TAKES 55 mins **SERVES** 4

Melt 30g (1oz) **butter** in a large saucepan, add
1 finely chopped **onion**, 2 finely chopped **celery
sticks**, and 1 crushed **garlic clove**, and fry for
3–4 minutes, or until softened. Stir in 450g (1lb)
roughly chopped **mixed mushrooms** and
continue to fry for 5–6 minutes. Add 200g (7oz)
peeled and diced **potatoes** and 1 litre (1¾ pints)
vegetable stock and bring to a boil. Reduce the
heat and simmer gently for 30 minutes. Use a
hand blender to whizz the soup until smooth,
working in batches if necessary. Sprinkle in
2 tbsp finely chopped **parsley**, season with **salt**
and freshly ground **black pepper**, and serve.

◀ Tofu and mushroom stroganoff

TAKES 35 mins **SERVES** 4

Heat 1 tbsp **sunflower oil** in a pan. Stir-fry 350g
(12oz) diced **tofu** over a high heat until golden. Set
aside. Add 1 tbsp oil, reduce the heat, and fry 1
sliced **red onion** and 2 crushed **garlic cloves**
until soft. Add 1 **red** and 1 **orange pepper**, sliced,
and 250g (9oz) **mixed mushrooms**, quartered.
Stir-fry for 5 minutes. Add 2 tbsp each **tomato
purée** and **smooth peanut butter** and the tofu.
Stir in 150ml (5fl oz) **vegetable stock** and 2 tsp
cornflour mixed to a paste with water. Cook for 3
minutes. Add 200g (7oz) **crème fraîche** and **salt**
and freshly ground **black pepper**. Simmer for 2
minutes, sprinkle with **chives**, and serve with **rice**.

Mushrooms come in a range of flavours, from the mild button type to full-bodied portobellos and nutty chanterelles. **All should be firm and earthy-smelling.** Always wipe them – but don't wash them – before use.

Mushrooms in garlic sauce ▶

TAKES 25 mins **SERVES** 4

Heat 4 tbsp **olive oil** in a frying pan. Add 400g (14oz) **chestnut mushrooms**, halved, 4 finely sliced **garlic cloves**, and 2 **red chillies**, deseeded and finely sliced. Fry for 2 minutes over a low heat. Add 4 tbsp **dry sherry**, crumble in 1 **vegetable stock** cube, and season with freshly ground **black pepper**. Cook over a medium heat for 10 minutes, or until the mushrooms have released their juices. Cook for a further 3 minutes, or until the juices have reduced by half, and then serve with some fresh **crusty bread**.

◀ Mushroom bruschetta

TAKES 30 mins **SERVES** 12

Preheat the oven to 180°C (350°F/Gas 4). Brush 12 slices of **ciabatta** with **olive oil**, then bake for 10 minutes. Melt 60g (2oz) **butter** in a pan, add 4 finely chopped **shallots** and 2 finely chopped **garlic cloves**, and fry gently for 5 minutes. Add 450g (1lb) sliced **field mushrooms** and fry until wilted. Add 4 tbsp **Marsala**, bring to a boil, then simmer until reduced to 1 tsp. Reduce the heat, add 100ml (3½fl oz) **double cream**, and simmer for 5 minutes. Add **salt** and freshly ground **black pepper**, and stir in 2 tbsp finely chopped **parsley** and 3 tbsp grated **Parmesan cheese**. Spoon the mixture over the toasted bread.

Antipasti salad

SERVES 4   **PREPARATION 30 MINS**   TO COOK **10 MINS**

A mix of lettuce varieties and spicy leaves such as rocket or mizuna really lifts the flavours of this salad, while the mozzarella, olives, and tomatoes add to its visual appeal.

INGREDIENTS

400g (14oz) French beans
salt and freshly ground
   black pepper
3 tbsp chopped parsley
2 tsp lemon thyme leaves
1 tbsp chopped fennel
2 tbsp extra virgin olive oil
125g (4½oz) mixed lettuce
   and spicy salad leaves
400g jar or can artichoke
   hearts, drained and halved
125g (4½oz) mozzarella pearls
   (baby mozzarella
   cheese balls)
16 black olives, pitted
   and chopped
125g (4½oz) cherry
   tomatoes, halved
2 spring onions, chopped
3 tbsp chopped chervil

For the dressing
5 tbsp extra virgin olive oil
½ garlic clove, crushed
1½ tbsp balsamic vinegar

1 Bring a pan of lightly salted water to a boil. Top and tail the French beans and blanch in the boiling water for 5–7 minutes. Refresh in cold water and drain.

2 Place the beans in a wide, shallow salad bowl and season lightly with salt and pepper. Scatter half the parsley, lemon thyme, and fennel over the beans. Drizzle the oil over, toss, and set aside.

3 Make the dressing by pouring the oil into a small jug. Season with salt and pepper, then whisk in the garlic and balsamic vinegar. Next, whisk in the remaining parsley, thyme, and fennel.

4 Scatter the salad leaves over the beans, then the artichoke hearts, mozzarella pearls, olives, tomatoes, and spring onions. Whisk the dressing and drizzle it over the salad. Toss, sprinkle over the chervil, and serve.

Soups and salads
Celery and apple salad with blue cheese dressing

SERVES 4 **PREPARATION 10 MINS** **TO COOK 2 MINS**

The strong tastes of celery and bitter leaves more than hold their own against the **pungency of a blue cheese dressing** in this salad. Walnuts add crunch and texture.

1 In a frying pan or wok, dry fry the walnuts for a couple of minutes until they are golden and crispy. Set aside to cool.

2 In a food processor, mix together 100g (3½oz) blue cheese, vinegar, oil, and a good grinding of pepper. Whizz it up to a smooth, creamy dressing, which should have a thick pouring consistency. Add up to 1 tbsp cold water to thin the dressing a little if it is too thick.

3 In a large bowl, mix the celery, apples, and watercress or rocket. Coat the salad with the dressing and taste for seasoning. Top with the walnuts and the rest of the blue cheese, crumbled or diced into bite-sized pieces.

INGREDIENTS

60g (2oz) walnuts, chopped
300g (10oz) blue cheese, such as Dolcelatte or Gorgonzola
4 tbsp cider vinegar
4 tbsp hazelnut or walnut oil
salt and freshly ground black pepper
4 celery sticks, trimmed and sliced diagonally into 1cm (½in) slices
2 green apples, cored and cut into thin wedges
4 large handfuls of watercress or rocket

Aubergine salad

SERVES 6   PREPARATION **15 MINS**   TO COOK **10 MINS**

Steaming rather than frying the aubergines in this recipe enables them **to absorb readily the flavour of the walnut oil** in the dressing.

INGREDIENTS

2 aubergines, peeled and cut
   into 2cm (¾in) cubes
60g (2oz) soft goat's
   cheese, crumbled
2 ripe tomatoes, deseeded
   and diced
1 small red onion, finely diced
handful of flat-leaf parsley,
   finely chopped
60g (2oz) walnuts, lightly
   toasted and chopped
1 tbsp sesame seeds,
   lightly toasted
sea salt and freshly ground
   black pepper

For the dressing
1 garlic clove, crushed
4 tbsp walnut oil
juice of 1 lemon

1 Cook the aubergine in a covered steamer basket placed over simmering water for 10 minutes. Leave to cool slightly, then gently squeeze the cubes to extract as much water as possible.

2 Combine all the ingredients in a mixing bowl and toss gently. Whisk together all the dressing ingredients and toss the dressing with the salad. Season well with salt and pepper.

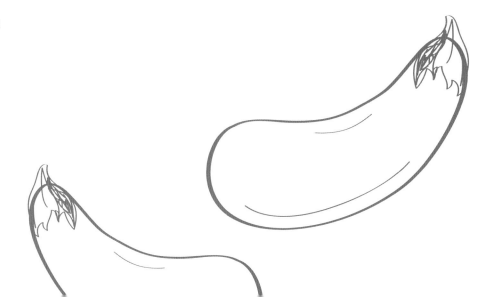

Chicory salad with spinach and pears

SERVES 4   **PREPARATION 10 MINS**

The crispness of the chicory and the mild, soft spinach in this salad work well with the creamy cheese, the sweetness of the pears, and the strong mustard dressing.

1 To make the vinaigrette, place the honey, mustard, oil, and vinegar in a screw-top jar and shake well. Season well with salt and pepper. Alternatively, whisk the ingredients together in a bowl.

2 Cut a cone-shaped core out of the base of the chicory to remove any bitterness, then cut the head into chunks and separate the leaves. Place the spinach, chicory, sliced pears, Dolcelatte, and shallots in a salad bowl. Drizzle the vinaigrette over the salad, toss gently, and serve.

INGREDIENTS

2 heads white chicory
200g (7oz) baby spinach leaves
2 firm, ripe pears,
   peeled and sliced
115g (4oz) Dolcelatte, cut into
   small cubes
3 shallots, finely sliced

For the vinaigrette
1 tbsp clear honey
½ tbsp Dijon mustard
6 tbsp extra virgin olive oil
2 tbsp red wine vinegar
salt and freshly ground
   black pepper

Aubergine, courgette, and flageolet salad with mozzarella and red pesto dressing

SERVES 4–6   **PREPARATION 10 MINS**   TO COOK **25 MINS**

Serve this colourful salad as a **light lunch for four or as a starter for six**. To prepare the onion, cut it into thin slices, discarding the ends, before peeling off the outer layer.

INGREDIENTS

2 small aubergines
2 courgettes
7 tbsp olive oil
400g can flageolet beans,
    rinsed and drained
1 garlic clove, crushed
salt and freshly ground
    black pepper
1–2 tbsp lime juice
115g (4oz) cherry
    tomatoes, halved
1 small red onion, thinly sliced
4 tbsp red pesto (see pp298–9
    or use ready-made)
125g (4½oz) ball fresh
    mozzarella cheese, torn
a few pimento-stuffed
    green olives, halved
crusty bread, to serve

1 Preheat a griddle pan. Trim the aubergines and courgettes and cut lengthways into 5mm (¼in) slices. Brush with some of the oil. Cook in batches on a hot griddle for 3 minutes on each side, pressing down with a fish slice, until tender and striped brown. Wrap in foil to keep warm and set aside.

2 Put the flageolet beans in a large saucepan. Drizzle with 2 tbsp oil and add the garlic, salt and pepper, and lime juice (leaving a little for the pesto), to taste. Heat through, stirring gently, then remove from the heat. Add the tomatoes and onion slices and toss gently.

3 Thin the pesto with 4 tbsp oil, or enough to form a spoonable dressing. Taste and sharpen with lime juice.

4 Gently mix the aubergines and courgettes into the beans. The mixture should now be just warm.

5 Stir in the mozzarella, then spoon the salad into serving bowls. Drizzle the pesto dressing over and scatter with the olives. Serve with crusty bread.

Thai vegetable salad with cabbage and peanuts

SERVES 4   **PREPARATION 15 MINS**

This is **a simpler version of the Thai salad som tam,** which has a hot, salty, sweet, and sour dressing. Add some cooled rice noodles to turn it into a main course.

INGREDIENTS

2 dessert apples
4 carrots, grated
1 small white cabbage, shredded
handful of sunflower seeds
handful of salted or dry-roasted peanuts

For the dressing
2 tbsp light soy sauce
1 green chilli, deseeded and finely chopped
1 garlic clove, grated
juice of 2 limes
1–2 tsp caster sugar
handful of coriander, finely chopped

1 To make the dressing, put all the dressing ingredients in a small bowl and mix thoroughly until the sugar has dissolved. Taste to check the flavour – if it needs sweetening, add more sugar, and if it needs saltiness, add a little more soy sauce.

2 Quarter and core the apples, then chop into bite-sized pieces. Put in a bowl with the carrot, cabbage, and sunflower seeds. Mix together thoroughly.

3 Drizzle the dressing over and toss together so that everything is well mixed. Transfer to a serving dish and scatter the peanuts over.

Squash with cranberries and chestnuts

SERVES 4   **PREPARATION 10 MINS**   TO COOK **30 MINS**

This gently spiced, flavoursome dish makes **excellent use of seasonal ingredients for a warm winter salad**. It is also good served as a side dish.

1 Heat the oil and butter in a large frying pan. Add the allspice, cinnamon, and squash. Season well with salt and pepper and cook over a low-medium heat, stirring occasionally, for 15 minutes, or until the squash begins to soften a little. Add a little more oil, if needed.

2 Add the chestnuts and stir so that they are coated with the oil. Cook over a low heat for 5–10 minutes, then add the cranberries and cook for a further 5 minutes.

3 Taste and season again, if needed, adding a little sugar if the cranberries are too tart (cook until the sugar has dissolved).

4 Pile a bed of rocket and watercress on a shallow dish and scatter the squash mixture over it. Serve warm.

INGREDIENTS

1–2 tbsp extra virgin olive oil
knob of butter
pinch of ground allspice
pinch of ground cinnamon
1 butternut squash, peeled, halved, deseeded, and cut into bite-sized pieces
salt and freshly ground black pepper
240g can ready-cooked chestnuts
50g (1¾oz) cranberries
sugar, to taste (optional)
100g (3½oz) mixed rocket and watercress

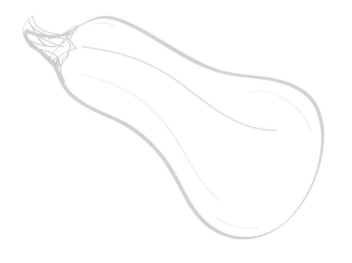
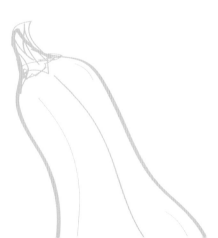

Warm pasta, kale, and duck egg salad with truffle oil

SERVES 4   **PREPARATION 20 MINS**   TO COOK **10 MINS**

If fresh wild mushrooms aren't available, use 140g (5oz) white or chestnut ones, thickly sliced, and a handful of dried **morels, chanterelles, or porcini,** reconstituted.

INGREDIENTS

4 large duck eggs, scrubbed
salt and freshly ground
   black pepper
225g (8oz) conchiglie pasta
200g (7oz) finely shredded
   curly kale, thick
   stalks removed
knob of butter
2 tbsp olive oil
200g (7oz) mixed wild
   mushrooms, cut up if large
2 tbsp chopped thyme,
   plus a few thyme leaves,
   to garnish
2 spring onions, chopped
4 tbsp truffle oil
2 tbsp white balsamic
   condiment
small black truffle, grated
   (optional), to garnish
warm ciabatta bread, to serve

1 Place the duck eggs in a steamer basket or large metal colander. Fill a bowl with cold water and set near the hob.

2 Add a generous pinch of salt to a large pan of water and bring to a boil, then add the pasta and stir. Bring back to a boil, top with the steamer containing the eggs, cover, and cook for 5 minutes. Add the kale to the steamer, cover, and cook for a further 5 minutes. Quickly take the steamer off the pan and immediately put the eggs in the bowl of cold water. Drain the pasta and rinse with cold water. Drain again and return to the pan.

3 While the kale is cooking, melt the butter and olive oil in a frying pan. Add the mushrooms and thyme and sauté, stirring, for 3 minutes. Season with salt and pepper. Add to the pasta with the kale and spring onions.

4 Whisk 2 tbsp truffle oil into the juices in the mushroom pan, along with the balsamic condiment, and a pinch of salt and a good grinding of pepper. Heat through, stirring, then pour into the pasta mixture. Toss gently.

5 Pile into dishes and drizzle with the remaining truffle oil. Carefully shell the duck eggs and place one on top of each salad. Cut open so that the yolk trickles out slightly. Add a grating of black truffle, if using, and a few thyme leaves. Serve with warm ciabatta.

Bulghur wheat with okra

SERVES 4   **PREPARATION 15 MINS**   **TO COOK 30 MINS**

Bulghur makes a wonderful base for a salad, served warm or cold. Try this piled on a bed of shredded crisp lettuce or spooned into whole leaves.

INGREDIENTS

200g (7oz) bulghur wheat
4 tbsp olive oil, plus extra
    for drizzling
1 large onion, finely chopped
200g (7oz) okra, trimmed and
    cut into chunks
100g (3^1/$_2$ oz) baby corn cobs,
    cut into short lengths
225g (8oz) shelled baby broad
    beans, blanched and popped
    out of their skins
3 garlic cloves, grated or
    finely chopped
^{1}/$_2$ glass dry white wine
handful of dill, chopped, plus
    small sprigs to garnish
salt and freshly ground
    black pepper
2 tomatoes, cut into wedges,
    to garnish

1 Preheat the oven to 150°C (300°F/Gas 2). Put the bulghur wheat in a bowl and pour in enough boiling water to cover it. Cover with a tea towel, leave for 5 minutes, then stir.

2 Meanwhile, heat the oil in a large heavy-based pan, add the onion, and cook over a medium heat for 5 minutes, or until it starts to soften. Add the okra, corn, and broad beans and cook for 2 minutes, then add the garlic and continue to cook, stirring frequently, for 2–3 minutes.

3 Stir in the wine and dill and cook for 2 minutes, then stir in the wheat. Transfer to an ovenproof dish, season with salt and pepper, and cover with foil. Cook in the oven for 20 minutes, stirring occasionally. Remove from the oven, fluff up with a fork, then cover again and leave until warm or completely cold. Drizzle with a little oil and serve garnished with tomato wedges and sprigs of dill.

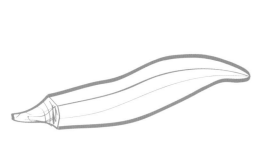
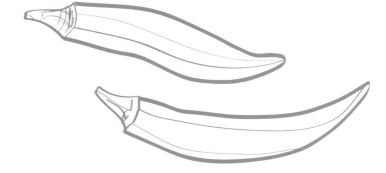

Quinoa, broad bean, and dill salad

SERVES 4   **PREPARATION 15 MINS**   TO COOK **20 MINS**

If possible, prepare this salad at least an hour in advance so that the individual flavours have plenty of time to develop.

1 Put the quinoa in a pan, cover with water, bring to a boil, and cook according to packet instructions. Drain well, rinse under cold running water, drain again, then transfer to a large serving dish.

2 Cook the broad beans in a pan of salted boiling water for 2 minutes until tender. Drain and rinse under cold water. If using fresh beans, peel the outer skin of any that are larger than your thumbnail. Add to the quinoa in the serving dish.

3 Heat the oil in a large frying pan, add the courgettes, and season well with salt and pepper. Stir in the garlic, chilli flakes, and lemon zest, and cook on a medium heat for 5–6 minutes until golden. Stir the courgettes into the quinoa and beans. Add the sultanas, if using, and dill, then mix well. Add the lemon juice and the fruity olive oil. Taste and season, if necessary. Serve with some bread.

INGREDIENTS

200g (7oz) quinoa
250g (9oz) broad beans, fresh
  or frozen (shelled weight)
salt and freshly ground
  black pepper
1 tbsp olive oil
3 small courgettes, trimmed,
  halved lengthways,
  and chopped
2 garlic cloves, finely chopped
pinch of dried chilli flakes
grated zest and juice
  of 1 lemon
handful of sultanas (optional)
bunch of dill, finely chopped
1 tbsp fruity extra virgin
  olive oil
bread, to serve

Fennel and goat's cheese salad

SERVES 6   **PREPARATION** **10 MINS, PLUS MARINATING**

The addition of **diced goat's cheese and a few slices of apple** turns this salad into a light lunch and also adds plenty of red-and-white visual appeal.

INGREDIENTS

1 fennel bulb, finely sliced
  and separated into shreds
½ tbsp balsamic vinegar
3 tbsp extra virgin olive oil
1 garlic clove, crushed
salt and freshly ground
  black pepper
150g (5½oz) mixed salad
  leaves, such as watercress,
  baby spinach, rocket, or
  lamb's lettuce
120g cylinder goat's
  cheese, diced
1 red dessert apple, quartered,
  cored, sliced, and tossed in
  lemon juice

1 In a bowl, toss the fennel with a few drops of vinegar, 1 tbsp oil, and garlic, then season with salt and pepper. Set aside to marinate for at least 1 hour before serving.

2 To serve, mix the salad leaves, fennel, and the remaining oil and vinegar, then season with salt and pepper and divide between individual serving plates. Scatter the goat's cheese and apple slices over the top.

Potato salad niçoise

SERVES 4   **PREPARATION 15 MINS**   TO COOK **15 MINS**

This substantial salad is a twist on a classic recipe. It also works well with baby broad beans, cooked and popped out of their shells, instead of green beans.

1 Boil the potatoes for 15 minutes until tender. Add the beans for the last 5 minutes of cooking time and the corn for the last minute. Drain, rinse with cold water, and drain again.

2 Meanwhile, hard-boil the eggs in simmering water for 8 minutes. Drain and plunge into cold water.

3 Put the cooked vegetables in a large bowl with the onion, separated into rings, tomatoes, cucumber, lettuce, basil, and olives.

4 Whisk the dressing ingredients together until thick and smooth. Pour over the salad and toss gently.

5 Shell the hard-boiled eggs and cut each into quarters. Pile the salad into bowls and top each with 4 quarters of egg.

INGREDIENTS

350g (12oz) baby
  salad potatoes
115g (4oz) green beans,
  topped, tailed, and cut
  into short lengths
115g (4oz) baby sweetcorn,
  cut into short lengths
4 eggs
1 small red onion, thinly sliced
12 cherry tomatoes, halved
¼ cucumber, cut into
  small chunks
1 Little Gem lettuce, torn
  in pieces
handful of basil leaves,
  shredded
handful of black olives,
  pitted if liked

For the dressing
3 tbsp extra virgin olive oil
1 tbsp white wine vinegar
1 tsp Dijon mustard
½ tsp caster sugar
salt and freshly ground
  black pepper

Pasta, noodles, and rice

Pasta with asparagus and courgettes

SERVES 4   **PREPARATION 10 MINS**   **TO COOK 20 MINS**

This easy pasta dish is a simple way to turn asparagus into a substantial supper, with **lemon zest and salty capers bringing out the freshness of the ingredients**.

INGREDIENTS

1 tbsp olive oil
1 onion, finely chopped
sea salt
4 small courgettes, 2 diced and 2 grated
3 garlic cloves, grated or finely chopped
bunch of fine asparagus spears, trimmed, and each cut into 3 pieces
1 small glass of white wine
1–2 tsp rinsed, dried, and chopped capers
grated zest of 1 lemon
350g (12oz) dried penne pasta
handful of flat-leaf parsley, finely chopped
Parmesan cheese, grated, to serve

1 Heat the oil in a large frying pan, add the onion and a pinch of salt, and cook over a low heat for 5 minutes, or until soft and translucent. Add all the courgettes and cook for 10 minutes, or until they have cooked down and softened, but not browned.

2 Stir in the garlic and asparagus spears. Add the wine, increase the heat, and boil for 2–3 minutes. Return it to a simmer and cook for 2–3 minutes more, or until the asparagus has softened. Remove from the heat and stir in the capers and lemon zest.

3 Meanwhile, cook the pasta in a large pan of salted boiling water for 10 minutes, or until it is cooked but still has a bit of bite to it – al dente. Drain, reserving a tiny amount of the cooking water. Return the pasta to the pan, add the courgette mixture and parsley, then toss it together. Sprinkle with the Parmesan and serve.

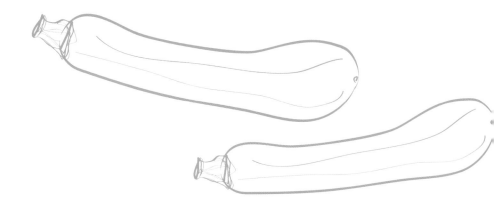

Pasta, noodles, and rice
Lemon and asparagus pasta

SERVES 4   **PREPARATION 5 MINS**   **TO COOK 10–12 MINS**

Try to get the freshest new season asparagus for this simple supper dish, in which lively flavours come from just a few well-chosen ingredients.

1 Bring a small pan of salted water to a boil. Blanch the asparagus spears in the boiling water for 2 minutes. Drain and refresh in cold water.

2 Place a griddle pan on the hob to heat up. Drizzle the blanched asparagus with a little of the oil and season well with salt and pepper. Cook the asparagus on the hot griddle for 5–6 minutes, turning it occasionally until chargrilled. Set aside.

3 Bring a large pan of salted water to a boil. Add the pasta to the pan and cook according to packet instructions, giving it a stir at the beginning to prevent it from sticking together.

4 Heat the remaining oil in a large frying pan and add the garlic, lemon zest, and chilli. Sauté for 30 seconds, then add the lemon juice, plenty of pepper, and the nutmeg. Remove from the heat.

5 Drain the pasta and add it to the frying pan along with the asparagus and parsley. Toss well to mix. Divide between plates and serve sprinkled with Parmesan.

INGREDIENTS

250g (9oz) asparagus spears, trimmed and halved
6 tbsp olive oil
salt and freshly ground black pepper
350g (12oz) tagliatelle
2 garlic cloves, crushed
grated zest and juice of 1 large lemon
1 red chilli, deseeded and finely chopped
½ tsp grated nutmeg
3 tbsp finely chopped flat-leaf parsley
Parmesan cheese, grated, to serve

Farfalle with spinach, avocado, baby plum tomatoes, and pumpkin seeds

SERVES 4   **PREPARATION 10 MINS**   TO COOK **16 MINS**

Available in vacuum packs, slow-roasted tomatoes are soft yet intensely flavoured. Semi-dried or sun-dried tomatoes, drained of oil, may be used instead.

INGREDIENTS

400g (14oz) dried farfalle pasta
2 tbsp olive oil
4 spring onions, cut into
   short lengths
1 garlic clove, finely chopped
1 tsp crushed dried chillies
350g (12oz) baby
   spinach leaves
150ml (5fl oz) vegetable stock
4 slow-roasted
   tomatoes, chopped
175g (6oz) baby plum
   tomatoes, halved
30g (1oz) pitted black
   olives, sliced
1½ tbsp pickled capers
2 avocados, peeled, stoned,
   and diced
squeeze of lemon juice
salt and freshly ground
   black pepper
3 tbsp pumpkin seeds
lemon wedges and a few torn
   basil leaves, to garnish

1 Cook the pasta according to the packet instructions. Drain. Heat the oil in a deep-sided sauté pan or wok. Add the spring onions and garlic and fry, stirring gently, for 1 minute. Stir in the chillies.

2 Add the spinach and stock and simmer, turning over gently for about 2 minutes until beginning to wilt. Gently fold in the pasta and the remaining ingredients. Simmer for 3 minutes until most of the liquid has been absorbed.

3 Pile into warmed, shallow bowls. Garnish with lemon wedges and a few torn basil leaves.

Pasta with butternut squash, chilli, and Parmesan cheese

SERVES 4   PREPARATION **20 MINS**   TO COOK **30 MINS**

Ripening pumpkins and squashes herald the onset of autumn. Perfect for those slightly cooler days, **this dish has the comfort of cream and the warmth of red chillies.**

INGREDIENTS

3 tbsp olive oil

200g (7oz) butternut squash, halved, deseeded, peeled and diced

salt and freshly ground black pepper

1 garlic clove, crushed

½ red chilli, deseeded and finely chopped

8 sage leaves

150ml (5fl oz) single cream

25g (scant 1oz) Parmesan cheese, grated, plus extra to serve

350g (12oz) conchiglie pasta

1 Heat 2 tbsp oil in a frying pan, add the squash, and toss in the oil. Add 3 tbsp water and some salt and pepper. Bring to a boil and reduce the heat to as low as possible. Cover and cook very gently for 10 minutes until soft, stirring occasionally. Leave to cool for a few minutes. Meanwhile, gently fry the garlic, chilli, and sage in a little oil for 2–3 minutes.

2 Once the squash has cooled slightly, put it into a blender or food processor. Add the cream and Parmesan, the cooked garlic, chilli, and sage mixture, and a little salt and plenty of pepper. Blend it all to a fine purée, adding 1–2 tbsp water if it looks too thick.

3 Cook the pasta until it is cooked but still has a bit of bite to it – al dente – and drain it. Quickly reheat the sauce in the pasta pan, adding more water if it seems a little stiff. Put the pasta back into the pan and mix it well, allowing the sauce to coat the pasta. Serve with plenty of fresh Parmesan.

Pasta, noodles, and rice
Ricotta and squash ravioli

SERVES 4   **PREPARATION 1 HOUR, PLUS CHILLING**   **TO COOK 4–5 MINS**

You can make the ravioli a day in advance, if you wish. Dust them with polenta, layer in a sealable plastic box with oiled cling film in between, cover, and chill.

1 Sift the flour into a bowl. Make a well in the centre and add the eggs. Gradually mix together to form a dough. Knead gently on a lightly floured surface for about 5 minutes until smooth and elastic. Wrap in cling film and chill for at least 30 minutes.

2 To make the ravioli filling, cook the squash as for the pasta dish on the opposite page. Cool slightly then blitz until smooth in a food processor. Leave to cool. Place the ricotta, Parmesan, garlic, and nutmeg in a bowl. Stir in the squash and season with salt and pepper. Chill.

3 Roll out the pasta dough very thinly on a lightly floured surface. Cut out 76–80 rounds using a 6cm (2½in) round fluted cutter, re-kneading and rolling the trimmings as necessary. Place ½ heaped tsp of filling on half the rounds. Brush the other rounds with water, place on top, dampened sides down, and pinch the edges together to seal. This will make 38–40 ravioli. Dust with polenta to prevent them from sticking together. Cover and chill until required.

4 Bring a large pan of salted water to a boil. Add the pasta and cook for 4–5 minutes, or until al dente. Drain and return to the pan.

5 For the sage butter, heat the oil, butter, lemon zest, and sage together, stirring until the butter melts, and season with plenty of pepper. Add to the pasta and toss well to mix. Serve in shallow bowls, sprinkled with some grated Parmesan.

INGREDIENTS

225g (8oz) tipo "00" pasta
  flour (or fine plain flour)
3 eggs, beaten
plain flour, for dusting
polenta, for dusting

For the filling
1 tbsp olive oil
175g (6oz) butternut squash,
  halved, deseeded, peeled
  and diced
salt and freshly ground
  black pepper
85g (3oz) ricotta cheese
30g (1oz) Parmesan cheese,
  grated, plus extra to serve
1 garlic clove, crushed
½ tsp grated nutmeg

For the sage butter
3 tbsp olive oil
60g (2oz) butter
grated zest of ½ lemon
2 tsp roughly chopped
  sage leaves

Pumpkin, spinach, and Gorgonzola lasagne

SERVES 4   **PREPARATION 25–30 MINS**   **TO COOK 1–1¼ HRS**

This vegetable lasagne is **rich and satisfying, with fresh sage and nutmeg bringing the flavours alive**. If pumpkin is not available, use butternut squash or sweet potato.

INGREDIENTS

small pumpkin or butternut
   squash (approx. 800g/1¾lb)
   peeled, halved, deseeded,
   and chopped into
   bite-sized pieces
1 tbsp olive oil
salt and freshly ground
   black pepper
8 sage leaves,
   roughly chopped
pinch of grated nutmeg
pinch of dried chilli
   flakes (optional)
pinch of allspice
200g (7oz) spinach
10 pre-cooked lasagne sheets
125g (4½oz) Gorgonzola
   cheese, chopped
lightly dressed green salad,
   to serve

For the sauce
60g (2oz) butter
60g (2oz) plain flour
900ml (1½ pints) milk
1 bay leaf

1 Preheat the oven to 200°C (400°F/Gas 6). Place the pumpkin in a large roasting tin, add the oil and plenty of salt and pepper, and toss to coat; the tin must be large or the pumpkin will steam rather than roast. Sprinkle over the sage, nutmeg, chilli, if using, and allspice and stir. Roast for 20–30 minutes, stirring halfway, until golden, then remove. Stir in the spinach, which will wilt in a few minutes. Set aside. Reduce the oven temperature to 190°C (375°F/Gas 5).

2 For the sauce, melt the butter in a medium pan. Remove from the heat and blend in the flour. Gradually blend in the milk, stirring continuously with a wooden spoon or wire whisk. Add the bay leaf. Return to the heat and bring to a boil, stirring all the time until thickened, then cook for 2 minutes, continuing to stir as before. Add salt and pepper to taste, discard the bay leaf, and set aside.

3 Spoon half the pumpkin mixture into a 20 × 30cm (8 × 12in) ovenproof dish. Seasoning well between each layer, add half the lasagne sheets, half the sauce, and half the Gorgonzola. Repeat to use up all the ingredients. Place on a baking tray and bake for 30–40 minutes until golden and bubbling. Serve with a green salad.

Pasta primavera

SERVES 4   **PREPARATION 15 MINS**   **TO COOK 30 MINS**

As the name suggests, **this light, fresh dish celebrates spring vegetables in Italy**. In cooler climates, it is more suited to serving in early summer.

INGREDIENTS

200g (7oz) green beans, trimmed
salt and freshly ground black pepper
bunch of fine asparagus spears, trimmed
350g (12oz) dried linguine or other pasta shapes
1 tbsp olive oil
3 courgettes, halved lengthways and chopped
pinch of saffron threads (optional)
4 tomatoes, roughly chopped
Parmesan or Pecorino cheese, grated, to serve

1 Place the beans in a pan of salted boiling water and cook for 4–5 minutes until tender, but still with some bite. Remove with a slotted spoon (reserve the water in the pan), refresh in cold water, and roughly chop. Add the asparagus spears to the reserved boiling water and cook for 6–8 minutes until almost tender. Drain, refresh, and roughly chop.

2 Put the pasta in a large pan of salted boiling water and cook according to packet instructions, giving it a stir at the beginning to prevent it from sticking together. Drain well, return to the pan with a little of the cooking water, and toss together to combine.

3 Meanwhile, heat the oil in a large frying pan, add the courgettes, and season with salt and pepper. Add the saffron threads (if using) and cook on a low-medium heat for about 10 minutes until the courgettes turn golden.

4 Add the beans, asparagus, and tomatoes to the frying pan. Stir and cook over a low heat for 5 minutes. Tip the vegetables into the pasta and toss to combine. Serve with the Parmesan or Pecorino and add more pepper, if you wish.

Spicy spaghetti with broccoli

SERVES 4   **PREPARATION 5 MINS**   **TO COOK 20 MINS**

Here is a quick and simple way to make the most of delicious young sprouting broccoli. The **spicy chilli and zesty lemon flavours** are perfect for the winter months.

1 Trim the sprouting broccoli and separate any multiple florets into single heads so that all are similar in size for even cooking. Slice any thicker stems in half and others diagonally.

2 Cook the spaghetti in a large pan of salted boiling water for about 10 minutes, or until cooked, but with a little bit of bite – al dente. Drain and return to the pan.

3 Meanwhile, heat the oil in a non-stick wok or large frying pan, then add the sprouting broccoli and spring onions and stir-fry over a medium heat for 5–10 minutes, or until tender.

4 Tip the broccoli and spring onions into the pan with the spaghetti. Add the chilli flakes and lemon juice, and season with salt and pepper. Toss lightly over a gentle heat. Serve immediately with a sprinkling of Parmesan cheese.

INGREDIENTS

200g (7oz) white or purple sprouting broccoli
400g (14oz) dried spaghetti
5 tbsp olive oil, for frying
bunch of spring onions, chopped
½ tsp dried chilli flakes
juice of ½ lemon
sea salt and freshly ground black pepper
25g (scant 1oz) Parmesan cheese, grated

Pasta, noodles, and rice
Linguine with baby broad beans, cherry tomatoes, and spring onions

SERVES 4   PREPARATION **15 MINS**   TO COOK **18 MINS**

Popping the beans out of their skins can be fiddly. Although not essential, it's worth doing as the **silky texture of the skinned beans enhances the dish**.

INGREDIENTS

450ml (15fl oz) vegetable stock
250g (9oz) fresh shelled or
  frozen baby broad beans
450g (1lb) dried linguine
30g (1oz) butter
bunch of spring
  onions, chopped
150g (5½oz) cherry
  tomatoes, halved
300ml (10fl oz) crème fraîche
2 tbsp chopped parsley
2 tbsp chopped sage
salt and freshly ground
  black pepper
30g (1oz) Parmesan
  cheese, grated

1 Bring the stock to a boil in a saucepan. Add the broad beans, then bring back to a boil and cook for about 8 minutes until tender. Drain, reserving the stock. When cool enough to handle, gently squeeze the beans out of their skins and set aside.

2 Meanwhile, in a pan, cook the linguine according to the packet instructions. Drain and return to the pan.

3 Melt the butter in the rinsed-out bean saucepan. Add the spring onions and fry, stirring, over a low heat for 3 minutes until softened, but not browned. Add the reserved stock, bring to a rapid boil, and continue to boil for about 4 minutes until well reduced and syrupy. Stir in the cherry tomatoes to heat just through, but not soften too much.

4 Stir in the crème fraîche, herbs, salt and pepper, and half the Parmesan cheese. Add the broad beans and mix gently to heat through. Tip the bean mixture into the pasta and toss over a gentle heat until every strand is coated. Pile into warmed bowls, sprinkle with the remaining Parmesan, and serve.

Pasta, noodles, and rice
Vegetable chow mein with black beans

SERVES 4–6   **PREPARATION 15 MINS**   TO COOK **12 MINS**

This simple but delicious stir-fry is a **colourful melange of textures and flavours**. Use cauliflower instead of broccoli, or cucumber instead of courgette, if you prefer.

1 Cook the noodles in boiling water according to the packet instructions, then drain and set aside.

2 Meanwhile, heat the oil in a wok or large frying pan. Add the garlic, ginger, spring onions, pepper, and carrot and stir-fry for 2 minutes. Add the courgette, broccoli, mangetout, and sweetcorn and stir-fry for a further 5 minutes.

3 Add the beans, sauces, and sherry and toss for 1–2 minutes until hot. Add the noodles and toss until well combined and piping hot. Pile into warmed bowls and serve.

INGREDIENTS

4 nests of dried medium
   Chinese egg noodles
2 tbsp sunflower oil
2 garlic cloves, finely chopped
1 tsp grated fresh root ginger
bunch of spring onions, cut
   into short diagonal lengths
1 red pepper, deseeded
   and diced
1 carrot, cut into thin strips
1 courgette, cut into thin strips
1 small head of broccoli
   (approx. 140g/5oz), cut
   into tiny florets
115g (4oz) mangetout
6 baby sweetcorn, cut into
   short lengths
2 × 400g cans black beans,
   drained and rinsed
6 tbsp black bean sauce
2 tbsp soy sauce
1 tbsp mirin or dry sherry

Mixed mushroom and pak choi stir-fry with soba noodles

SERVES 4   **PREPARATION 10 MINS**   **TO COOK 8 MINS**

This dish uses cultivated mushrooms that originate from Japan. They are widely available in supermarkets, but chestnut mushrooms can be substituted, if necessary.

INGREDIENTS

250g (9oz) dried soba or
  brown udon noodles
6 tbsp tamari or light
  soy sauce
1 tbsp lemon juice
2 tsp grated fresh root ginger
2 garlic cloves, crushed
1 tsp chopped lemongrass
  or lemongrass purée
1 tbsp caster sugar
¼–½ tsp wasabi paste
225g (8oz) fresh shelled
  or frozen soya beans
3 tbsp sunflower oil
1 bunch of spring onions,
  trimmed and sliced
2 celery sticks, cut
  into matchsticks
100g (3½oz) shiitake
  mushrooms, sliced
100g (3½oz) oyster
  mushrooms, sliced
100g (3½oz) enoki
  mushrooms, trimmed
  of base and separated
2 heads pak choi (approx.
  200g/7oz), coarsely shredded
2 tbsp sesame seeds,
  to garnish

1 Cook the noodles according to the packet instructions. Drain and set aside.

2 Whisk the tamari sauce, lemon juice, ginger, garlic, lemongrass, sugar, and wasabi paste in a small bowl with 2 tbsp water and set aside. Boil the soya beans in water for 3 minutes. Drain and set aside.

3 Heat the oil in a large frying pan or wok. Add the spring onions and celery and stir-fry for 2 minutes. Add all the mushrooms and stir-fry for 3 minutes. Add the pak choi and soya beans and stir-fry for 1 minute.

4 Add the noodles and the bowl of tamari sauce. Toss until everything is hot through and coated. Spoon into bowls and sprinkle with sesame seeds before serving.

Thai noodle stir-fry

SERVES 4   **PREPARATION 15 MINS**   **TO COOK 20 MINS**

Perfect in stir-fries, **oriental greens add colour and a fresh flavour to the finished dish.** The rice noodles used here are quite delicate – be careful not to overcook them.

INGREDIENTS

175g (6oz) dried thin rice
  noodles
3 tbsp sunflower oil
1 onion, sliced
1 stalk of lemongrass, outer
  leaves removed, woody end
  trimmed, and finely chopped
1 tsp finely grated fresh
  root ginger
1 red chilli, deseeded and
  finely chopped
1 orange pepper, deseeded
  and sliced
115g (4oz) sugarsnap
  peas, trimmed
225g (8oz) shiitake
  mushrooms, sliced
3 heads pak choi, shredded
3 tbsp light soy sauce
1 tsp sweet chilli sauce

1 Soak the noodles in a bowl of boiling water until softened, or as directed on the packet. Drain and set aside.

2 Heat the oil in a wok and stir-fry the onion for 2–3 minutes. Add the lemongrass, ginger, chilli, pepper, sugarsnap peas, and mushrooms, and stir-fry for 2 minutes.

3 Add the pak choi and stir-fry for a further 2 minutes, then add the noodles. Pour in the soy sauce and sweet chilli sauce. Toss everything together over the heat for 2–3 minutes, or until piping hot. Serve at once.

Split pea, noodle, and vegetable pot

SERVES 4   **PREPARATION 15 MINS**   TO COOK **1 HR**

The split peas will gradually absorb all the wonderful flavours of the spices, herbs, and coconut in this simple-to-cook noodle dish.

1 Soak the noodles in boiling water for 5 minutes, or as directed on the packet, then drain and set aside.

2 Heat the oil in a large, heavy-based pan. Add the onion and cook on a low heat for 2–3 minutes. Season well with salt and pepper. Stir in the garlic, turmeric, and coriander and cook for 2 minutes.

3 Add the carrots and courgettes, turn to coat, and cook for 5 minutes. Stir in the split peas and add the coconut milk. Increase the heat and allow to bubble for 1 minute, then add the stock and bring to a boil.

4 Reduce to a simmer and cook on a low heat, partially covered, for 40–50 minutes, or until the split peas begin to soften. Top up with hot water as needed – there should be plenty of liquid. Add the noodles for the last 5 minutes of cooking to heat through. Season well and serve garnished with the chopped coriander.

INGREDIENTS

85g (3oz) dried thin rice noodles
1 tbsp olive oil
1 onion, finely chopped
salt and freshly ground black pepper
2 garlic cloves, finely chopped
1 tsp turmeric
1 tsp coriander seeds, crushed
3 carrots, diced
2 courgettes, diced
225g (8oz) yellow split peas, rinsed
200ml (7fl oz) coconut milk
1 litre (1¾ pints) hot vegetable stock
large handful of coriander leaves, roughly chopped, to garnish

Four ways with
Asparagus

Pancakes with asparagus ▶

TAKES 20 mins **MAKES** 8

Mix 125g (4½oz) **plain flour** and a pinch of **salt** in a bowl. Make a well, crack 1 **egg** in, and stir in a little of 300ml (10fl oz) **milk**. Stir in the remaining milk until mixed. Chill for 30 minutes. Cut 8–12 **asparagus spears** into thirds and boil in salted water for 4 minutes. Refresh in cold water, then mix with chopped **dill**, 250g (9oz) crumbled **feta cheese**, and freshly ground **black pepper**. Heat a little **olive oil**, swirl it around the pan, then tip out. Stir the batter, then spoon in 2 tbsp, swirling it around the pan. Cook for 2 minutes, then turn and cook the other side for 1 minute. Slide onto a plate. Spoon filling onto half the pancake and roll it up.

◀ Asparagus with mustard sauce

TAKES 20 mins **SERVES** 4

Take a large frying pan and add water to a depth of 1.5cm (½in). Bring to a boil over a high heat and add 675g (1½lb) **asparagus spears**. Reduce the heat to low, cover, and cook for 3–4 minutes. Drain the asparagus, rinse, pat dry, and chill. In a bowl, whisk together 4 tbsp **olive oil** and 1 tbsp each **white wine vinegar** and **Dijon mustard**. Beat in 2 tbsp **Greek-style yogurt** and season with **salt** and freshly ground **black pepper**. Spoon the mustard sauce over the asparagus and sprinkle with some chopped **red onion** to finish.

Green and purple asparagus have a **fragrant, grassy flavour**, while white asparagus, which is grown in the dark to blanch it, is sweeter. **Choose stems with tight buds.** Trim the stalks, then peel them if they are thick.

Chargrilled asparagus and Gorgonzola ▶

TAKES 30 mins **SERVES** 4

Heat the barbecue or griddle pan until hot. Trim 16 **asparagus spears** and cook in boiling salted water for 2–3 minutes. Drain and place on the barbecue or griddle. Grill over a medium heat for about 5 minutes, brushing the asparagus with a little **extra virgin olive oil** as it is cooking, and turning as it chars. To serve, divide the asparagus among 4 serving plates. Gently slice or crumble 150g (5½oz) **Gorgonzola cheese** over the asparagus. Sprinkle with freshly ground **black pepper** and drizzle with olive oil. Serve immediately.

◀ Asparagus frittata on crostini

TAKES 40 mins **SERVES** 4

Preheat the oven to 200°C (400°F/Gas 6). Coat 4 slices of **sourdough bread** in **olive oil**, season with **salt** and freshly ground **black pepper**, and bake for 15 minutes. Rub with 1 **garlic clove**. Blanch 8 **asparagus spears** in salted boiling water for 3 minutes. Refresh, drain, and halve lengthways. Heat 2 tbsp olive oil and cook 2 tbsp chopped **onion** for 5 minutes. Add the asparagus and cook for 2 minutes. Whisk 4 **eggs**, 120ml (4fl oz) **double cream**, and 60g (2oz) grated **Parmesan**. Season and pour over the asparagus. Cook until almost set, then brown under a hot grill. Tear into 4 pieces and place on the crostini with **flat-leaf parsley**.

Spicy mixed greens and pea stir-fry with hoisin sauce and toasted sesame seeds

SERVES 4   **PREPARATION 15 MINS**   TO COOK **13 MINS**

This beautiful combination of **fresh-tasting greens with toasted sesame seeds and nuts** is simple to make. For a little heat, add a teaspoon of crushed dried chillies.

INGREDIENTS

2 × 300g packs ready-to-wok thick udon noodles, or 250g pack dried noodles

4 tbsp sesame seeds

2 tbsp sunflower oil

2 onions, halved and sliced

½ small head Chinese leaves, shredded

200g (7oz) Brussels sprouts, sliced

2 heads pak choi, shredded

115g (4oz) shiitake mushrooms, sliced

115g (4oz) frozen peas, thawed

large handful of roasted, unsalted peanuts or cashew nuts

2 tbsp soy sauce

2 tbsp hoisin sauce

90ml (3fl oz) vegetable stock

2 tbsp sesame oil, for drizzling

1 If using dried noodles, cook them according to the packet instructions. Drain and set aside. Toast the sesame seeds in a large frying pan or wok. Tip into a bowl and set aside.

2 Heat the sunflower oil in the frying pan or wok, add the onions, and stir-fry for 3 minutes until softened and lightly golden. Add all the greens, mushrooms, and peas and stir-fry for 2 minutes until the greens are wilted, but still crunchy.

3 Add the nuts, sauces, and stock and simmer for 2 minutes. Add the noodles and half the sesame seeds and toss well.

4 Pile into bowls, drizzle with sesame oil, and sprinkle with the remaining sesame seeds. Serve hot.

Pasta, noodles, and rice
Stir-fried ribbon vegetables with coconut noodles

SERVES 4   **PREPARATION 15 MINS**   TO COOK **8 MINS**

The coconut noodles add a delicious base to this quick-to-cook stir-fry. They also taste great with spiced griddled aubergine and courgette slices.

1 Cook the noodles for half the time stated on the packet instructions. Drain and return to the pan. Add the coconut milk, salt, and half the coriander. Bring to a boil, then cover and set aside.

2 For the ribbon vegetables, pare the courgettes, carrots, and daikon into thin strips using a potato peeler or mandolin. If using a turnip, cut any wide strips in half lengthways.

3 Heat the oils in a wok or large frying pan. Add the vegetables, chillies, ginger, and garlic and stir-fry for 1–2 minutes so they are soft, but still retain some crunch. Add the soy sauce, cashew nuts, and the remaining coriander and toss well.

4 Heat the noodles in the coconut milk until boiling again, then spoon into large bowls. Pile the vegetables on top and serve with extra soy sauce, if required.

INGREDIENTS

250g (9oz) dried brown
   udon noodles
410g can coconut milk
salt
4 tbsp chopped coriander
2 small courgettes
4 carrots
½ small daikon, or
   1 large turnip
1 tbsp sunflower oil
1 tbsp sesame oil
2 fat red chillies, deseeded
   and cut into thin strips
2 tsp grated fresh root ginger
   or galangal
2 garlic cloves, crushed
2 tbsp soy sauce, plus extra
   to serve
handful of raw cashew nuts

Baked vegetable and chickpea pilau

SERVES 4   **PREPARATION 10 MINS**   **TO COOK 25 MINS, PLUS STANDING**

This is a complete meal, but to add a little relish on the side, **serve with mint raita** – just add some dried mint to thick, plain yogurt and season to taste.

INGREDIENTS

2 tbsp sunflower oil
1 onion, finely chopped
2 carrots, finely diced
2 courgettes, finely diced
1 red pepper, deseeded
  and finely diced
½ tsp ground turmeric
2 garlic cloves, crushed
400g can chickpeas, drained
250g (9oz) Basmati rice
500ml (16fl oz) hot
  vegetable stock
85g (3oz) fresh shelled
  or thawed frozen peas
pinch of salt
1 bay leaf
5cm (2in) piece of
  cinnamon stick
4 cardamom pods, split

1 Preheat the oven to 220°C (425°F/Gas 7). Heat the oil in a flameproof casserole and fry the onion, carrots, courgettes, and pepper over a low heat, stirring, for 4 minutes until softened, but not browned.

2 Stir in the turmeric, garlic, chickpeas, and rice until all the grains are glistening. Add the stock, peas, salt, bay leaf, and spices. Bring to a boil, stir, cover, and cook in the oven for 20 minutes.

3 Remove from the oven, but do not uncover. Leave to stand for 10 minutes, then fluff up with a fork. Remove the bay leaf and spices, if liked, before serving.

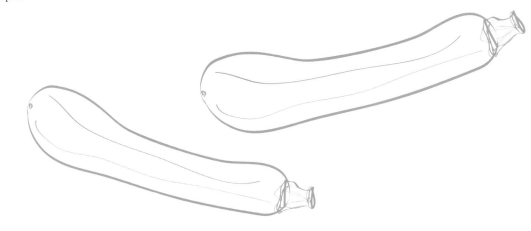

Cinnamon, almond, and raisin brown rice pilaf with griddled aubergine

SERVES 4   **PREPARATION 10 MINS**   TO COOK **45 MINS, PLUS STANDING**

There's a real taste of the Middle East in this sweet-spiced pilaf. Use white rice instead of brown, if you prefer – but cook it for 20 minutes only.

1 Pare the strings off the celery with a potato peeler, then chop. Heat the oil in a large saucepan. Add the celery, leek, carrots, and garlic and fry, stirring, for 3 minutes. Stir in the rice and spices and cook, stirring, until every grain is glistening.

2 Add the oregano, stock, raisins, mushrooms, almonds, and salt and pepper. Bring to a boil, stirring, then reduce the heat to low. Cover and cook for 40 minutes, then remove from the heat and leave to stand for 5 minutes.

3 While the rice is cooking, heat a griddle pan. Brush the aubergine slices with oil and griddle in batches for 2–3 minutes on each side until striped brown and tender, pressing down with a fish slice as they cook. Set aside and keep warm.

4 Fluff up the rice, taste, and adjust the seasoning, if necessary. Gently stir in the aubergine slices and feta, pile onto warmed plates, and garnish with a few sliced olives.

INGREDIENTS

2 celery sticks
2 tbsp sunflower oil, plus extra for brushing
1 leek, chopped
2 carrots, chopped
1 garlic clove, crushed
225g (8oz) brown Basmati rice
1 tsp ground cinnamon
1 tsp grated fresh root ginger
½ tsp ground cumin
1 tsp dried oregano
750ml (1¼ pints) vegetable stock
4 tbsp raisins
115g (4oz) chestnut mushrooms, sliced
115g (4oz) whole blanched almonds
salt and freshly ground black pepper
2 aubergines, cut lengthways into 5mm (¼in) thick slices
200g (7oz) feta cheese, diced
a few sliced black and green olives, to garnish

Vegetable ramen noodle bowl

SERVES 4   **PREPARATION 10 MINS, PLUS SOAKING**   TO COOK **10 MINS**

Miso paste enhances the flavour of this dish, but omit it if preferred and season with more tamari. **Use dashi powder to make the vegetable stock,** if it is available.

INGREDIENTS

2 × 10cm (4in) pieces wakame

2 heaped tbsp dried shiitake mushrooms

250g (9oz) dried ramen noodles (or brown rice noodles)

1 litre (1¾ pints) vegetable stock

2 tbsp tamari or light soy sauce

2 tsp soft light brown sugar

3 tbsp mirin (or dry sherry)

4 spring onions, chopped

1 red pepper, deseeded and finely sliced

2 heads of pak choi, cut into thick shreds

1 courgette, cut into matchsticks

4 radishes, sliced

225g can bamboo shoots, drained

1 tsp crushed dried chillies (optional)

1 tbsp red miso paste

250g block firm tofu, cut into 8 slices

sweet chilli sauce, to drizzle

1 Soak the wakame and mushrooms in 300ml (10fl oz) warm water for 30 minutes. Lift out the wakame and cut out any thick stalk, if necessary. If the wakame is large, cut into pieces before returning to the soaking water with the mushrooms.

2 Cook the noodles according to the packet instructions. Drain. Put the stock in a large saucepan with the remaining ingredients, except the miso paste and tofu. Add the wakame, mushrooms, and soaking water. Bring to a boil, reduce the heat, and simmer for 3 minutes.

3 Blend a ladleful of the stock with the miso paste until smooth. Pour back into the pan and stir gently. Taste and add more tamari, if necessary. Make sure the soup is very hot, but not boiling.

4 Divide the noodles between 4 large open soup bowls. Add 2 slices of tofu to each bowl and ladle the very hot soup over. Serve at once with sweet chilli sauce to drizzle over, if using.

Fiery peanut and pepper noodles

SERVES 4   **PREPARATION 20 MINS**   TO COOK **4–5 MINS**

This is **a great meal to put together in a hurry.** If fresh noodles aren't to hand, use 250g (9oz) dried noodles, reconstituted according to packet instructions.

INGREDIENTS

1 red pepper
1 green pepper
1 tbsp sunflower oil
4 spring onions, chopped
1 garlic clove, finely chopped
1 courgette, finely chopped
1–2 green jalapeño chillies,
    deseeded and chopped
1 tsp grated root ginger
1 tbsp chopped
    flat-leaf parsley
1 tbsp chopped coriander,
    plus a few torn leaves,
    to garnish
grated zest and juice of 1 lime
4 tbsp crunchy wholegrain
    peanut butter
3 tbsp soy sauce
1 tbsp dry sherry
500g (1lb 2oz) fresh
    egg noodles
60g (2oz) roasted peanuts,
    chopped, to garnish

1 Grill the peppers for about 15 minutes, turning once or twice, until blackened in places. Put in a plastic bag and leave until cold. Rub off the skins and dice the flesh, discarding the stalk and seeds.

2 Heat the oil in a wok or large frying pan. Add the spring onions, garlic, and courgette and stir-fry for 1 minute. Add the peppers, chillies, ginger, herbs, lime zest and juice, peanut butter, soy sauce, sherry, and 9 tbsp water. Stir until the peanut butter melts. Add the noodles, then toss for 2 minutes until piping hot. Pile into warmed bowls and sprinkle with peanuts and a few torn coriander leaves.

Mushroom orzotto

SERVES 4   **PREPARATION 10 MINS, PLUS SOAKING**   TO COOK **45 MINS**

Barley makes a fabulous, risotto-type dish that is easy to cook. Unlike rice, it can produce a creamy, nutty-textured result with the liquid added all in one go.

1 Soak the dried mushrooms in boiling water for 30 minutes until tender. Drain, chop, and set aside.

2 In a pan, soften the onion and garlic in the butter, stirring, for 2 minutes. Add the fresh mushrooms and wine. Simmer for 2 minutes. Stir in the barley and thyme. Add the stock and season with salt and pepper. Bring to a boil, then simmer for about 40 minutes, stirring twice, until the barley is tender, but with a bit of bite, and the liquid is almost absorbed.

3 Add the chopped mushrooms and cream to the mixture and heat through, but do not boil. Garnish with thyme leaves and serve with the Parmesan cheese.

INGREDIENTS

1 tbsp dried mushrooms
1 onion, chopped
1 garlic clove, crushed
15g (½oz) butter
225g (8oz) chestnut
  mushrooms, sliced
150ml (5fl oz) dry white wine
200g (7oz) pearl barley
2 tsp chopped thyme, plus
  a few leaves, to garnish
750ml (1¼ pints)
  vegetable stock
salt and freshly ground
  black pepper
2–3 tbsp single cream
Parmesan cheese, grated,
  to serve

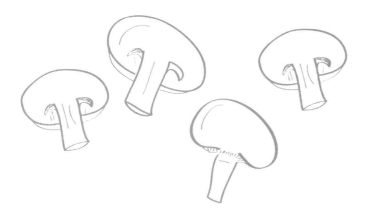

Cashew nut paella

SERVES 4   PREPARATION **10 MINS**   TO COOK **25 MINS**

Cashews are expensive nuts, but they make a delicious paella. Try substituting chopped cooked chestnuts or even toasted hazelnuts for a change.

INGREDIENTS

large pinch of saffron strands
750ml (1¼ pints) hot
   vegetable stock
2 tbsp olive oil
1 leek, chopped
1 onion, chopped
2 garlic cloves, crushed
1 red pepper, deseeded
   and chopped
1 carrot, chopped
250g (9oz) paella rice
150ml (5fl oz) dry white wine
115g (4oz) chestnut
   mushrooms, sliced
115g (4oz) roasted, unsalted
   cashew nuts
salt and freshly ground
   black pepper
115g (4oz) fresh shelled
   or frozen peas
1½ tbsp chopped thyme
4 tomatoes, quartered
½ tsp smoked paprika
sprig of flat-leaf parsley and
   lemon wedges, to garnish
crusty bread and green
   salad, to serve

1 Put the saffron in the stock to infuse. Heat the oil in a paella pan or large frying pan and fry the leek, onion, garlic, red pepper, and carrot, stirring, for 3 minutes until softened, but not browned. Add the rice and stir until coated in oil and glistening.

2 Add the wine and boil until it has been absorbed, stirring. Stir in the saffron-infused stock, mushrooms, nuts, and some salt and pepper. Bring to a boil, stirring once, then reduce the heat, cover, and simmer very gently for 10 minutes.

3 Add the peas and thyme, stir gently, then distribute the tomatoes over the top. Cover and simmer very gently for a further 10 minutes until the rice is just tender and has absorbed most of the liquid, but is still creamy.

4 Sprinkle the paprika over and stir through gently, taking care not to break up the tomatoes. Taste and adjust the seasoning, if necessary.

5 Garnish with a sprig of parsley and lemon wedges and serve hot with crusty bread and a green salad.

Beetroot risotto

SERVES 4   **PREPARATION 30 MINS**   TO COOK **1 HR**

The deep, earthy flavour of the beetroot and the sharp tang of goat's cheese combine beautifully in this deep purple, rich risotto, laced with fragrant sage.

INGREDIENTS

500g (1lb 2oz) beetroot, peeled and diced

2 tbsp extra virgin olive oil, plus extra for tossing

salt and freshly ground black pepper

6 tbsp sunflower oil

20 sage leaves

2 onions, finely diced

2 garlic cloves, crushed

350g (12oz) risotto rice

1 litre (1¾ pints) vegetable stock

60g (2oz) Parmesan cheese, grated

200g (7oz) firm goat's cheese, cut into 1cm (½in) cubes

1 Preheat the oven to 200°C (400°F/Gas 6). Toss the beetroot in a little olive oil and some salt and pepper. Wrap in foil and cook in the oven for 30–40 minutes until soft.

2 In a small pan, heat the sunflower oil over a high heat until smoking. Drop in most of the sage leaves, a few at a time, and deep-fry for 5 seconds, or until they stop fizzing. Remove and drain.

3 Remove the beetroot from the oven and purée in a food processor with 4 tbsp water, the remaining sage leaves, and some salt and pepper. Set aside.

4 In a large, heavy-based pan, fry the onions in olive oil over a medium heat for 3 minutes until soft. Add the garlic and cook for 1 minute. Pour in the rice and stir so that the grains are coated in oil. Meanwhile, bring the stock to a low simmer in a separate pan.

5 Keeping the stock on a low simmer, add a ladle at a time to the rice, stirring continuously until each ladleful is absorbed, for about 15 minutes until the rice is almost cooked. Add the beetroot purée to the risotto and cook for another 5–10 minutes until the rice is just tender.

6 Remove the rice from the heat and season. Stir in two-thirds of the Parmesan and fold in the goat's cheese. Serve garnished with the deep-fried sage leaves and the remaining Parmesan.

Traffic-light risotto

SERVES 4–6   **PREPARATION 12 MINS**   TO COOK **30 MINS**

This is **a fantastic, colourful dish that is very easy to prepare**. It is quite filling, so will serve up to six people, depending upon their appetites.

1 Cut the squash into 1cm (½in) cubes and discard the seeds and skin. Melt the butter in a large pan and fry the onions until transparent. Add the red pepper and squash and continue to cook for a further 2 minutes.

2 Add the rice and stir until the grains are coated in butter, then add the wine, if using, or a cup of stock, and stir. Add the herbs and salt and pepper, and simmer until the wine (or stock) has evaporated.

3 Stir in 2 ladlefuls of stock and simmer until the liquid has evaporated again. Continue adding 2 ladlefuls of stock at a time, allowing it to evaporate until the rice is tender but al dente – about 20 minutes.

4 Add a further ladle of stock, the spinach, and tomatoes, and simmer for a further 2 minutes. Stir, taste, and season again, if necessary. Serve the grated cheese separately, if using.

INGREDIENTS

675g (1½lb) any winter squash

75g (2½oz) butter

2 onions, chopped

2 red peppers, deseeded
  and chopped

350g (12oz) arborio rice

1 large glass white
  wine (optional)

1.2 litres (2 pints) hot
  vegetable stock

large sprig of thyme, leaves
  picked and chopped

8 sage leaves,
  roughly chopped

salt and freshly ground
  black pepper

150g (5½oz) spinach, chopped

8 cherry tomatoes, chopped
  into quarters

2 tbsp grated Parmesan or
  hard goat's cheese (optional)

Pasta, noodles, and rice
Green peas pilau

SERVES 4   **PREPARATION 10 MINS, PLUS SOAKING**   TO COOK **20 MINS**

Always use the right amount of water for pilau rice so it is all absorbed when the rice is done. This dish is great served with cucumber raita, a side salad, and naan bread.

INGREDIENTS

400g (14oz) Basmati rice
75g (2½oz) butter or ghee
   (clarified butter)
1 tsp cumin seeds
½ tsp cloves
1 cinnamon leaf or bay leaf
4 green cardamom pods
1 cinnamon stick
2 red onions, finely sliced
225g (8oz) frozen petit pois
   or peas, thawed
1 tbsp salt
10g (¼oz) mint leaves,
   shredded
10g (¼oz) coriander
   leaves, chopped

1 Wash the rice in cold running water, then soak in cold water for 20–25 minutes, if you have time. Soaking the rice reduces the cooking time and prevents the grains from breaking while cooking.

2 Heat the butter or ghee in a heavy-based casserole over a medium heat and add the whole spices. When they pop, add the onions and sauté until they are golden brown. Add the peas and sauté for 2–3 minutes. Pour in 750ml (1¼ pints) water. Add the salt, cover, and bring to a boil.

3 Drain the rice and add to the casserole. Bring back to a boil and cook, uncovered, for 8 minutes over a medium heat until nearly all the liquid has been absorbed, stirring once – stirring it too much can break up the rice grains.

4 When small holes start to appear on the surface of the rice, sprinkle the mint and coriander over. Cover the casserole tightly and turn the heat to as low as possible. Cook for a further 10 minutes. Alternatively, finish cooking the rice in a preheated 130°C (250°F/Gas ½) oven for a further 10 minutes.

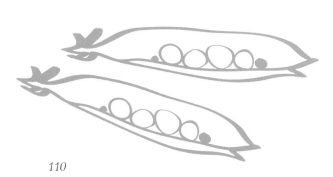

Vegetable biryani

SERVES 6   **PREPARATION 15 MINS, PLUS SOAKING**   TO COOK **1 HR 5 MINS**

Use any combination of vegetables in season for this colourful, mild curried rice dish. It is equally delicious hot or cold, which is an added bonus.

1 Wash the rice thoroughly in cold running water, then put in a pan, pour in enough water to cover, and leave to soak for at least 1 hour. Drain the rice and cook in plenty of salted boiling water for 8 minutes. Drain again and set aside.

2 Heat the oil in a saucepan and fry the onions for about 5 minutes, stirring, until golden brown and soft. Remove half and set aside for garnish. Add the ginger and garlic and cook for 1 minute, then stir in the tomatoes, all the spices, the bay leaves, some salt, and the yogurt. Cook for about 10 minutes or until the oil separates.

3 Add the potatoes, courgettes, carrots, and peas with 120ml (4fl oz) water and cook for 5–8 minutes, or until the vegetables are tender. Remove from the heat.

4 Spread half the cooked rice over the bottom of a large saucepan. Put the cooked vegetables on this layer of rice and sprinkle with coriander. Cover with the remaining rice.

5 Cover the saucepan with a damp, clean tea towel, then with a tightly fitting lid. Stand the saucepan in a frying pan to reduce the heat further and cook over a very low heat for 30 minutes.

6 Mix the rice gently with the vegetables, then spoon into a large, flat dish. Garnish with the reserved onions and serve.

INGREDIENTS

500g (1lb 2oz) Basmati rice
120ml (4fl oz) sunflower oil
4 large onions, sliced
1 tsp grated root ginger
1 garlic clove, crushed
4 tomatoes, skinned and
    finely chopped
1 tsp red chilli powder
1 tsp ground turmeric
1 tsp ground coriander
2 cinnamon sticks
4 black cardamom pods
1 tsp cumin seeds
1 tsp black peppercorns
1 tsp cloves
4 star anise
2 bay leaves
salt
250g (9oz) Greek-style yogurt
2 potatoes, peeled and diced
2 courgettes, diced
150g (5½oz) carrots, diced
150g (5½oz) shelled fresh or
    frozen peas
4 tbsp chopped coriander

Pan-fries
and fritters

Chinese pumpkin fritters

MAKES 20   **PREPARATION 15 MINS, PLUS CHILLING**   TO COOK **40 MINS**

These crisp, bite-sized fritters, fried in a beer batter, make a light supper accompanied by rice. Use only plain flour for the batter, if preferred.

INGREDIENTS

500g (1lb 2oz) pumpkin or
  butternut squash, peeled,
  halved, seeded, and grated
5cm (2in) piece fresh root
  ginger, grated
½ tsp turmeric
1 red chilli, deseeded and
  finely chopped
1 tbsp plain flour, plus extra
  for dusting
salt and freshly ground
  black pepper
sunflower oil, for deep-frying
soy sauce and rice, to serve

For the batter

100ml (3½fl oz) beer
50g (1¾oz) plain flour
50g (1¾oz) gram
  (chickpea) flour
3 tbsp carbonated water

1 Put the pumpkin in a colander or steamer basket and sit it over a pan of simmering water, covered, for 10–15 minutes until the pumpkin is tender. Remove, leave to cool slightly, then squeeze out any excess water. Place in a bowl and mix in the ginger, turmeric, chilli, and plain flour. Season with salt and pepper.

2 Dust your hands with flour, then take a tablespoonful of the pumpkin mixture and shape it into a ball. Repeat to make 19 more round balls. Place them on a lightly floured baking tray and chill in the refrigerator for at least 30 minutes to firm.

3 For the batter, place all the ingredients in a bowl and season. Stir until combined, but still lumpy. If the batter is thin, add more of the flours in equal amounts – it should be the consistency of thick cream.

4 Pour the oil to a depth of 5cm (2in) into a wok or a large, deep-sided, non-stick frying pan and place over a medium-high heat until hot. Don't leave the wok or pan unattended. Take off the heat when not using, and keep a fire blanket nearby in case of fire.

5 Dip the pumpkin balls into the batter one at a time, making sure they are well coated. Fry them in the hot oil, about 5 at a time, cooking each side for 2–3 minutes until golden and crisp. Remove and place on kitchen paper to drain. Serve with a small bowl of soy sauce and some rice.

Sweetcorn fritters with tomato salsa

SERVES 4   **PREPARATION 20 MINS**   TO COOK **10 MINS**

If you're lucky enough to obtain **newly harvested corn cobs**, there is no need to blanch them – they will be sweet and tender enough used fresh.

1 If using fresh corn cobs, remove the husks and silk and cut off the kernels (see p321). Blanch the kernels in boiling water for 3 minutes. Drain, rinse with cold water, and drain again.

2 Sift the flour and baking powder into a bowl. Mix the eggs and milk together in a jug and gradually whisk them into the flour to make a thick batter. Add the corn, paprika, the white parts of the spring onions, 2 tbsp coriander, and the chilli, if using. Mix well and season with salt and pepper.

3 Heat the sunflower oil in a large frying pan and add the batter mixture one tablespoonful at a time. Use the back of the spoon to spread the fritters out slightly, and fry for 2–3 minutes on each side until puffed up and golden brown. Fry in batches until all the mixture is cooked, adding a little more sunflower oil if necessary.

4 Put the tomatoes, the remaining coriander and spring onion, the olive oil, and the Tabasco or chilli sauce into a food processor or blender, and process until blended but still quite chunky. Check the salsa for seasoning. Serve the hot fritters with the salsa on the side.

INGREDIENTS

2 large corn cobs, or 250g (9oz) fresh or frozen kernels
100g (3½oz) self-raising flour
1 tsp baking powder
2 large eggs
4 tbsp milk
1 tsp smoked paprika
2 spring onions, finely chopped, green and white parts separated
4 tbsp chopped coriander
1 red chilli, deseeded and finely chopped (optional)
salt and freshly ground black pepper
2 tbsp sunflower oil
2 ripe tomatoes, skinned and roughly chopped
2 tbsp extra virgin olive oil
dash of Tabasco or chilli sauce

Thai-style beansprout and shredded vegetable fritters

MAKES 8   **PREPARATION** **15 MINS**   TO COOK **25 MINS**

If egg rings (or large metal pastry cutters) are not available, mix the vegetables into the batter and drop ladlefuls into the hot oil. Serve two for a light lunch.

INGREDIENTS

½ carrot
60g (2oz) asparagus tips (approx. 15cm/6in long)
½ small red pepper, deseeded and cut into thin strips
125g (4½oz) plain flour
1 tsp baking powder
¼ tsp ground turmeric
¾ tsp salt
1 tsp grated fresh root ginger
1 tsp finely chopped lemongrass or lemongrass purée
1 garlic clove, crushed
1 thin red chilli, deseeded and finely chopped
4 spring onions, chopped
100g (3½oz) beansprouts
1 tbsp chopped coriander
sunflower oil, for frying
1 tbsp snipped chives, plus extra to garnish
noodle and beansprout salad and sweet chilli sauce, to serve

1 Pare the carrot into thin ribbons with a potato peeler or a mandolin. Cut the asparagus spears in half lengthways and then widthways. Set both aside with the red pepper.

2 Mix the flour with the baking powder, turmeric, salt, ginger, lemongrass, garlic, and chilli. Whisk in 250ml (8fl oz) cold water to form a batter the consistency of thick cream. Stir in the spring onions, beansprouts, and coriander.

3 Place 4 egg rings in a large frying pan. Add about 5mm (¼in) oil and heat until hot, but not smoking.

4 Add about an eighth of the batter (a small ladleful) to one of the egg rings and quickly top with a few strips of each vegetable, pressing gently into the uncooked batter. Repeat with the other rings, using half the ingredients in all. Fry for 2–3 minutes until the batter is puffed up, set, and brown underneath.

5 Lift off the rings with tongs. Flip the fritters over with a fish slice and fry for a further 2 minutes to brown and cook the vegetables. Lift out with a fish slice and drain, vegetable side up, on kitchen paper. Keep warm while cooking the remaining fritters in the same way.

6 Transfer the fritters to serving plates and garnish with a few snipped chives. Serve with a noodle and beansprout salad and some sweet chilli sauce for dipping.

Pan-fries and fritters
Cauliflower pakoras with carrot raita

SERVES 4–6 **PREPARATION 20 MINS** TO COOK **8 MINS**

These delicious morsels make a great starter or, served with a salad, a light meal. For a variation, use chopped broccoli, onions, or mushrooms instead of cauliflower.

INGREDIENTS

½ small cauliflower, white part
  only (approx. 300g/10oz)
115g (4oz) gram (chickpea)
  or wholemeal flour
1 tsp ground cumin
1 tsp ground coriander
¼ tsp bicarbonate of soda
2 spring onions,
  finely chopped
1 large green chilli, deseeded
  and finely chopped
sunflower oil, for frying

For the raita
1 tsp cumin seeds
200g (7oz) thick plain yogurt
1 large carrot, coarsely grated
2 tbsp chopped coriander
1 small green chilli, deseeded
  and finely chopped
generous pinch of sugar
salt and freshly ground
  black pepper

1 First, make the raita. Toast the seeds in a dry frying pan for 30 seconds until fragrant. Tip into a small bowl and add the yogurt. Stir in the carrot, coriander, chilli, and sugar and season with salt and pepper. Chill until ready to serve.

2 To make the pakoras, cut the cauliflower into slices about 5mm (¼in) thick, then chop them into cubes measuring about 1cm (½in). Mix the flour with the cumin, coriander, bicarbonate of soda, ½ tsp salt, and 150ml (5fl oz) water to form a thick batter. Stir in the cauliflower, spring onions, and chilli.

3 Heat about 1cm (½in) oil in a deep-sided frying pan to 180°C (350°F), or until a tiny portion of batter dropped into it sizzles furiously and rises to the surface immediately. Using about a third of the batter, drop heaped teaspoonfuls of the mixture into the oil and fry for 2–3 minutes until golden, turning once. Remove with a slotted spoon and drain on kitchen paper. Keep warm while cooking the remainder. Pile on a plate and serve hot with the raita.

Crushed pea fritters in beer batter with a tomato tartare sauce

SERVES 4–8   **PREPARATION 20 MINS**   TO COOK **10 MINS**

Serve these crispy, fresh-tasting little balls with chips or as a starter. For a nibble with drinks, make each ball a bit smaller and use the sauce as a dip.

1 Cook the potatoes in lightly salted boiling water for 5 minutes. Add the peas and mint and cook for a further 4–5 minutes until both vegetables are really tender. Drain thoroughly, return to the pan, and mash the vegetables with a potato masher. Season with salt and pepper and set aside to cool.

2 To make the sauce, finely chop the tomatoes and mix with the mayonnaise, capers, and sugar, then season with salt and pepper. Transfer to a small bowl and chill until ready to serve.

3 Shape the cooled pea mixture into 24 small balls, each about the size of a golf ball, and coat in the plain flour.

4 In a deep-sided frying pan, heat the oil to 180°C (350°F), or until a tiny portion of the batter dropped into the oil sizzles furiously and rises to the surface immediately.

5 Make the batter while the oil is heating. Mix the self-raising flour and cornflour with a generous pinch of salt and chilled lager. Whisk the egg white until stiff and fold into the batter.

6 Dip the pea balls in the batter to coat completely. Gently drop into the hot oil, in batches, and fry for about 3 minutes until crisp and golden, turning once. Drain on kitchen paper and serve immediately with the tomato tartare sauce.

INGREDIENTS

2 large potatoes, peeled and
    cut into small chunks
350g (12oz) fresh shelled or
    frozen peas
1 large sprig of mint, chopped
salt and freshly ground
    black pepper
4 tbsp plain flour
sunflower or corn oil,
    for deep-frying
60g (2oz) self-raising flour
60g (2oz) cornflour
150ml (5fl oz) chilled lager
1 egg white

For the tomato
tartare sauce
4 tomatoes, skinned
    and deseeded
6 tbsp mayonnaise
2 tsp pickled capers, chopped
pinch of sugar

Pan-fries and fritters
Bean patties

MAKES 8   **PREPARATION 20 MINS, PLUS CHILLING**   **TO COOK 50 MINS**

These mashed bean patties are delicious and satisfying. **If making for children, omit the chilli** and replace half the onion with grated carrot for sweetness.

INGREDIENTS

1 onion, quartered
2 tbsp chopped
  flat-leaf parsley
400g can butter beans,
  drained and rinsed
400g can borlotti beans,
  drained and rinsed
1 tsp cayenne pepper
2 tbsp plain flour
1 egg, lightly beaten
salt and freshly ground
  black pepper
3 tbsp olive oil
green salad, to serve

For the avocado salsa

2 ripe avocados, stoned
  and diced (see pp324–5)
1 large garlic clove, grated
1 red chilli, deseeded and
  finely chopped
2 tbsp olive oil
1 tbsp finely chopped
  coriander leaves
juice of 1 lime
1 tsp sugar

1 Place the onion in a food processor and pulse until roughly chopped. Add the parsley and pulse again a couple of times, then add the beans and pulse again. Transfer to a large bowl and stir in the cayenne pepper, flour, and egg. Season with salt and pepper and mix well. Shape the mixture into 8 patties and chill in the refrigerator until firm.

2 For the salsa, place all the ingredients in a bowl and combine well. Leave for 15 minutes, then stir and season to taste.

3 Heat the oil in a large frying pan on a medium-high heat. Add the patties, cooking in 2 batches if necessary and adding more oil as required. Fry for 5 minutes on each side until crisp and golden, then drain on kitchen paper. Serve with a green salad and the salsa on the side.

Mushroom burgers with chips and dip

MAKES 4   **PREPARATION 20 MINS, PLUS CHILLING**   TO COOK **50 MINS**

Served with miso-roasted sweet potato chips and tahini dip, these burgers have **plenty of gutsy flavours**. Mini versions can be made for children.

1 Preheat the oven to 200°C (400°F/Gas 6). Heat 1 tbsp oil in a large frying pan, add the onion, and cook on a low heat for 3–4 minutes. Add the mushrooms and cook for 6 minutes, or until they start to release their juices. Add the mushroom ketchup and soy sauce to taste and cook for 1 minute. Transfer to a large bowl. Add the breadcrumbs, then trickle in the egg until the mixture binds well. Add some more breadcrumbs if it's too wet and season well with salt and pepper.

2 Make 4 large balls from the mixture and form into burgers. Sit them on a baking sheet lined with baking parchment and chill for 30 minutes.

3 For the chips, toss the potatoes with the oil and soy sauce and spread out in a roasting tin. Roast in the oven for 20 minutes until the chips begin to turn golden and the thinner ones are crisp.

4 For the tahini dip, grind the garlic and salt with a pestle and mortar. Add the soy sauce and mix. Add about 2 tbsp water to loosen it. Stir through the lemon juice.

5 To cook the burgers, heat 1 tbsp oil in a large frying pan on a medium heat. Add the burgers, 2 at a time if necessary, and cook for 3–5 minutes on each side until golden. Drain on kitchen paper. Serve with the sweet potato chips and tahini dip.

INGREDIENTS

2 tbsp olive oil
1 onion, finely chopped
500g (1lb 2oz) chestnut
    mushrooms, pulsed in
    a food processor
1 tbsp mushroom ketchup
2–3 tbsp soy sauce
125g (4½oz) breadcrumbs
1 egg, lightly beaten
salt and freshly ground
    black pepper

For the miso chips
4 sweet potatoes, peeled
    and cut into thin slices
1 tbsp olive oil
1 tbsp soy sauce

For the tahini dip
2 garlic cloves, grated
pinch of salt
3 tbsp soy sauce
juice of 1 lemon

Falafel with dill and cucumber dip

SERVES 4   **PREPARATION 20 MINS**   TO COOK **9 MINS**

These falafel balls are particularly appetizing when served with plenty of salad in split, warm pitta breads, with the dip spooned in, too.

INGREDIENTS

1 onion, roughly chopped
400g can chickpeas, drained
1 small garlic clove, crushed
1 tsp ground cumin
1 tsp ground coriander
2 tbsp roughly
  chopped parsley
salt and freshly ground
  black pepper
½ tsp baking powder
1 egg, separated
splash of milk, if needed
85g (3oz) fresh breadcrumbs
sunflower oil, for frying

For the dip
150g (5½oz) Greek-style
  yogurt
5cm (2in) piece cucumber,
  peeled, deseeded, and grated
1 tsp white balsamic
  condiment
¼ tsp caster sugar
2 tbsp chopped dill

1 To make the falafel, put the onion, chickpeas, garlic, spices, parsley, salt and pepper, and baking powder in a food processor and blend to a thick paste, stopping and scraping down the sides as necessary.

2 Mix in the egg yolk to bind. Add a splash of milk, if necessary, but don't make the mixture too wet.

3 Shape the mixture into 12 small balls and flatten slightly. Coat in lightly beaten egg white, then in the breadcrumbs. Chill, if time allows, until ready to cook.

4 Meanwhile, mix the dip ingredients together and chill until ready to serve.

5 Shallow-fry the falafel in hot oil for about 3 minutes, turning once, until crisp and golden. Drain on kitchen paper. Serve warm or cold with the dip.

Lentil and carrot rissoles

MAKES 8   PREPARATION **20 MINS**   TO COOK **8–12 MINS**

In these tasty rissoles, other roots can be used instead of carrots. **Try a large parsnip to add a sweet earthiness,** or a small celeriac for a subtle celery flavour.

1 Using a food processor or hand blender, purée the lentils to a rough paste.

2 Heat the oil in a saucepan. Add the onion, garlic, and carrots and fry, stirring, for 3 minutes until softened and the onion is lightly golden.

3 Remove from the heat, add the lentils and sage, mix well, and season with salt and pepper.

4 Whisk the egg and yogurt together and add to the mixture to bind. It will be quite wet. Shape the mixture into 8 patties and coat thoroughly in the breadcrumbs, pressing them on firmly as you shape the patties. Place on a plate and chill for at least 30 minutes or overnight, if possible, to firm.

5 Heat about 5mm (¼in) oil in a large frying pan and shallow-fry the patties for 2–3 minutes on each side until crisp and golden, turning once. Cook in two batches.

6 Drain on kitchen paper and serve hot with chutney and a large mixed salad.

INGREDIENTS

2 × 400g cans green lentils, rinsed and drained
1 tbsp sunflower oil, plus extra for frying
1 small onion, finely chopped
1 large garlic clove, crushed
2 large carrots, grated
2 tbsp chopped sage
salt and freshly ground black pepper
1 egg
1 tbsp plain yogurt
100g (3½oz) fresh breadcrumbs
chutney and large mixed salad, to serve

Veggie burgers with melting cheese

MAKES 4   **PREPARATION 15 MINS, PLUS CHILLING**   TO COOK **10 MINS**

It's best to use ready-sliced Gruyère or Emmental cheese for this dish – the slices will **melt perfectly to a lovely gooey finish and add a sweet, nutty tang**.

INGREDIENTS

400g can aduki beans, drained
2 carrots, grated
1 small onion, grated
30g (1oz) chopped mixed nuts
85g (3oz) fresh breadcrumbs
1 tsp dried mixed herbs
1 tbsp mushroom ketchup
   or Worcestershire sauce
salt and freshly ground
   black pepper
1 small egg, beaten
sunflower oil, for frying
4 burger buns, cut in half
tomato ketchup or sweet
   chilli sauce
4 slices Swiss cheese
2 tomatoes, sliced
a little shredded lettuce
French fries and coleslaw,
   to serve

1 Mash the beans well in a bowl with a potato masher or fork. Add the carrots, onion, nuts, breadcrumbs, mixed herbs, mushroom ketchup, and some salt and pepper. Combine thoroughly, then mix with just enough of the beaten egg to bind the mixture together.

2 Shape the mixture into 4 burgers, place on baking parchment on a plate, and chill for 30 minutes to firm up.

3 Heat enough oil to cover the base of a large non-stick frying pan. Fry the burgers over a moderate heat for 6–7 minutes on each side until golden brown. Drain on kitchen paper.

4 Preheat the grill. Toast the buns on the cut sides only. Spread with some tomato ketchup. Remove the bun tops from the grill pan, place the burgers on top of the bases, then add a slice of cheese. Flash under the grill until the cheese starts to melt. Top with some sliced tomatoes and a little shredded lettuce.

5 Quickly place the bun tops in place, either completely on top or at a jaunty angle, and serve with French fries and coleslaw.

Pancakes with mushrooms, garlic, and cheese

MAKES 8   **PREPARATION** **15 MINS, PLUS STANDING**   TO COOK **15 MINS**

These flavoursome pancakes make a delicious light lunch or supper. For added colour, try substituting halved cherry tomatoes for some of the mushrooms.

INGREDIENTS

125g (4½oz) plain flour
pinch of salt
1 egg
300ml (10fl oz) milk
a little olive oil, for frying
salad, to serve

For the filling
2 tbsp olive oil
2 large garlic cloves, crushed
450g (1lb) button
   mushrooms, sliced
200g (7oz) white soft cheese
2–3 tbsp milk
2 tbsp chopped parsley
salt and freshly ground
   black pepper

1 To make the pancake batter, sift the flour and salt into a bowl. Add the egg, then gradually work in the milk and beat to form a smooth batter. Leave to stand for 30 minutes.

2 Meanwhile, make the filling. Heat the oil in a saucepan. Add the garlic and mushrooms and fry, stirring, for 2 minutes. Cover, reduce the heat, and cook gently for 5 minutes. Remove the lid and boil rapidly until only about 1 tbsp liquid is left.

3 Stir in the cheese until melted, thinning with enough milk to coat the mushrooms in a smooth sauce. Stir in the parsley and season with salt and pepper. Set aside, ready to heat through when the pancakes are cooked.

4 To make the pancakes, heat a little oil in a non-stick crêpe pan or omelette pan and pour off excess into a bowl to reuse. Add about 3 tbsp batter and swirl around to coat the base. Cook for 1–2 minutes until the base is golden and the top is set. Flip over and briefly cook the other side. Slide out onto a plate and keep warm while cooking the remaining pancakes, reheating and oiling the pan between each one.

5 Reheat the filling, stirring gently. Spoon an eighth of the mushroom mixture on one quarter of a pancake, then fold it in four. Repeat with the remaining pancakes. Serve hot with salad.

Pan-fries and fritters
Courgette, carrot, and Gruyère pancakes

MAKES 8   **PREPARATION 10 MINS, PLUS STANDING**   TO COOK **25 MINS**

For variety, use any melting cheese for these pancakes and **experiment** with a quarter of a small celeriac, grated, cooked with the courgettes instead of the carrots.

1 Make the pancake batter (see p126, step 1) and leave to stand for 30 minutes. Meanwhile, heat the oil in a saucepan. Add the courgettes and carrots and fry on a medium heat for 5–8 minutes, stirring, until softened and lightly golden. Stir in the crème fraîche, cheese, thyme, and salt and pepper to taste. Set aside, ready to heat through when the pancakes are cooked.

2 Make the pancakes (see p126, step 4). Reheat the filling, stirring gently. Spoon an eighth of the filling on one quarter of a pancake, then fold it in four. Repeat with the remaining pancakes. Serve hot with a tomato salad.

INGREDIENTS

1 quantity pancake batter (see p126)
2 tbsp olive oil, plus a little extra for frying
2 small courgettes, grated
2 young carrots, grated
100g (3^1/$_2$oz) crème fraîche
150g (5^1/$_2$oz) Gruyère cheese, grated
1 tbsp chopped thyme
salt and freshly ground black pepper
tomato salad, to serve

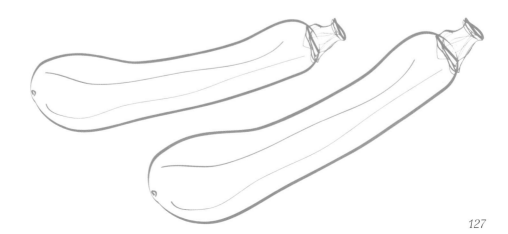

Four ways with
Potatoes

Dauphinoise potatoes ▶

TAKES 2 hrs **SERVES** 4

Preheat the oven to 180°C (350°F/Gas 4). Put 900g
(2lb) **waxy potatoes**, peeled and cut into slices
3mm (⅛in) thick, 300ml (10fl oz) **double cream**,
and 300ml (10fl oz) **milk** in a large pan. Season with
salt and freshly ground **black pepper**. Bring to a
boil, cover, and simmer for 10–15 minutes, or until
the potatoes begin to soften. Using a slotted spoon,
transfer the potatoes to a shallow 2.3 litre (4 pint)
ovenproof dish. Sprinkle over 3 grated **garlic
cloves** and season. Strain the cream and milk
mixture, then pour over the potatoes. Cover with
foil and bake for 1 hour. Remove the foil and cook
for 30 minutes more, or until the top turns golden.

◀ Egg and fennel potato salad

TAKES 25 mins **SERVES** 4

Boil 4 **eggs** for 8 minutes – less if you prefer
a runnier yolk. Cook 250g (9oz) **new potatoes**
in a large pan of lightly salted boiling water
for 15–20 minutes, or until soft. Drain them well
and transfer to a serving plate. Drizzle over
some **olive oil** while the potatoes are still hot,
then season with **salt** and freshly ground
black pepper. Mix in a handful of finely
chopped **flat-leaf parsley** and 1 trimmed and
finely chopped **fennel bulb**. Shell and quarter
the hard-boiled eggs and add to the potato
salad. Serve immediately.

Choose floury potatoes for **mash, chips, baking, and roasting,** and waxy varieties **for gratins, salads, boiling, and steaming.** All-purpose potatoes are mid-way in texture, which makes them **extremely versatile.**

Cajun-spiced potato wedges ▶

TAKES 45 mins–1 hr **SERVES** 6

Preheat the oven to 200°C (400°F/Gas 6). Cut 4 unpeeled **floury potatoes** into thick wedges. Cook in boiling salted water for 3 minutes; drain. Place in a roasting tin with 1 **lemon**, cut into 6 wedges, 12 **garlic cloves**, 3 **red onions**, cut into 8 wedges, and 4 **bay leaves**. Whisk together 3 tbsp **lemon juice**, 1 tbsp **tomato purée**, **salt** and freshly ground **black pepper**, ½ tsp each **cayenne pepper** and **ground cumin**, 1 tsp each **paprika**, **dried oregano,** and **dried thyme**, and 6 tbsp each **olive oil** and water. Pour evenly over the potatoes and toss. Roast for 30–40 minutes, turning the potatoes frequently. Serve hot.

◀ Potato cakes

TAKES 35 mins **SERVES** 4

Boil 450g (1lb) peeled **floury potatoes** in a pan of salted water for 15–20 minutes until soft. Drain, then mash. Mix the mashed potatoes with 1 peeled and grated **onion**, a handful of fresh **chives**, finely chopped, 125g (4½oz) **feta cheese**, crumbled, and 1 lightly beaten **egg**. Season with **salt** and freshly ground **black pepper**. Heat 1 tbsp **olive oil** in a non-stick frying pan over a medium heat. Using floured hands, scoop up large balls of the potato mixture, roll, and flatten slightly. Carefully add to the hot oil and fry for 2–3 minutes on each side until golden, topping up the pan with more oil, if needed. Serve hot.

Potato, celery, and walnut cakes with mushrooms

MAKES 12   PREPARATION **15 MINS**   TO COOK **1 HR 30 MINS**

These golden, crisp cakes are delicious served with celeriac remoulade (see p284), or just with pickled beetroot instead of the mayonnaise and mushrooms.

INGREDIENTS

3 baking potatoes
salt and freshly ground
   black pepper
olive oil, for frying
butter, for frying
1 onion, peeled and
   finely chopped
2 celery sticks, finely chopped
45g (1½oz) walnuts,
   finely chopped
2 tbsp plain flour
2 eggs
pinch of nutmeg
1 garlic clove, chopped
225g (8oz) mixed
   mushrooms, sliced
dash of lemon juice
2 tbsp thyme leaves
2 tbsp chopped parsley
4 tbsp mayonnaise, to serve

1 Place the potatoes in a large pan of cold salted water and cover. Bring to a boil, then simmer for 3 minutes. Drain, cool, and peel off the skins. Grate the potato and put into a bowl. Set aside.

2 Heat a little oil and butter in a frying pan and fry the onion for 5 minutes. Add the celery and cook gently for 5 minutes to soften. Allow to cool, then add the potatoes along with the walnuts, flour, eggs, and nutmeg, and season with salt and pepper. Mix together well.

3 In a non-stick frying pan, melt a knob of butter and some oil. When sizzling hot, add heaped tablespoons of the mixture, pressing down to flatten into round discs. Cook for 5 minutes on each side, turning once. Drain on kitchen paper and keep warm in a low oven until needed. Repeat this process until 12 cakes are made.

4 Heat a little more oil and butter in the wiped-out frying pan. Add the garlic and cook over a low heat until softened, then add the mushrooms and cook for 5 minutes, or until soft and sizzling hot. Season well and add the lemon juice, thyme, and parsley.

5 Divide the cakes between 4 plates, then spoon over the mushrooms and top with a dollop of mayonnaise.

Warm pea pancakes with grilled asparagus

SERVES 4   **PREPARATION 10 MINS**   TO COOK **30 MINS**

A deceptively simple dish to prepare, with the **bright colours of the peas and asparagus** contrasting beautifully with the golden yolk of the poached egg.

1 Put the peas in a pan and blanch in boiling water for 1–2 minutes. Drain and leave to cool.

2 Put the peas and mint into a food processor and whizz together to get a rough texture. Add the melted butter, flour, cream, Parmesan, 2 eggs, and season with salt and pepper. Process the mixture to a stiff paste.

3 Heat some butter or oil in a large frying pan and add 2 tablespoonfuls of the mixture for each pancake. Cook over a medium heat and use the back of a spoon to smooth the top of the mixture. After 3–4 minutes, the edges of the pancakes will change colour. Carefully turn them over and cook for another 2 minutes.

4 Meanwhile, bring a large pan of water to a boil and lightly poach the remaining eggs until just set. Remove them with a slotted spoon.

5 As the eggs are cooking, chargrill the asparagus spears in a hot griddle pan with oil for 4–6 minutes until tender, seasoning with salt and pepper while cooking.

INGREDIENTS

400g (14oz) fresh peas (podded weight) or frozen
large handful of mint leaves, chopped
50g (1¾oz) melted butter, plus extra for frying
4 tbsp plain flour
4 tbsp double cream
2 tbsp grated Parmesan cheese
6 large eggs
sea salt and freshly ground black pepper
large bunch of asparagus spears, woody ends removed
1 tsp extra virgin olive oil

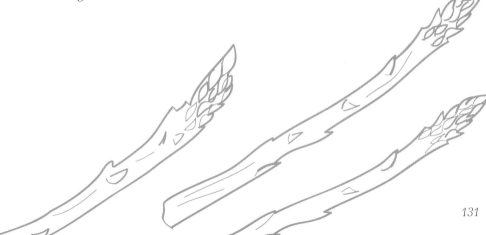

American-style parsnip and walnut pancakes with maple butter

MAKES 8   **PREPARATION 20 MINS**   TO COOK **30 MINS**

These are perfect for breakfast or brunch. For speed, cook and purée the parsnips the night before so that they are ready for making the pancakes in the morning.

INGREDIENTS

1 large parsnip (approx. 225g/8oz), cut into small chunks
salt
125g (4½oz) self-raising flour
1 tsp baking powder
2 tbsp caster sugar
1 egg
250ml (9fl oz) milk
60g (2oz) walnuts, finely chopped
sunflower oil, for frying

For the maple butter
45g (1½oz) butter
3 tbsp maple syrup

1 Cook the parsnips in lightly salted boiling water for about 10 minutes or until soft. Drain and return to the pan, then purée with a hand blender or mash well and beat with a wooden spoon until smooth. Allow to cool a little.

2 In a bowl, mix the flour, baking powder, sugar, and a generous pinch of salt. Gradually beat in the egg and milk and continue to beat until smooth. Stir in the walnuts, then beat in the puréed parsnip.

3 Put the butter and syrup in a small saucepan and melt, whisking until thoroughly blended. Set aside.

4 Heat a little oil in a non-stick frying pan until very hot, then pour off the excess. Ladle in 3–4 tbsp batter to make a pancake about 12cm (5in) in diameter. Reduce the heat to medium and cook for 1½–2 minutes until bubbles pop on the surface and the pancake is golden brown underneath and almost set. Flip over and brown the other side. Slide out onto a plate and keep warm while cooking the remaining pancakes in the same way, oiling and heating the pan between batches.

5 Reheat and whisk the maple butter again. Serve the pancakes hot with the maple butter drizzled over.

Buckwheat galettes with cheese and caramelized onions

MAKES 8   **PREPARATION** 10 MINS, PLUS STANDING   TO COOK 35 MINS

Cook the onions first, then reheat them just before serving. They will keep in the refrigerator for several days. **For the best results, use ready-sliced cheese.**

1 First, cook the onions. Heat the oil and butter in a saucepan. Add the onions and fry, stirring, for 2 minutes. Reduce the heat to low, cover, and cook for 15 minutes, stirring occasionally, until softened and lightly golden. Increase the heat, add the sugar, and cook, stirring for a few minutes, until richly golden. Add 6 tbsp water and cook, stirring, until it evaporates. Remove from the heat, season with a little salt and pepper, and set aside.

2 Mix the flour with a generous pinch of salt in a bowl. Make a well in the centre and add the egg and half the milk. Beat well until smooth. Stir in the melted butter and remaining milk. Leave to stand for 30 minutes, if time allows.

3 Reheat the onions gently. Heat a little oil in a non-stick frying pan and pour off the excess. Add about 3 tbsp batter to make a thin pancake covering the base of the pan, swirling the pan quickly to spread out the batter. Fry for 1–2 minutes until holes appear in the surface and the pancake is almost set and golden brown underneath. Flip over and cook the other side.

4 Slide out of the pan, top with a slice of cheese, then a spoonful (about an eighth) of the hot onions. Fold in the sides to wrap like a parcel and invert on a warmed plate. Keep warm while cooking and filling the remainder in the same way. Serve warm.

INGREDIENTS

115g (4oz) buckwheat flour
1 egg, beaten
300ml (10fl oz) milk
45g (1½oz) butter, melted
sunflower oil, for frying
8 thin slices Leerdammer
  or Emmental cheese

For the onions

1 tbsp sunflower oil
knob of butter
4 large red onions, halved
  and thinly sliced
2 tsp caster sugar
salt and freshly ground
  black pepper

Beetroot and caraway blinis with soured cream

SERVES 4–6   **PREPARATION 20 MINS**   TO COOK **40 MINS**

Blinis are usually made with yeast, but **these are just as light and much quicker to make**. They are best eaten fresh, but can be made in advance and reheated.

INGREDIENTS

115g (4oz) plain flour
pinch of salt
2 tsp caster sugar
2 eggs, separated
250ml (9fl oz) milk
1 tbsp caraway seeds
3 large or 6 small cooked
   beetroot, grated
1 large onion, finely chopped
1 tbsp chopped coriander
   or tarragon
200ml (7fl oz) soured cream
   or crème fraîche
sunflower oil, for frying

1 Sift the flour, salt, and sugar into a bowl. Add the egg yolks and half the milk and beat well until smooth.

2 Stir in the remaining milk and add the caraway seeds and a quarter of the beetroot. Whisk the egg whites until stiff and fold in with a metal spoon.

3 Mix the onion with the coriander and place in a small serving dish. Put the remaining beetroot in a second serving dish and the soured cream in a third. Chill until ready to serve.

4 Heat a little oil in a non-stick frying pan. Pour off the excess. Add 3 tbsp batter and spread out to make a pancake about 10cm (4in) in diameter (you may be able to make 2 or 3, depending on the size of the pan). Cook over a medium-high heat for 1–2 minutes or until golden underneath and bubbles have risen and popped to the surface. Flip over and briefly cook the other side. Remove and keep warm while cooking the remainder.

5 Serve the stack of blinis with the beetroot, onion, and coriander mixture and soured cream. To eat, take a blini, add a spoonful of beetroot, then a little onion mixture, and top with a dollop of soured cream. The blinis may also be made much smaller to serve as canapés.

Stuffed pancakes with spinach, ricotta, and pine nuts

MAKES 8 **PREPARATION 30 MINS, PLUS STANDING** TO COOK **35–40 MINS**

Here, the **classic combination of spinach and ricotta is enhanced** with the sweet tang of semi-dried tomatoes and the crunch of toasted pine nuts.

INGREDIENTS

1 quantity pancake batter
  (see p126)
400g (14oz) spinach
250g (9oz) ricotta cheese
1–2 tbsp chopped rosemary
grated nutmeg
4 tbsp toasted pine nuts
squeeze of lemon juice
4 semi-dried tomatoes in oil,
  drained and chopped
salt and freshly ground
  black pepper
115g (4oz) Cheddar
  cheese, grated

1 Make the pancake batter (see p126, step 1) and leave to stand for 30 minutes. Meanwhile, preheat the oven to 190°C (375°F/Gas 5). Wash the spinach well and shake off excess water. Place in a large saucepan and cook, stirring, for about 2 minutes until the spinach has wilted. Drain in a colander, then squeeze to remove as much moisture as possible and chop, using scissors.

2 Tip the spinach into a bowl and mix with the ricotta cheese, rosemary, plenty of nutmeg, nuts, lemon juice, tomatoes, and salt and pepper to taste.

3 Make the pancakes (see p126, step 4), then divide the spinach mixture among them. Roll up and pack into a lightly greased, shallow, ovenproof dish that will hold the pancakes in a single layer. Sprinkle with Cheddar cheese and bake for about 30 minutes until the cheese melts and is slightly golden, and the pancakes are hot through and crisp at the edges.

Pan-fries and fritters
Ratatouille in tomato pancakes

MAKES 8   **PREPARATION 20 MINS, PLUS STANDING**   TO COOK **25–35 MINS**

To prepare these pancakes in advance, roll them up and place in a baking dish. Sprinkle with grated Cheddar cheese and reheat in a medium-hot oven.

1 Make the pancake batter (see p126, step 1) and whisk in the tomato purée, 2 tbsp water, and the dried basil. Leave to stand for 30 minutes.

2 Meanwhile, heat the oil in a large saucepan. Add the onion, garlic, red and green peppers, aubergine, and courgettes. Fry, stirring, for 5–10 minutes until they begin to soften, then add the tomatoes, tomato purée, wine or 2 tbsp water, sugar, and salt and pepper to taste. Cover and cook over a medium heat for 10 minutes, stirring occasionally, then stir in the chopped basil.

3 Make the pancakes (see p126, step 4). Reheat the ratatouille and use to fill the pancakes. Roll up and serve straight away, dusted with grated Parmesan cheese.

INGREDIENTS

1 quantity pancake batter
   (see p126)
2 tbsp tomato purée
1 tsp dried basil
4 tbsp olive oil, plus extra
   for frying the pancakes
1 onion, halved and sliced
1 large garlic clove, crushed
1 red pepper, halved,
   deseeded, and cut
   into thin strips
1 green pepper, halved,
   deseeded, and cut into
   thin strips
1 aubergine, sliced
2 courgettes, sliced
2 large tomatoes, chopped
1 tbsp tomato purée
2 tbsp red wine
generous pinch of
   caster sugar
salt and freshly ground
   black pepper
2 tbsp chopped basil
4 tbsp grated
   Parmesan cheese

Potato pancakes with apple sauce and chive yogurt

SERVES 4   **PREPARATION 20 MINS**   TO COOK **40 MINS**

Enjoy these pancakes as a delicious light lunch on their own or, for a more substantial meal, **add some grilled halloumi slices** and serve with a tomato salad.

INGREDIENTS

1 small onion, grated
2 large potatoes, peeled
   and grated
1 tbsp fennel seeds
3 tbsp plain flour
2 eggs, beaten
sunflower oil, for frying

For the apple sauce

2 dessert apples, peeled,
   cored, and chopped
1 tbsp lemon juice
knob of butter
caster sugar, to taste

For the chive yogurt

150g (5½oz) Greek-style
   yogurt
2 tbsp snipped chives
salt and freshly ground
   black pepper

1 First, make the apple sauce. Put the apples in a saucepan with the lemon juice and 3 tbsp water. Bring to a boil, reduce the heat, cover, and cook gently for 10 minutes until really tender, stirring occasionally. Beat in the butter, then sweeten to taste with sugar. Put in a small bowl and set aside.

2 Mix the yogurt with the chives and season with salt and pepper. Put in a separate small bowl and set aside.

3 Mix the onion and potatoes together in a bowl. Put into a colander, then squeeze out excess moisture with your hands. Return to the bowl and stir in the fennel seeds, flour, and some salt and pepper, then mix in the eggs.

4 Heat enough oil to coat, just, the base of a large frying pan over a medium heat. Divide the mixture into 12 portions. Add 4 portions of the mixture to the pan and press out to make pancakes about 10cm (4in) in diameter. Cook for 3–4 minutes on each side until golden brown and cooked through. Drain on kitchen paper and keep warm while cooking the remainder in the same way. Serve with the apple sauce and the chive yogurt.

Mediterranean vegetable fritters with aioli

SERVES 4–6   PREPARATION **15 MINS, PLUS STANDING**   TO COOK **20 MINS**

These vegetables have a wonderful summery flavour. **Blanching the pepper ensures it is tender when cooked,** but if you prefer a little more crunch, omit this step.

1 Place the aubergine and courgette in a colander and sprinkle with salt. Toss well and leave to stand for 15 minutes to remove excess moisture. Rinse and dry well on plenty of kitchen paper.

2 Meanwhile, mix the aioli ingredients together, season with salt and pepper, and chill until ready to serve.

3 Blanch the red and yellow pepper pieces in boiling water for 1 minute. Drain and pat dry on kitchen paper.

4 Mix the plain flour with plenty of pepper and use to coat all the vegetables.

5 Heat the oil for deep-frying. Meanwhile, mix the self-raising flour with a generous pinch of salt and 150ml (5fl oz) very cold water to form a creamy batter. The oil is ready when a tiny portion of the batter dropped in rises immediately to the surface and sizzles furiously.

6 Dip pieces of vegetable in the batter, allow excess to drain off, and fry for about 4 minutes until crisp and golden, turning occasionally. Cook in batches and reheat the oil between batches. Drain on kitchen paper and keep warm while cooking the remainder. Serve the fritters hot with the bowl of aioli for dipping.

INGREDIENTS

1 small aubergine, halved
   and sliced
1 large courgette, sliced
salt and freshly ground
   black pepper
1 red pepper, halved,
   deseeded, and cut
   into chunks
1 yellow pepper, halved,
   deseeded, and cut
   into chunks
4 tbsp plain flour
sunflower oil, for deep-frying
115g (4oz) self-raising flour

For the aioli
3 garlic cloves, crushed
150g (5½oz) mayonnaise

Vegetable spring rolls

MAKES 10   **PREPARATION 30 MINS**   TO COOK **15–20 MINS**

Fry these spring rolls ahead of time and crisp them in a hot oven to serve. Rice pancakes can be obtained in Asian stores. Use bought chilli sauce if preferred.

INGREDIENTS

15g (½oz) dried shiitake
   mushrooms, soaked in
   boiling water for 30 mins
1 small carrot, cut
   into matchsticks
3 spring onions, cut
   into matchsticks
85g (3oz) white cabbage,
   shredded
2 garlic cloves, crushed
2cm (¾in) piece fresh root
   ginger, grated
2 tbsp soy sauce
1 tbsp Chinese cooking wine
½ tsp Chinese five-spice
   powder
1 tbsp sunflower oil, plus extra
   for deep-frying
60g (2oz) beansprouts
20 rice pancakes

For the chilli sauce

60g (2oz) caster sugar
90ml (3fl oz) rice wine vinegar
2 garlic cloves, chopped
2 red chillies, deseeded and
   finely chopped

1 Drain and finely chop the mushrooms and mix together with the carrot, spring onions, cabbage, garlic, and ginger. In a small jug, mix the soy sauce, wine, and five-spice powder. Heat the oil in a frying pan or wok. Add the vegetable mix and beansprouts and stir-fry for 1 minute. Add the soy sauce mix and simmer for 30 seconds. Remove from the heat and leave to cool.

2 For the chilli sauce, place all the ingredients in a medium saucepan with 4 tbsp water, bring to a boil, then simmer for 5 minutes, or until slightly thickened. Cool.

3 Dip a pancake in a bowl of warm water for 10–15 seconds, or until soft. Lay it on a damp tea towel and blot until slightly sticky. Place a heaped dessertspoonful of filling in the centre. Fold the bottom of the pancake up over the filling, then fold in the sides, rolling up the pancake tightly. Soak a second pancake. Wrap it around the first layer and set aside. Repeat until the filling is used up.

4 Heat some oil in a deep-fat fryer or large pan until it reaches 180°C (350°F). Cook the spring rolls in the hot oil, 2 at a time, for 3–4 minutes or until golden. Remove with a slotted spoon and drain on kitchen paper. Keep the rolls warm while frying the remainder. Serve hot with the chilli dipping sauce.

Mixed root tempura with dipping sauce

SERVES 4–6   **PREPARATION 25 MINS**   TO COOK **12–18 MINS**

Here sturdy Western root vegetables and leeks are given a Japanese treatment and served as tempura with a hot, sweet, and piquant dipping sauce.

1 Mix all the dipping sauce ingredients together in a small saucepan. Heat gently, stirring, until the honey dissolves, then bring to a boil. Pour into a small bowl and leave to cool.

2 Blanch all the prepared vegetables in boiling water for 2 minutes. Drain and dry well on kitchen paper. Put in a large bowl. Sprinkle with the cornflour and toss to coat.

3 Whisk all the batter ingredients together in a bowl until fairly smooth (the mixture will be quite runny). Heat the oil for deep-frying until a cube of day-old bread browns in 30 seconds when added to it.

4 Dip about a sixth of the vegetables into the batter. Drain off any excess from each piece before carefully dropping it into the oil – it should have only a thin coating. Fry for 2–3 minutes until tender, crisp, and golden, turning over as necessary. Drain on kitchen paper on a large baking sheet and keep warm while frying the remaining batches. Skim off any floating pieces of batter between batches. Serve with the dipping sauce.

INGREDIENTS

1 parsnip, cut into
   short fingers
½ small swede
½ small celeriac, cut into
   small chunks
1 large carrot, cut into
   short fingers
1 leek, cut into thick slices
2 tbsp cornflour
sunflower oil, for deep-frying

For the dipping sauce
3 tbsp clear honey
3 tbsp balsamic vinegar
1 tsp grated root ginger
1 garlic clove, finely chopped
¼–½ tsp dried chilli flakes
3 tbsp soy sauce

For the batter
85g (3oz) self-raising flour
85g (3oz) cornflour
200ml (7fl oz) sparkling
   mineral water
2 tsp sunflower oil
½ tsp salt
¾ tsp cumin seeds

Curries, stews, and casseroles

Kadhai paneer with peppers

SERVES 4–6   **PREPARATION 25 MINS**   TO COOK **30 MINS**

A kadhai is an Indian wok, and **this is the Indian answer to a stir-fry**. The sauce can be used with any vegetables and pulses, so make extra and keep it in the refrigerator.

INGREDIENTS

1 tbsp ghee (clarified butter) or sunflower oil
½ tsp crushed dried chillies
2 red peppers, deseeded and cut into strips
1 red onion, thickly sliced
500g (1lb 2oz) paneer, cut into 1cm (½in) batons
1 bunch of coriander, chopped
juice of 1 lemon
5cm (2in) piece fresh root ginger, cut into julienne

For the kadhai sauce

3 tbsp ghee or sunflower oil
2 garlic cloves, finely chopped
2 tsp coriander seeds, crushed
2 red chillies, deseeded and finely chopped
2 onions, finely chopped
2 tsp grated fresh root ginger
450g (1lb) tomatoes, chopped
1 tbsp crushed dried fenugreek leaves
salt
1 tsp sugar (optional)

1 To make the sauce, heat the ghee or oil in a pan, add the garlic, and let it colour but not burn. Stir, then add the coriander seeds and red chillies. When they release their aromas, add the onions and cook until they begin to turn light golden. Stir in the grated ginger and tomatoes. Reduce the heat to low and cook until excess moisture has evaporated and the fat starts to separate, stirring frequently. Add the fenugreek. Taste and add salt and some sugar if needed.

2 For the stir-fry, heat the ghee or oil in a kadhai, wok, or large frying pan. Add the crushed chillies, pepper strips, and red onion. Stir and sauté on a high heat for 2 minutes. Add the paneer and stir for another minute. Now add the sauce and mix well. Once everything is heated through, check for seasoning, adding a touch of salt if required. Finish with the coriander and lemon juice. Garnish with the ginger and serve.

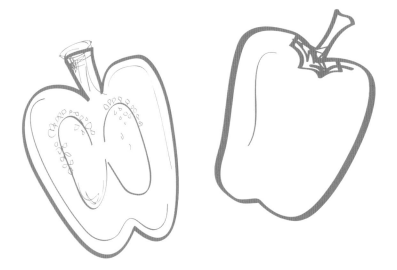

Curries, stews, and casseroles

Seasonal vegetables in spinach and garlic sauce

SERVES 4–6   **PREPARATION 25 MINS**   TO COOK **20 MINS**

For this dish, **parboil hard vegetables first and add the delicate and green ones later.** Cut all the vegetables to more or less the same shape and size.

1 Parboil the carrots, cauliflower, and green beans until al dente (3 minutes for the cauliflower and green beans, 4 minutes for the carrots). Drain well, refresh in iced water, and drain again.

2 Blanch the spinach in boiling salted water until wilted, then drain and cool quickly in iced water. Squeeze dry. Blend in a food processor to make a smooth paste, adding a little water if required.

3 In a heavy-based pan, heat the ghee or oil over a medium heat. Stir in the cumin seeds for 30 seconds until fragrant, then add the garlic and sauté until golden. Add the onion, reduce the heat to low, and cook, stirring, until soft and golden brown. Stir in the ginger and chillies and sauté for 2–3 minutes.

4 Stir in the carrots and cauliflower and cook for 2–4 minutes before adding the coriander and salt. Then add the mushrooms and sauté, stirring, for 2–3 minutes or until they soften. Add the baby corn and sauté for 1–2 minutes. Next add the beans and peas, mixing together well. Add the chickpea flour and stir for 2–3 minutes, then add the spinach paste and bring to a boil, stirring in the butter and cream.

5 As soon as the vegetables are boiling, check for seasoning and correct if necessary. Finish with the fenugreek leaves and garam masala. Do not cook for too long after adding the spinach paste as it will discolour and make the dish look unappetizing. Serve with rice.

INGREDIENTS

2 young carrots, diced
¼ cauliflower, cut into
  small florets
100g (3½oz) fine green beans,
  cut into short lengths
1kg (2¼lb) baby spinach leaves
5 tbsp ghee or sunflower oil
2 tsp cumin seeds
2 garlic cloves, finely chopped
1 large onion, finely chopped
2.5cm (1in) piece fresh root
  ginger, finely chopped
6 green chillies, deseeded
  and finely chopped
1½ tsp ground coriander
2 tsp salt
100g (3½oz) button
  mushrooms
50g (1¾oz) baby sweetcorn,
  cut into short lengths
60g (2oz) fresh or frozen peas
1 tbsp gram (chickpea) flour
25g (scant 1oz) butter
4 tbsp single cream
1 tsp crushed, dried
  fenugreek leaves
1 tsp garam masala

Mangetout, sweet potato, and cashew nut red curry

SERVES 4   **PREPARATION 10 MINS**   TO COOK **20 MINS**

Cooking the green vegetables quickly retains their colour and texture. Butternut squash or pumpkin can be substituted for sweet potato, and tofu for cashew nuts.

INGREDIENTS

2 tbsp sunflower oil
1 bunch spring onions,
    cut into short lengths
1 sweet potato (approx.
    600g/1lb 5oz), peeled and
    cut into walnut-sized pieces
1 garlic clove, crushed
1 tsp grated fresh root ginger
    or galangal
1 tsp finely chopped
    lemongrass
    (or lemongrass purée)
3 tbsp Thai red curry paste
400ml can coconut milk
175g (6oz) mangetout,
    topped and tailed
2 courgettes, cut into
    batonettes (see p320)
12 cherry tomatoes
115g (4oz) raw cashew nuts
1 tbsp chopped coriander
squeeze of lime juice
jasmine rice, to serve
1 fat red chilli, deseeded
    and cut into thin strips,
    to garnish

1 Heat the oil in a large saucepan or wok. Add the spring onions and stir-fry gently for 2 minutes until softened but not coloured. Add the sweet potato and cook, stirring, for 1 minute.

2 Stir in the garlic, ginger, lemongrass, curry paste, and coconut milk. Bring to a boil, reduce the heat, cover, and simmer gently for 10 minutes or until the sweet potato is tender.

3 Meanwhile, cook the mangetout and courgette batonettes in boiling water for 2–3 minutes until just tender. Drain.

4 Stir the mangetout and courgettes into the curry with the tomatoes, nuts, and coriander. Spike with a squeeze of lime juice and simmer for 2 minutes until the tomatoes are softened slightly but still hold their shape. Spoon the curry over jasmine rice served in bowls and garnish with strips of red chilli.

Mixed vegetable curry

SERVES 4   PREPARATION **15 MINS**   TO COOK **25–30 MINS**

In this popular South Indian dish, mixed vegetables are cooked in a delightful spicy tomato masala. The coconut milk makes it creamy and slightly sweet.

INGREDIENTS

1 large carrot
1 potato
100g (3½oz) green beans,
  fresh or frozen
3 tbsp sunflower oil
2 onions, cut into small pieces
1 green chilli, slit lengthways
  and deseeded
½ tsp chilli powder
½ tsp ground coriander
½ tsp ground turmeric
salt
¼ small cauliflower, separated
  into florets
100ml (3½fl oz) coconut milk

For the spice paste
2 garlic cloves, peeled
2cm (¾in) piece fresh root
  ginger, finely chopped
1 green chilli, deseeded
  and finely chopped
½ tsp fennel seeds
100g (3½oz) tomatoes,
  chopped

1 Grind all the ingredients for the spice paste in a pestle and mortar or a blender until fine. Set aside.

2 Cut the carrots, potatoes, and green beans into 2.5cm (1in) pieces and set aside.

3 Heat the oil in a large pan, add the onions and green chilli and cook for about 5 minutes until the onions are soft. Add the carrots, chilli powder, coriander, turmeric, and salt to taste. Mix well. Lower the heat and add the potatoes and 3 tbsp water. Cover and cook very gently for 10 minutes.

4 Add the cauliflower and beans together with the spice paste and mix well. Cook, covered, for a further 10–15 minutes, adding a dash of water, if necessary, to prevent the mixture sticking to the pan.

5 Remove the pan from the heat and slowly add the coconut milk, stirring to blend well. Serve hot.

Spinach and yogurt curry

SERVES 4   PREPARATION **10 MINS**   TO COOK **15 MINS**

This is a **mild dish, but can be made spicier** if preferred. Avoid boiling it after adding the yogurt or it will curdle. A yogurt curry is best eaten with rice.

1 Heat the oil in a large saucepan and add the mustard seeds. As they begin to pop, add the fenugreek seeds. Then add the garlic, dried chillies, and curry leaves and sauté for 1 minute. Add the shallots, green chillies, and ginger and cook, stirring occasionally, until the shallots turn brown.

2 Add the green lentils, tomatoes, turmeric, and some salt to taste. Mix thoroughly, then add the spinach and cook for 5 minutes, stirring occasionally.

3 Remove the pan from the heat and gradually add the yogurt, stirring slowly and constantly. Set the pan on a low heat and warm gently for 3 minutes, stirring constantly. Serve the curry warm with Basmati rice.

INGREDIENTS

2 tbsp sunflower oil
½ tsp mustard seeds
pinch of fenugreek seeds
2 garlic cloves, finely chopped
3 dried red chillies
10 curry leaves
100g (3½oz) shallots, chopped
3 green chillies, slit
    lengthways and deseeded
2.5cm (1in) piece fresh root
    ginger, finely chopped
2 × 400g cans green lentils
2 tomatoes, finely chopped
½ tsp ground turmeric
salt
100g (3½oz) spinach, chopped
300g (10oz) plain yogurt

Vegetable dahl with tandoori paneer

SERVES 4 **PREPARATION 20 MINS, PLUS MARINATING** TO COOK **35 MINS**

Presentation is key to this dish. Choose the loosest iceberg you can find, cut off the stump, then carefully peel off four good, bowl-shaped leaves.

INGREDIENTS

900ml (1½ pints) vegetable
  stock
225g (8oz) red lentils
1 tsp ground cumin
1 tsp ground turmeric
½ tsp ground coriander
1 piece of cinnamon stick
2 tbsp sunflower oil
1 onion, chopped
1 garlic clove, crushed
2 tbsp Madras curry paste
2 carrots, diced
2 potatoes, diced
150g (5½oz) green beans,
  cut in short lengths
2 tomatoes, roughly chopped
4 large iceberg lettuce leaves
paprika, to garnish
mango chutney, to serve

For the paneer

250g (9oz) block paneer
2 tbsp tandoori paste
115g (4oz) plain yogurt
1 large garlic clove, crushed
1 tbsp chopped coriander
salt and freshly ground
  black pepper

1 First, prepare the paneer. Cut the block into 4 strips widthways, then cut each strip in half horizontally to make 8 thinner slabs. Make slashes on each side with a sharp knife, just cutting the surface. Mix the tandoori paste with the yogurt, garlic, coriander, and a pinch of salt. Add the paneer, turn to coat completely, then cover and chill for 2 hours.

2 About 40 minutes before you intend to eat, pour the stock into a saucepan. Bring to a boil and add the lentils and spices. Season well. Bring to a boil, reduce the heat, and simmer for 25–30 minutes until the lentils are tender, stirring occasionally. If necessary, boil rapidly for 1–2 minutes to evaporate any remaining liquid.

3 Meanwhile, in a separate pan, heat the oil and fry the onion and garlic for 3 minutes, stirring, until softened and slightly browned. Add the curry paste and fry for 30 seconds, then gently stir in the carrots, potatoes, and beans. Add 150ml (5fl oz) water and salt and pepper. Bring to a boil, reduce the heat, cover, and simmer gently for 10–15 minutes until the vegetables are tender. Remove the lid and boil rapidly to evaporate any remaining liquid, if necessary.

4 Stir the vegetable mixture into the cooked lentils and season to taste. Gently fold in the tomatoes. Cover and keep warm.

5 Oil and preheat a griddle. Shake excess marinade off the paneer. Griddle for 1–2 minutes on each side, pressing down with a fish slice, until striped and brown in places. Remove from the griddle.

6 Spoon the curry into the lettuce on serving plates. Add the paneer. Dust the plates with paprika and serve with mango chutney.

Black-eyed beans with spinach and tomato curry

SERVES 4   **PREPARATION 10 MINS**   TO COOK **12 MINS**

A refreshing and light curry, this is **easy to make and very versatile**. Double the quantity of beans for a more substantial meal. Take care not to overcook the yogurt.

INGREDIENTS

3 tbsp sunflower oil
½ tsp mustard seeds
2 garlic cloves, finely chopped
10 curry leaves
1 large onion, chopped
2 green chillies, slit
   lengthways and deseeded
½ tsp chilli powder
1 tsp ground coriander
½ tsp ground turmeric
3 tomatoes, chopped
100g (3½oz) spinach, chopped
400g can black-eyed beans,
   rinsed and drained
salt
300g (10oz) plain yogurt
naan breads, to serve

1 Heat the oil in a large saucepan and add the mustard seeds. When they start to pop, add the garlic, curry leaves, and onion. Cook over a medium heat for 5 minutes, or until the onion is soft.

2 Add the green chillies, chilli powder, coriander, and turmeric. Mix well and add the tomato pieces. Stir, then add the spinach. Cook over a low heat for 5 minutes.

3 Add the black-eyed beans with salt to taste. Cook for another minute, or until everything is hot. Remove the pan from the heat and slowly add the yogurt, stirring well. Serve warm with plenty of naan breads.

Okra and aubergine spicy masala

SERVES 4   **PREPARATION 10 MINS**   TO COOK **20–25 MINS**

Okra and aubergine blend well here with aromatic spices for a fairly mild curry. This can be eaten as a main dish with chapattis or as a fantastic side dish.

1 Heat the oil in a saucepan and add the fenugreek seeds, fennel seeds, cardamom pods, cinnamon stick, bay leaf, garlic, and onions. Cook, stirring occasionally, until the onions are golden brown.

2 Add the turmeric, chilli powder, coriander, and tomato purée and stir well. Cook for another minute. Stir in the tomatoes and 500ml (16fl oz) water. Bring to a boil, then reduce the heat and simmer for about 10 minutes, or until the sauce is thick.

3 Add the okra and aubergine to the sauce with salt to taste and stir thoroughly. Cover and cook on a low heat for 5 minutes, or until the aubergine and okra become tender. Garnish with chopped coriander and serve hot.

INGREDIENTS

3 tbsp sunflower oil
pinch of fenugreek seeds
pinch of fennel seeds
2–3 cardamom pods
2cm (¾in) cinnamon stick
1 bay leaf
3 garlic cloves, chopped
2 onions, finely chopped
½ tsp ground turmeric
½ tsp chilli powder
1 tsp ground coriander
1 tbsp tomato purée
2 tomatoes, finely chopped
150g (5½oz) okra, cut
  into pieces
150g (5½oz) aubergine,
  cut into pieces
salt
2 tbsp chopped coriander
  leaves, to garnish

Potato and green bean stew

SERVES 4   PREPARATION **10 MINS**   TO COOK **35 MINS**

This is a wonderful dish, **so easy to make and with a lovely flavour.** The vegetables can be replaced according to seasonality and to make the dish more colourful.

INGREDIENTS

2 tbsp sunflower oil
1 tsp mustard seeds
2 dried red chillies
a few curry leaves
2 onions, chopped
½ tsp ground coriander
½ tsp ground garam masala
½ tsp ground turmeric
¼ tsp chilli powder
2 tomatoes, quartered
2 potatoes, peeled and cut
  into wedges or cubes
100g (3½oz) green beans,
  fresh or frozen, cut into
  2.5cm (1in) pieces
salt
200ml (7fl oz) coconut milk
pinch of crushed black
  peppercorns, to garnish

1 Heat the oil in a large saucepan and add the mustard seeds. When they begin to pop, add the dried chillies and curry leaves and sauté for 2 minutes. Stir in the onions and cook over a moderate heat for 5 minutes, or until the onions are soft.

2 Stir in the coriander, garam masala, turmeric, and chilli powder. Add the tomatoes and cook for 5 minutes. Add the potatoes and mix well, then cook over a gentle heat for a further 5 minutes.

3 Add the beans and salt to taste. Cook for another minute, then reduce the heat to very low. Pour in the coconut milk and 100ml (3½fl oz) water. Stir well to combine. Cook for 15–20 minutes, or until all the vegetables are tender. Garnish with the black peppercorns and serve hot.

Vegetables with lentils

SERVES 4   PREPARATION **15 MINS, PLUS SOAKING**   TO COOK **35–40 MINS**

The lentils add substance and a delicious texture to this curry from South India. Also try it with baby corn or broad beans instead of green beans.

1 To make the spice paste, toast the coconut and spices in a dry frying pan, stirring for 1–2 minutes until brown. Leave to cool, then grind in a food processor, gradually adding about 250ml (9fl oz) water to make a fine paste. Set aside.

2 Bring 300ml (10fl oz) water to a boil in a saucepan and add the lentils, turmeric, chilli powder, and onions. Simmer for 15–20 minutes until the lentils are well cooked.

3 Add the carrots, beans, tomatoes, and potatoes and stir well. Cover and cook for 10 minutes, or until the vegetables are tender.

4 Add the tamarind paste and salt to the vegetables. Cover and cook for a further 5 minutes. Stir in the spice paste. Bring to a boil, then reduce the heat to medium and cook, uncovered, for 5 minutes, stirring occasionally. Taste and add more salt, if necessary.

5 For tempering (heating the spices), heat the oil in a frying pan and add the mustard seeds. As they begin to pop, add the curry leaves and dried red chillies. Pour this over the curry and gently stir through. Serve hot with rice and/or naan breads.

INGREDIENTS

100g (3½oz) split yellow lentils
1 tsp ground turmeric
1 tsp chilli powder
2 onions, cut into small pieces
1 large carrot, cut into
   2.5cm (1in) pieces
100g (3½oz) green beans,
   frozen or fresh, cut into
   2.5cm (1in) pieces
3 tomatoes, quartered
100g (3½oz) potatoes, peeled
   and cut into cubes
1 tbsp tamarind paste
pinch of salt
rice and/or naan breads,
   to serve

For the spice paste
8 tbsp desiccated coconut
2 tsp coriander seeds
1 dried red chilli

For tempering
1 tbsp sunflower oil
1 tsp mustard seeds
10 curry leaves
3 dried red chillies

Chickpea and spinach masala with bhatura

SERVES 4   **PREPARATION 10 MINS**   **TO COOK 30 MINS**

Bhatura is a puffy fried bread traditionally served with chole – spicy chickpeas. **It tastes good with any spiced dish** and makes a lovely change from naans or chapattis.

INGREDIENTS

sunflower oil
2 large onions, chopped
1 large garlic clove, crushed
1 tsp ground cumin
1 tsp ground coriander
1 tsp grated fresh root ginger
¼ tsp ground cloves
½ tsp chilli powder
400ml (14fl oz) vegetable stock
1 tsp caster sugar
3 potatoes, cut into large cubes
2 × 400g cans chickpeas, drained
salt and freshly ground black pepper
400g (14oz) spinach
4 tomatoes, cut into wedges
4 tbsp plain yogurt and 1 tbsp snipped chives, to garnish

For the bhatura

85g (3oz) wholemeal flour
85g (3oz) plain flour, plus extra for dusting
1 tsp baking powder
¼ tsp bicarbonate of soda
½ tsp caster sugar
4 tbsp plain yogurt
2–3 tbsp milk

1 Heat 2 tbsp oil in a pan, add the onions, and stir-fry for 2 minutes. Add the garlic and all the spices and fry for 30 seconds.

2 Pour in the stock and stir in the remaining ingredients except the spinach and tomatoes. Season with salt and pepper. Bring to a boil, stir, partially cover, and simmer for 15 minutes. Stir in the spinach until beginning to wilt, then add the tomatoes, partially cover, and cook for 5 minutes, until the spinach is tender and everything is bathed in a rich sauce. Taste and adjust the seasoning if necessary.

3 Meanwhile, make the bhatura. Mix the ingredients together with ¼ tsp salt and 2 tsp oil, using enough milk to form a soft but not sticky dough. Working quickly, knead the dough gently on a floured surface and shape into 4 balls. Roll out each to a 10cm (4in) round.

4 Heat the oil for deep-frying to 180°C (350°F), or until a cube of day-old bread browns in 30 seconds. Slide a bhatura into the hot oil and fry for about 2 minutes, turning once, until puffy and golden. Remove from the pan with tongs or a fish slice, drain on kitchen paper, then keep warm while cooking the remainder in the same way, reheating the oil each time.

5 Spoon the chickpea masala into bowls. Top each with a spoonful of yogurt, then sprinkle with the chives. Serve with the bhatura.

Potato and tomato curry

SERVES 4   **PREPARATION 15 MINS**   TO COOK **30 MINS**

Potato curry is an extremely versatile dish – it can be eaten for breakfast, lunch, or dinner, either alone or with bread or rice. Leftovers are great cold, too.

INGREDIENTS

2 tbsp sunflower oil

1 large onion, finely chopped

2 large plum tomatoes, skinned and chopped

2–3 red chillies, deseeded and chopped

½ tsp red chilli powder

1 tsp cumin seeds

salt

500g (1lb 2oz) potatoes, peeled and cut into bite-sized chunks, or whole new potatoes

chopped coriander leaves, to garnish

1 Heat the oil in a saucepan, add the onion, and cook for 3 minutes or until slightly browned. Add the chopped tomatoes, then stir in the chillies, chilli powder, cumin seeds, and salt to taste. Add 120ml (4fl oz) water and cook, stirring, until the excess liquid has evaporated.

2 Add the potatoes, together with another 120ml (4fl oz) water. Stir well to coat the potatoes with the spice mixture, then put the lid on the pan. Cook for 15–20 minutes, or until the potatoes are tender but not breaking up.

3 Remove the lid and continue cooking until the oil separates out. Garnish with chopped coriander and serve hot.

Red curry of oyster mushrooms and tofu

SERVES 4   **PREPARATION 10 MINS**   **TO COOK 12 MINS**

Tamarind and kaffir limes add tartness to this rustic curry. Reduce the amount of both for a milder flavour, and try the dish with shiitake mushrooms instead.

1 In a saucepan, simmer the red curry paste in the coconut cream, stirring, for 3–5 minutes until fragrant. Season with the sugar, salt, soy sauce, and tamarind paste. Add the coconut milk, bring to a boil, then add the mushrooms, tofu, spinach, and kaffir lime leaves.

2 Cut the kaffir limes in half and deseed. Squeeze them and add to the curry along with their juice. Simmer for 5 minutes until the mushrooms and spinach are cooked. Check the seasoning and adjust according to taste, then remove the lime shells and serve the curry spooned over jasmine rice.

INGREDIENTS

2½ tbsp Thai red curry paste
120ml (4fl oz) coconut cream
1 heaped tbsp palm sugar or
    demerara sugar
pinch of salt
2 tsp light soy sauce
2 tbsp tamarind paste
400ml can coconut milk
200g (7oz) oyster mushrooms,
    cut up if large
250g (9oz) firm tofu, drained
    and diced
115g (4oz) baby spinach leaves
7 kaffir lime leaves
2 small kaffir
    (or ordinary) limes
jasmine rice, to serve

Heart of palm green curry

SERVES 4   **PREPARATION 10 MINS**   TO COOK **10 MINS**

Heart of palm has a **crunch that offers a wonderful textural contrast to the creamy spicy sauce**. For added colour, throw in some cherry tomatoes at step 2.

INGREDIENTS

5 tbsp coconut cream
4 tbsp Thai green curry paste
400g can hearts of palm,
    drained and cut into
    bite-sized pieces
4–5 baby sweetcorn, each
    cut in half lengthways
light soy sauce, to taste
400ml can coconut milk
a few picked pea
    aubergines (optional)
3 kaffir lime leaves, torn
3 green chillies, deseeded
    and thinly sliced at an angle
handful of Thai (or ordinary)
    basil leaves, torn
jasmine rice, to serve

1 Heat the coconut cream in a saucepan, add the curry paste, and cook over a high heat for 3 minutes, stirring regularly. Add the hearts of palm and corn, and fry for a further 3 minutes or until the paste looks scrambled and smells cooked. Season with soy sauce.

2 Pour in the coconut milk, stirring gently. Bring to a boil and add the remaining ingredients except the basil. Check the seasoning and adjust if necessary. Simmer for 2 minutes, then stir in the basil. Spoon over jasmine rice in bowls and serve.

Aromatic curry of pumpkin

SERVES 4   PREPARATION **10 MINS**   TO COOK **20 MINS**

Try sweet potato and carrot as alternatives to pumpkin and potato. Cooking the paste first releases its wonderful flavour. Serve this dish over noodles or sticky rice.

1 Blanch the potato in boiling water for 3 minutes, then drain and set aside. Heat the coconut cream in a saucepan, add the curry paste, and cook over a medium heat for about 3 minutes, or until it is quite fragrant. Stir regularly to prevent the paste from scorching. Season with the palm sugar and soy sauce.

2 Stir in the coconut milk, salt, pumpkin, and potato, and bring to a boil. Mix in a little water, as this helps to prevent the coconut milk from splitting as the pumpkin cooks. Simmer gently over a medium heat for about 10 minutes, or until the vegetables are tender.

3 Meanwhile, heat the oil in a frying pan and fry the onions, stirring over a medium heat for about 5 minutes until golden and tender. Drain on kitchen paper. Serve the curry topped with the onions.

INGREDIENTS

1 large potato, peeled and cut into bite-sized chunks
4 tbsp coconut cream
4 tbsp Thai red curry paste
2 tsp palm sugar or demerara sugar
2 tbsp light soy sauce
2 × 400ml cans coconut milk
pinch of salt
½ small pumpkin, peeled and cut into bite-sized chunks (approx. 350g/12oz prepared weight)
2 tbsp sunflower oil
2 red onions, sliced

Four ways with
Avocados

Quesadilla with avocado, spring onion, and chilli ▶

TAKES 25 mins **MAKES** 1

Put 4 finely chopped **spring onions**, 1–2 **hot red chillies**, deseeded and finely chopped, and juice of ½ **lime** in a bowl. Season with **salt** and freshly ground **black pepper** and mix. Heat 1½ tbsp **olive oil** in a non-stick frying pan, then fry 1 **wheat** or **corn tortilla** for 1 minute. Scatter over ½ sliced **avocado**, leaving some space around the edge. Spoon on the spring onion mixture and sprinkle with 50g (1¾oz) **Cheddar cheese**. Top with another tortilla; press down with the back of a fish slice. Turn the quesadilla over and cook the other side for 1 minute. Slice in half or quarters and serve.

◀ Avocado with roasted cherry tomatoes and paprika dressing

TAKES 20 mins **SERVES** 4

Preheat the oven to 200°C (400°F/Gas 6). Toss 350g (12oz) **cherry tomatoes** with 1 tbsp **olive oil** in a roasting tin. Add some **thyme** leaves and season with **salt** and freshly ground **black pepper**. Roast for 12–15 minutes. Whisk together 90ml (3fl oz) olive oil, 3 tbsp **white wine vinegar**, 1 tsp **paprika**, a pinch of **caster sugar**, and ½ tsp **mayonnaise**. Season. Halve, stone, and peel 2 ripe **avocados**. Slice lengthways without cutting all the way through, then fan out. Place a fan on each plate with some **wild rocket** leaves and the tomatoes. Spoon the dressing over and serve.

The most widely available types of avocado are the dark, knobbly-skinned Hass and the green, smooth-skinned Fuerte. Both have a **nutty flavour, creamy-yellow colour, and oily texture**; the latter are easier to peel.

Avocado mousse with lime ▶

TAKES 15 mins, plus chilling **SERVES** 4

Halve and stone 2 large ripe **avocados**. Scoop the flesh into a bowl, add the grated zest and juice of 1 **lime**, and mash until smooth. Beat in 100g (3½oz) **low-fat cream cheese** and season with **salt** and freshly ground **black pepper**. Sprinkle 2 tsp powdered **gelatine** over 2 tbsp water in a small heatproof bowl. Leave for 1 minute, then place the bowl in a pan of hot water and stir the gelatine until it dissolves. Whisk 1 **egg white** in a bowl to form soft peaks. Drizzle the dissolved gelatine into the avocado mixture and stir. Fold in the egg white without knocking out the air. Spoon into ramekins, cover with cling film, and chill for 2 hours.

◀ Avocado, tomato, and mozzarella salad

TAKES 20 mins **SERVES** 4

Preheat the grill to the highest setting. Put 200g (7oz) small **plum tomatoes** on a baking tray. Add **salt** and freshly gound **black pepper**, 2 sliced **garlic cloves**, and 2 chopped **spring onions**. Drizzle with 4 tbsp **extra virgin olive oil**. Grill for 4–5 minutes. Place in a bowl with the juices. Add 2 tbsp **balsamic vinegar**, 2 tbsp **capers**, rinsed, 150g (5½oz) torn **buffalo mozzarella**, and shredded **basil leaves**. Toss gently. Peel, stone, and quarter 2 ripe **avocados**. Place 2 quarters on each plate. Spoon the tomato mixture over and drizzle with balsamic vinegar. Serve immediately.

Vietnamese vegetable and tofu curry

SERVES 4   PREPARATION **10 MINS**   TO COOK **25 MINS**

This recipe combines smooth tofu, crunchy bamboo, and slightly smoky aubergine to make a subtle, mild curry. Try it over brown jasmine rice for a change.

INGREDIENTS

1½ tbsp sunflower oil
1 large garlic clove, crushed
1 shallot, thinly sliced
1 tbsp curry powder
2 tsp palm sugar or
    demerara sugar
400ml can coconut milk
juice of ½ lime
1 tsp annatto seed extract
    or ground turmeric
1 stalk lemongrass, finely
    chopped, or 2 tsp purée
1 kaffir lime leaf, bruised
salt
500g (1lb 2oz) firm tofu, cut
    into 2.5cm (1in) cubes
225g can bamboo
    shoots, drained
1 aubergine, halved
    lengthways and cut
    into 2.5cm (1in) pieces
a few coriander leaves or Thai
    basil leaves, to garnish

1 Heat the oil in a saucepan over a high heat and stir-fry the garlic and shallot for about 5 minutes, or until they are golden. Add the curry powder and sugar and continue to stir-fry for 1 minute, or until fragrant.

2 Add the coconut milk, lime juice, annatto seed extract or turmeric, lemongrass, and kaffir lime leaf. Bring to a boil, then reduce the heat to low. Adjust the seasoning with salt and add the tofu, bamboo shoots, and aubergine. Simmer, covered, for 10–15 minutes, or until the aubergine is tender. Discard the lemongrass. Serve garnished with coriander or Thai basil.

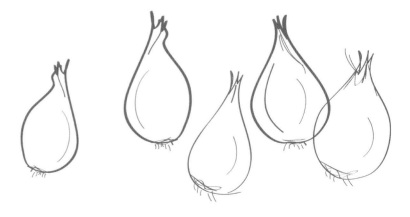

Thai-style baby aubergine curry

SERVES 4   **PREPARATION 20–25 MINS**   TO COOK **40 MINS**

In this **light curry with hot, sweet, and sour flavours**, Thai basil makes a good alternative to coriander. Non-vegetarians can add Thai fish sauce instead of soy sauce.

1 Heat half the oil in a large, heavy-based pan, add the onion, and cook on a low heat for 2–3 minutes. Stir in the garlic, cinnamon stick, star anise, chilli, lemongrass, and lime leaves, and season with salt and pepper. Add the remaining oil and aubergine. Cook over a medium heat for 5 minutes, or until the aubergine begins to turn slightly golden.

2 Add a little coconut milk, sprinkle in the sugar, stir, and bring to a boil. Add the remaining coconut milk and the stock, and bring to a boil. Reduce the heat, add a splash of light soy sauce, and simmer, uncovered, for 20 minutes. In a separate bowl, cook the noodles according to the packet instructions. Drain.

3 Taste the curry and add more soy sauce or sugar if needed. Remove the star anise and cinnamon stick. Chop half the coriander and stir in. Divide the noodles between 4 bowls and ladle the curry over. Top with the remaining coriander and serve with the lime wedges.

INGREDIENTS

2 tbsp sunflower oil
1 onion, finely chopped
3 garlic cloves, finely chopped
1 cinnamon stick
1 star anise
1 red chilli, deseeded and
  finely chopped
1 stalk lemongrass, finely
  chopped, or 2 tsp purée
4 kaffir lime leaves, bruised
salt and freshly ground
  black pepper
8 baby aubergines, sliced into
  quarters lengthways, or
  2 regular aubergines,
  roughly chopped
400ml can coconut milk
½ tsp palm sugar or
  demerara sugar
600ml (1 pint) vegetable stock
light soy sauce, to taste
200g (7oz) dried rice noodles
handful of coriander leaves
lime wedges, to serve

Spring vegetable stew with fresh herb dumplings

SERVES 4–6   **PREPARATION 20 MINS**   **TO COOK 35 MINS**

This colourful mixture of fresh vegetables, **topped with fluffy dumplings**, has two kinds of dried beans for protein as well as some grated cheese.

INGREDIENTS

30g (1oz) butter

1 tbsp sunflower oil

1 bunch spring onions, cut into short lengths

2 leeks, cut into chunky pieces

2 large waxy potatoes, peeled and cut into bite-sized pieces

4 young carrots, cut into chunks

1 large turnip, cut into bite-sized pieces

400g can chopped tomatoes

600ml (1 pint) vegetable stock

400g can haricot beans, drained

400g can borlotti beans, drained

1 large bay leaf

salt and freshly ground black pepper

1 head spring greens, finely shredded

grated Cheddar or Gruyère cheese, to serve

For the dumplings

115g (4oz) self-raising flour

60g (2oz) butter

2 tbsp chopped parsley

2 tsp chopped thyme

2 tsp chopped sage

1 Melt the butter in a large saucepan with the oil. Add the spring onions, leeks, potatoes, carrots, and turnip and fry gently, stirring, for 5 minutes until slightly softened, but not browned.

2 Add the tomatoes, stock, beans, bay leaf, and some salt and pepper. Bring to a boil, reduce the heat, cover, and simmer gently for 15 minutes. Discard the bay leaf. Taste and adjust the seasoning, if necessary.

3 To make the dumplings, mix the flour with a pinch of salt in a bowl. Rub in the butter until the mixture resembles breadcrumbs, then stir in the herbs. Using a round-bladed knife, mix in enough cold water to form a soft but not sticky dough. Quickly roll the dough into 8 balls.

4 Add the greens to the stew and press down well. Bring back to a boil, reduce the heat, and drop the dumplings around the top. Cover and simmer for 15 minutes until the dumplings are fluffy and cooked through. Serve hot with grated cheese to sprinkle over.

Chickpea and vegetable goulash

SERVES 4   **PREPARATION 20 MINS**   **TO COOK 30 MINS**

In winter, use root vegetables and shredded white cabbage for a seasonal twist. For a more substantial meal, add some diced sweet potato, too.

1 Heat the oil in a large non-stick saucepan. Add the onion and fry, stirring, for 2 minutes to soften. Add the aubergine, yellow and red peppers, and courgettes and cook, stirring, for 2 minutes.

2 Stir in the garlic and both types of paprika, then add the tomatoes, chickpeas, tomato purée, sugar, stock, bay leaf, and a little salt and a generous grinding of pepper. Bring to a boil, reduce the heat, partially cover, and simmer for 30 minutes, stirring occasionally, until everything is tender. If necessary, remove the lid and boil rapidly for a few minutes to thicken the liquid so everything is bathed in a rich, thick sauce. Discard the bay leaf. Stir in the parsley. Taste and adjust the seasoning, if necessary.

3 Spoon the goulash into warmed bowls and top with a dollop of yogurt and a sprinkling of caraway seeds. Serve with plenty of crusty bread and a green salad.

INGREDIENTS

2 tbsp olive oil
1 large onion, chopped
1 large aubergine, diced
1 yellow pepper, deseeded
  and diced
1 red pepper, deseeded
  and diced
2 courgettes, thickly sliced
1 large garlic clove, crushed
1 tsp smoked paprika
1 tbsp sweet paprika
400g can chopped tomatoes
2 × 400g cans chickpeas,
  drained
2 tbsp tomato purée
½ tsp caster sugar
150ml (5fl oz) vegetable stock
1 bay leaf
salt and freshly ground
  black pepper
2 tbsp chopped parsley
4 tbsp thick plain yogurt
2 tsp caraway seeds
crusty bread and green
  salad, to serve

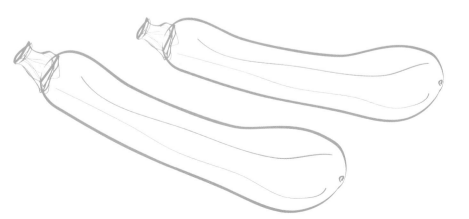

Red bean and chestnut bourguignon

SERVES 4–6   **PREPARATION 25 MINS**   **TO COOK 1¼–1½ HRS**

The chestnuts add a wonderful texture to this rich and flavoursome casserole – elegant enough for a dinner party, but good with homely jacket potatoes, too.

INGREDIENTS

1 tbsp olive oil
30g (1oz) butter
2 red onions, quartered
1 garlic clove, crushed
16 baby Chantenay carrots
  (approx. 115g/4oz),
  topped and tailed
8 baby turnips, peeled but
  left whole, or 2 larger ones,
  cut into chunks
150g (5½oz) crimini or white
  button mushrooms
2 tbsp plain flour
300ml (10fl oz) red wine
300ml (10fl oz) vegetable stock
2 tbsp brandy
1 tbsp tomato purée
good pinch of caster sugar
240g can cooked,
  peeled chestnuts
400g can red kidney beans,
  rinsed and drained
1 bouquet garni sachet
salt and freshly ground
  black pepper
fluffy mash or jacket potatoes
  and broccoli, to serve

1 Preheat the oven to 180°C (350°F/Gas 4). Heat the oil and butter in a flameproof casserole and fry the onions for 5 minutes, stirring, until richly browned.

2 Add the garlic, carrots, turnips, and mushrooms and fry for 2 minutes. Stir in the flour and cook for 1 minute. Gradually blend in the wine, stock, brandy, and tomato purée. Bring to a boil, stirring, until slightly thickened.

3 Stir in the sugar, chestnuts, beans, bouquet garni, and salt and pepper to taste. Cover the surface with wet baking parchment, then add the lid and cook in the oven for 1¼–1½ hours until the vegetables are really tender. Discard the bouquet garni, stir gently, then taste and adjust the seasoning if necessary. Serve hot with fluffy mash or jacket potatoes and broccoli.

Creamy mixed bean ragout with shredded kale

SERVES 4   **PREPARATION 15 MINS**   **TO COOK 25 MINS**

The slightly bitter flavour of kale blends beautifully with the earthy beans and the sweet taste of celeriac. Try different roots such as parsnips, carrots, or turnips, too.

INGREDIENTS

2 tbsp olive oil
1 leek, sliced
2 garlic cloves, chopped
1 tsp ground cumin
1 tsp crushed dried chillies
½ tsp ground turmeric
2 star anise
750ml (1¼ pints) vegetable
    stock
2 × 400g cans mixed
    pulses, drained
1 small celeriac, diced
115g (4oz) button mushrooms
1 bay leaf
salt and freshly ground
    black pepper
250g (9oz) kale, finely
    shredded, discarding
    thick stumps
handful of coriander, chopped
2 tbsp tahini paste
200g (7oz) crème fraîche
dash of lemon juice

1 Heat the oil in a large saucepan. Add the leek and fry, stirring, for 1 minute. Add the garlic and spices and fry for 30 seconds. Stir in the stock, mixed pulses, celeriac, and mushrooms. Add the bay leaf, and a little salt and a generous grinding of pepper. Bring to a boil, reduce the heat, partially cover, and simmer gently for 15 minutes.

2 Add the kale, stir, and bring back to a boil. Reduce the heat, cover, and simmer for a further 8 minutes until everything is really tender. Discard the bay leaf and star anise.

3 Gently stir in the coriander, tahini paste, and all but 2 tsp of the crème fraîche. Add lemon juice to taste and adjust the seasoning, if necessary.

4 Ladle into warmed bowls and add a swirl of the reserved crème fraîche.

Sweet potato, roasted pepper, and white bean hotpot

SERVES 4 **PREPARATION 20 MINS** TO COOK **1 HR 10 MINS**

In this simple casserole, the **sweet potatoes are cooked on top for added texture and flavour.** They can be diced and added to the mixture before cooking, if preferred.

1 Preheat the oven to 190°C (375°F/Gas 5). Heat the oil in a flameproof casserole and fry the onion for 3 minutes, stirring, until softened, but not browned. Add the garlic and carrots and fry for 1 minute.

2 Add the wine, bring to a rapid boil and cook for about 2 minutes until the wine is well reduced.

3 Add the remaining ingredients except the sweet potatoes and butter. Stir well and season with salt and pepper. Bring to a boil.

4 Layer the sweet potatoes on top and brush liberally with the butter. Cover with the lid or foil and bake in the oven for 30 minutes. Increase the temperature to 220°C (425°F/Gas 7) and cook for a further 20–30 minutes until the potatoes are golden and tender. Serve hot with broccoli and jacket potatoes.

INGREDIENTS

2 tbsp olive oil
1 large onion, chopped
2 garlic cloves, crushed
2 carrots, sliced
150ml (5fl oz) dry white wine
2 red peppers, roasted (see p326) and chopped
115g (4oz) closed-cup mushrooms, quartered
2 × 400g cans haricot beans, drained
400g can chopped tomatoes
120ml (4fl oz) vegetable stock
2 tbsp oat bran
1 tbsp chopped thyme
generous pinch of caster sugar
salt and freshly ground black pepper
2 sweet potatoes, cut into 5mm (¼in) slices
20g (¾oz) butter, melted
broccoli and jacket potatoes, to serve

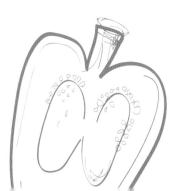

Chilli bean and vegetable braise with fried eggs

SERVES 4   **PREPARATION 15 MINS**   TO COOK **20 MINS**

Large, plump borlotti beans in a spicy sauce make a substantial meal when topped with fried eggs and served with rice. Use pinto or red kidney beans as an alternative.

INGREDIENTS

olive oil, for frying

1 large onion, chopped

1 large garlic clove, crushed

1 large green pepper, deseeded and diced

1 large yellow pepper, deseeded and diced

½ butternut squash, diced

2 fat red or green chillies, deseeded and finely chopped

½ tsp ground turmeric

1 tsp ground cumin

¼ tsp ground cloves

2 × 400g cans borlotti beans, rinsed and drained

400g can chopped tomatoes

120ml (4fl oz) vegetable stock

2 tbsp tomato purée

1 tsp caster sugar

a few pitted black or green olives, halved

handful of raisins

2 tsp red wine vinegar

4 eggs

plain rice and a green salad, to serve

chopped coriander and lime wedges, to garnish

1 Heat 2 tbsp of oil in a large frying pan or wok. Add the onion and fry, stirring, for 3 minutes until starting to soften and lightly golden. Add the garlic, green and yellow peppers, and squash, and fry for a further 2–3 minutes until starting to soften.

2 Add the remaining ingredients except the eggs. Bring to a boil, then reduce the heat to medium. Partially cover and simmer, stirring occasionally, for 15 minutes or until thick and pulpy and the vegetables are tender. Taste and adjust the seasoning, if necessary.

3 In a frying pan, fry the eggs in a little oil until cooked to your liking. Spoon the bean mixture onto plain rice in shallow bowls. Top with the eggs. Garnish with a sprinkling of coriander and lime wedges and serve with a green salad.

Curries, stews, and casseroles
Mushroom and black-eyed bean stroganoff

SERVES 4–6   **PREPARATION 10 MINS**   TO COOK **20 MINS**

Use mixed wild mushrooms when available, but chestnut or white cultivated varieties also work well. Avoid large, flat ones as they will discolour the sauce.

INGREDIENTS

2 tbsp sunflower oil
knob of butter
1 large onion, chopped
1 leek, chopped
2 garlic cloves, crushed
675g (1½lb) mushrooms,
    quartered
2 tbsp brandy
400g can black-eyed beans,
    drained and rinsed
400g (14oz) crème fraîche
salt and freshly ground
    black pepper
handful of chopped parsley
plain rice and green salad,
    to serve

1 Heat the oil and butter in a large pan and fry the onion and leek gently for 5 minutes, stirring, until golden.

2 Add the garlic and mushrooms and cook, stirring, for 1 minute. Cover and cook gently for 10 minutes.

3 Add the brandy and boil, uncovered, until most of the liquid has evaporated. Add the beans and heat through, stirring gently, for 2 minutes.

4 Stir in the crème fraîche and season with salt and pepper. Heat through, then stir in half the parsley.

5 Spoon the stroganoff over plain rice and sprinkle with the remaining parsley. Serve with a green salad.

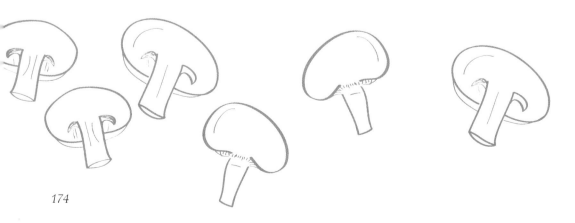

Creamy butternut squash and butter bean stew

SERVES 4   **PREPARATION 15 MINS**   **TO COOK 20–25 MINS**

Pumpkin or sweet potato can be used instead of the butternut squash, and **any shredded green cabbage will taste good** in this stew when cavolo nero isn't available.

1 Heat the oil and butter in a large saucepan. Add the onion and fry gently, stirring, for 3–4 minutes until soft, but not brown.

2 Add all the remaining ingredients except the cavolo nero, Calvados or brandy, and cream, seasoning with a little salt and plenty of pepper. Bring to a boil, reduce the heat, partially cover, and simmer gently for 8–15 minutes until the potato is tender. Add the cavolo nero and Calvados or brandy and press down in the liquid. Bring back to a boil, partially cover, and simmer for a further 4–5 minutes until everything is tender.

3 Gently stir in the cream and heat through for 1 minute. Ladle into bowls and serve hot with plenty of crusty bread.

INGREDIENTS

1 tbsp sunflower oil
large knob of butter
1 onion, chopped
1 turnip, cut into
  bite-sized chunks
1 large potato, peeled and
  cut into bite-sized chunks
1 butternut squash (approx.
  675g/1½lb), peeled,
  deseeded, and cut into
  bite-sized chunks
2 × 400g cans butter beans,
  drained and rinsed
300ml (10fl oz) medium cider
600ml (1 pint) vegetable stock
1 bay leaf
small handful of chopped
  thyme, plus extra to garnish
1 sharp dessert apple, peeled,
  cored, and chopped
salt and freshly ground
  black pepper
6 cavolo nero leaves, shredded
2 tbsp Calvados or brandy
120ml (4fl oz) double cream
crusty bread, to serve

Vegetable choucroute garni

SERVES 4–6   **PREPARATION 15 MINS**   TO COOK **1 HR 20 MINS**

This version of a traditionally meat-based dish has an **abundance of flavour and colour**. Use frozen chargrilled vegetables when time is short.

INGREDIENTS

1 aubergine, sliced

3 tbsp olive oil

1 large red pepper, deseeded and cut into 6–8 thick strips

1 large green pepper, deseeded and cut into 6–8 thick strips

250g (9oz) halloumi cheese, drained and cut into cubes

2 tsp smoked paprika

4 carrots, thickly sliced

2 turnips (or ½ daikon), cut into small chunks

950g jar sauerkraut

¼ tsp ground cloves

12 juniper berries, crushed

150ml (5fl oz) dry white wine

150ml (5fl oz) vegetable stock

1 large bay leaf

salt and freshly ground black pepper

large handful of chopped parsley

plain boiled potatoes and mustard, to serve

1 Preheat a griddle pan. Brush the aubergine slices with a little oil, then toss the red and green peppers in the remainder. Cook in batches for 3 minutes each side, pressing down with a fish slice, until charred brown in places and tender.

2 Mix the halloumi with the paprika and set aside. Blanch the carrots and turnips in boiling water for 3 minutes, then drain. Preheat the oven to 180°C (350°F/Gas 4). Rinse and drain the sauerkraut and place in a large casserole dish. Stir in the cloves and juniper berries, then add all the remaining ingredients except the parsley, seasoning well with salt and pepper. Stir gently.

3 Place a piece of baking parchment over the mixture, then cover the casserole with the lid and bake in the oven for 1 hour. Discard the bay leaf. Taste and adjust the seasoning, if necessary. Sprinkle with parsley and serve with plain boiled potatoes and mustard.

Cauliflower, broccoli, and tomato braise with cheese crumble

SERVES 4–6   **PREPARATION 20 MINS**   TO COOK **15–20 MINS**

Broccoli and cauliflower are always a good combination, and simmered in a light tomato sauce under a blanket of golden cheesy crumbs, they make a perfect light meal.

1 Cut the cauliflower and broccoli into even-sized florets, discarding the thick stumps. Tear off any green leaves from the cauliflower stalks to cook with the florets, if liked.

2 Heat the oil in a flameproof casserole and fry the onion, stirring, for 3 minutes until softened, but not browned. Add the stock and bring to a boil.

3 Tip in the cauliflower and broccoli, cover, and cook for 3–5 minutes. Add the tomatoes, cover, and cook for a further 2 minutes or until the vegetables are tender. Stir in the remaining ingredients, season with salt and pepper, and simmer for a further 1 minute.

4 Meanwhile, preheat the grill. Mix the crumble ingredients together and spoon over the braised vegetables. Place the casserole under the grill and cook for about 5 minutes until golden and the cheese is bubbling. (If need be, turn the vegetables into a shallow ovenproof dish to fit under the grill.) Serve hot with crusty bread and a green salad.

INGREDIENTS

1 small cauliflower
head of broccoli
   (approx. 300g/10oz)
1 tbsp sunflower oil
1 onion, chopped
400ml (14fl oz) vegetable stock
4 ripe beef tomatoes, skinned
   and chopped
2 tbsp tomato purée
generous pinch of
   caster sugar
2 tbsp chopped basil
5 tbsp ground almonds
salt and freshly ground
   black pepper
crusty bread and green
   salad, to serve

For the crumble

30g (1oz) butter, melted
60g (2oz) wholemeal
   breadcrumbs
85g (3oz) strong Cheddar
   cheese, grated
30g (1oz) Parmesan
   cheese, grated

Pizzas, wraps, and quesadillas

Cheese, tomato, and mushroom pizza

MAKES 2 LARGE OR 4 SMALL PIZZAS   **PREPARATION 20 MINS, PLUS PROVING**   TO COOK **35 MINS**

This pizza is delicious with the addition of a **handful of rocket on top to add a cool, peppery finish** to each bite. For a classic Margherita pizza, omit the mushrooms.

INGREDIENTS

450g (1lb) strong plain flour, plus extra for dusting

1 tsp salt

1 tsp caster sugar

2 tsp fast-action dried yeast

2 tbsp olive oil, plus extra for greasing and drizzling

For the topping

2 tbsp olive oil

1 small onion, finely chopped

2 garlic cloves, crushed

400g can chopped tomatoes

1 tbsp tomato purée

2 tsp dried oregano

pinch of sugar

salt and freshly ground black pepper

115g (4oz) crimini mushrooms, sliced

300g (10oz) mozzarella cheese, drained and torn into pieces

large handful of black olives

a few basil leaves

1 Mix the flour, salt, sugar, and yeast together in a large bowl. Gradually add 300ml (10fl oz) warm water and 2 tbsp oil and stir until combined. Mix with your hands to bring it into a ball, then tip out onto a lightly floured surface and knead for at least 5 minutes, adding a little more flour if needed, until the dough is springy to the touch, but not sticky. Shape into a ball and place in a large lightly oiled bowl. Cover with lightly oiled cling film and leave to prove for 1 hour in a warm place, or until it has doubled in size.

2 Meanwhile, make the topping. Heat the oil in a saucepan, then add the onion and sauté over a medium heat for 5 minutes. Stir in the garlic and cook for 1 minute. Add the tomatoes, tomato purée, oregano, and sugar. Season with salt and pepper and simmer uncovered for 10 minutes until pulpy. Set aside.

3 Preheat the oven to 220°C (425°F/Gas 7). Knead the risen dough again, then roll out to two 30–35cm (12–14in) rounds or 4 smaller rounds (about 20cm/8in). Place on oiled pizza plates or baking sheets and press out the rounds again with floured fingers. Alternatively, roll out to 2 large rectangles that just fit the baking sheets and press them into shape once transferred.

4 Divide the tomato sauce, sliced mushrooms, mozzarella, and olives between the pizzas. Season with pepper and drizzle with a little oil. Bake each pizza for 18–20 minutes until crisp and golden around the edges. Scatter with a few basil leaves before serving.

Spinach, fresh tomato, and blue cheese pizza

MAKES 2 LARGE OR 4 SMALL PIZZAS   **PREPARATION 20 MINS, PLUS PROVING**   TO COOK **20 MINS**

Try topping each pizza with six quail's eggs 5 minutes before the end of the cooking time, making tiny wells in the surface of the pizza first.

1 Make and prove the pizza dough (see p180, step 1). While the dough is proving, put the tomatoes in a bowl and cover with boiling water. Leave for 30 seconds, drain, plunge in cold water, then remove the skins and chop the flesh. Mix with the tomato purée, sugar, and some salt and pepper.

2 Shake the excess water from the spinach. Cook the spinach in a pan with no extra water for about 3 minutes until wilted, stirring. Drain thoroughly. Leave to cool, then squeeze out the excess liquid.

3 Preheat the oven to 220°C (425°F/Gas 7). Knead the risen dough again, then roll out to two 30–35cm (12–14in) rounds or 4 smaller rounds (about 20cm/8in). Place on oiled pizza plates or baking sheets and press out the rounds again with floured fingers. Alternatively, roll out to 2 large rectangles that just fit the baking sheets and press them into shape once transferred.

4 Spread the tomato mixture over the dough, not quite to the edges. Scatter the spinach and cheeses over. Sprinkle with the chopped sage, drizzle with a little more oil, and season with pepper. Bake each pizza for 18–20 minutes until crisp and golden around the edges.

INGREDIENTS

1 quantity pizza dough (see p180)
8 ripe tomatoes
6 tbsp tomato purée
1 tsp caster sugar
salt and freshly ground black pepper
450g (1lb) spinach, well washed
200g (7oz) blue cheese, crumbled
200g (7oz) mozzarella cheese, grated
12 sage leaves, chopped

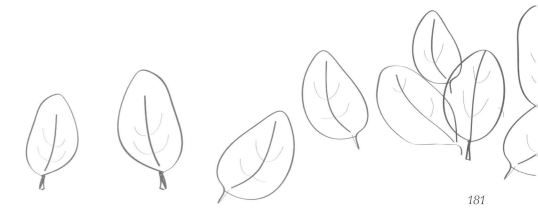

Beetroot, courgette, and goat's cheese pizzas

MAKES 2 LARGE OR 4 SMALL PIZZAS   PREPARATION **30 MINS, PLUS PROVING**   TO COOK **20 MINS**

When time is short, use two 290g (10oz) pizza base mixes. Try this with peppers instead of courgettes and slices of baby Camembert for a variation on goat's cheese.

INGREDIENTS

1 quantity pizza dough (see p180)
5 tbsp olive oil
4 small courgettes, sliced
1 red onion, halved and thinly sliced
1 large garlic clove, finely chopped
2 tbsp chopped rosemary
150ml (5fl oz) passata
2 tbsp tomato purée
2 cooked beetroots (in natural juices), diced
4 handfuls of wild rocket, plus extra to garnish
2 × 120g cylinders goat's cheese, sliced
coarse sea salt
freshly ground black pepper

1 Make and prove the pizza dough (see p180, step 1). While it is proving, heat 3 tbsp oil in a frying pan. Add the courgettes, onion, garlic, and rosemary and cook, stirring, for 3 minutes until softened, but not browned. Set aside.

2 When the dough has proved, preheat the oven to 220°C (425°F/ Gas 7). Knead the risen dough. Roll out to two 30–35cm (12–14in) rounds or four 20cm (8in) rounds and place on oiled pizza plates or baking sheets. Press out the rounds again with floured fingers, then place in the oven and bake for 10 minutes to cook them partially.

3 Mix the passata with the tomato purée. Remove the pizzas from the oven and spread the tomato mixture over, followed by the courgette and onion mixture. Scatter with the beetroot and rocket, then arrange the goat's cheese slices on top. Sprinkle with a little salt and add a good grinding of pepper to each.

4 Bake in the oven for a further 10 minutes until the crust is golden brown, the cheese is melting, and everything is hot through.

5 Top with a little rocket and drizzle each pizza with the remaining oil before serving.

Vegetable-stuffed pizzas

MAKES 4   **PREPARATION 25 MINS, PLUS PROVING**   TO COOK **20 MINS**

Vary the vegetables according to what you have to hand – cooked carrots, potatoes, or shredded greens could be added, or use peas instead of sweetcorn.

INGREDIENTS

1 quantity pizza dough
   (see p180)
4 tbsp tomato purée
250g (9oz) mozzarella cheese,
   torn into pieces
4 tbsp grated
   Parmesan cheese
4 small tomatoes, chopped
4 white cup or chestnut
   mushrooms, chopped
200g can sweetcorn, drained
1 tbsp pickled capers
   (optional)
4 generous pinches
   of dried basil
1 tsp smoked paprika
salt and freshly ground
   black pepper
2 tbsp olive oil, plus extra
   for greasing
150ml (5fl oz) passata, to serve

1 Make and prove the dough (see p180, step 1). Preheat the oven to 220°C (425°F/Gas 7). Cut the dough evenly into 4 and shape into balls. Roll out each ball into a circle about 20cm (8in) in diameter. Spread a little tomato purée on each circle, leaving a 3cm (1¼in) border all around. Divide the mozzarella cheese between the circles and sprinkle each with ½ tbsp Parmesan cheese.

2 Top with the tomatoes, mushrooms, sweetcorn, capers (if using), and basil. Season with paprika and salt and pepper, then drizzle with half the oil.

3 Brush the edges with water, draw the dough up over the filling, and press the edges together to seal. Invert on an oiled baking sheet. Brush with the remaining oil and bake in the oven for about 20 minutes until crisp and golden.

4 Meanwhile, heat the passata in a saucepan. Place the stuffed pizzas on warmed plates. Spoon the passata over and sprinkle with the remaining grated Parmesan.

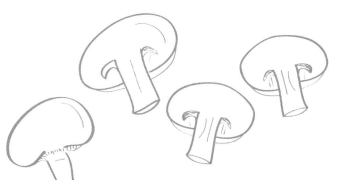

Sprouting broccoli, ricotta, and rosemary calzones

MAKES 4   **PREPARATION 30 MINS, PLUS PROVING**   TO COOK **25 MINS**

A calzone is the pizza equivalent of a pasty. The dough is folded over the filling and the edge sealed before baking so **all the flavour is encased in the dough**.

1 Make and prove the dough (see p180, step 1). Preheat the oven to 220°C (425°F/Gas 7). Steam or boil the sprouting broccoli for 3–4 minutes until it is just tender. Drain, rinse with cold water, and drain again. Chop into bite-sized pieces and set aside.

2 Cut the dough into 4 equal pieces and roll out to 20cm (8in) rounds on a lightly floured surface. Mash the butter, garlic, rosemary, ricotta, and salt and pepper together and spread over the rounds of dough, leaving a 3cm (1¼in) border all around.

3 Add the chopped broccoli, tomatoes, mozzarella, and olives, leaving the border clear. Drizzle with half the oil.

4 Brush the edges with water. Using lightly floured hands, fold the calzones in half and press the edges together, then roll over the edge to seal. Transfer to an oiled baking sheet and brush the tops with oil. Bake in the oven for 18–20 minutes, or until crisp and golden. Garnish with a dusting of grated Parmesan cheese.

INGREDIENTS

1 quantity pizza dough (see p180)
200g (7oz) sprouting broccoli, thick stalks removed
flour, for dusting
60g (2oz) butter, softened
2 large garlic cloves, crushed
2 tbsp chopped rosemary
150g (5½oz) ricotta cheese
salt and freshly ground black pepper
2 large tomatoes, chopped
85g (3oz) mozzarella cheese, torn into pieces
4 tbsp sliced black olives
2 tbsp olive oil, plus extra for greasing
2 tbsp grated Parmesan cheese, to garnish

Griddled asparagus, mushroom, and garlic sauce pizzas

MAKES 2 LARGE OR 4 SMALL PIZZAS   PREPARATION **30 MINS, PLUS PROVING**   TO COOK **30 MINS**

When asparagus isn't in season, **try this pizza with strips of aubergine sliced lengthways and griddled**. Fresh, green garlic works particularly well here, too.

INGREDIENTS

1 quantity pizza dough
  (see p180)
150g (5½oz) thin asparagus
  spears, trimmed
5–6 tbsp olive oil
2 shallots, chopped
250g (9oz) mixed speciality
  mushrooms such as
  shiitake, enoki, and
  nomeku, sliced if large
4 leaves spring greens or
  other green cabbage,
  (approx. 100g/3½oz),
  finely shredded, discarding
  any thick stalks
30g (1oz) butter
3 tbsp plain flour
250ml (9fl oz) milk
2 large garlic cloves, crushed
85g (3oz) Cheddar
  cheese, grated
salt and freshly ground
  black pepper
2 tbsp chopped tarragon
  or basil
125g (4½oz) mozzarella
  cheese, grated
2 tbsp snipped chives

1 Make and prove the pizza dough (see p180, step 1). While the dough is proving, preheat a griddle. Brush the asparagus spears with a little oil and cook on a griddle for 2 minutes on each side, until bright green with brown stripes and just tender. Cut in diagonal short lengths. Set aside.

2 Heat 2 tbsp oil and sauté the shallots and mushrooms for 2 minutes until softened. Remove from the pan and set aside. Add a further 1 tbsp oil to the pan and stir-fry the greens for 2 minutes, stirring until slightly softened. Set aside.

3 When the dough has proved, preheat the oven to 220°C (425°F/ Gas 7). Knead the risen dough. Roll out to two 30–35cm (12–14in) rounds or four 20cm (8in) rounds and place on oiled pizza plates or baking sheets. Press out the rounds again with floured fingers, then place in the oven and bake for 10 minutes to cook them partially.

4 Meanwhile, melt the butter in a small saucepan. Work in the flour with a wire whisk and cook, stirring, for 1 minute. Remove the pan from the heat and whisk in the milk. Return to the heat, bring to a boil, and cook for 2 minutes, whisking constantly until thickened. Stir in the garlic, Cheddar cheese, and salt and pepper to taste.

5 Spread the garlic sauce over the pizzas. Top with the greens, mushrooms, and asparagus. Sprinkle with the tarragon or basil, then the mozzarella. Drizzle with a little oil and sprinkle with the chives. Bake for 15–20 minutes until the pizzas are golden around the edges and crisp. Serve hot, cut into wedges.

Spicy lentil and pepper pizzas

MAKES 2 LARGE OR 4 SMALL PIZZAS   PREPARATION **30 MINS, PLUS PROVING**   TO COOK **25 MINS**

The roast pepper adds a lovely sweetness to the spices and lentils. If time is short, use a pimiento from a jar or simply a raw fresh pepper.

INGREDIENTS

1 quantity pizza dough
(see p180)
1 large red pepper, roasted, skinned, and deseeded (see p326)
2 tbsp olive oil, plus extra for greasing and drizzling
1 garlic clove, chopped
1 small onion, finely chopped
4 tomatoes, chopped
4 tbsp tomato purée
400g can green lentils, rinsed and drained
2 tsp smoked paprika
½ tsp chilli powder
½ tsp caster sugar
salt and freshly ground black pepper
2 tbsp pickled jalapeño peppers, sliced
1 tsp dried oregano
125g (4½oz) mozzarella cheese, grated
a few black olives

1 Make and prove the pizza dough (see p180, step 1). While the dough is proving, cut the pepper into thin strips.

2 Heat the oil in a saucepan. Add the garlic and onion and fry gently, stirring, for 2 minutes to soften. Add the tomatoes, tomato purée, lentils, paprika, and chilli powder and cook, stirring, for 2 minutes. Add the sugar and season with salt and pepper to taste.

3 Preheat the oven to 220°C (425°F/Gas 7). Knead the risen dough again, then roll out to two 30–35cm (12–14in) rounds or 4 smaller rounds (about 20cm/8in). Place on oiled pizza plates or baking sheets and press out the rounds again with floured fingers. Alternatively, roll out to 2 large rectangles that just fit the baking sheets and press them into shape once transferred.

4 Spread the lentil mixture over the dough, leaving a 1cm (½in) border all around. Sprinkle with the pepper strips, jalapeños, oregano, and mozzarella. Dot with a few black olives and drizzle with a little oil.

5 Bake for 18–20 minutes, or until the dough is crisp and lightly golden brown and the cheese has melted.

Pizza primavera

MAKES 2 LARGE OR 4 SMALL PIZZAS   PREPARATION **30 MINS, PLUS PROVING**   TO COOK **20 MINS**

These are **sumptuous pizzas packed with vegetables**. The vegetables are cooked first, then added to the part-baked pizza so they retain all their goodness, colour, and flavour.

1 Make and prove the pizza dough (see p180, step 1). While the dough is proving, heat the oil and butter in a large saucepan or wok. Add the garlic and onion and fry, stirring, for 2 minutes. Add the cauliflower, carrots, mushrooms, and a splash of water and stir-fry for about 3 minutes until softened, but still with some bite.

2 Add the courgette slices and stir-fry for another 1–2 minutes. Add a pinch of salt, plenty of pepper, rosemary, and a good squeeze of lemon juice and mix well. Set aside.

3 Preheat the oven to 220°C (425°F/Gas 7). Knead the risen dough again, then roll out to two 30–35cm (12–14in) rounds or 4 smaller rounds (about 20cm/8in). Place on oiled pizza plates or baking sheets and press out the rounds again with floured fingers. Alternatively, roll out to 2 large rectangles that just fit the baking sheets and press them into shape once transferred. Bake for 10 minutes.

4 Remove from the oven and spread quickly with the tomato purée, then top with the tomato slices and sprinkle with oregano. Divide the vegetable mixture between the trays and spread out evenly. Sprinkle the cheeses over. Return to the oven for 10 minutes until golden around the edges and the cheese is melted and slightly brown.

INGREDIENTS

1 quantity pizza dough (see p180)
4 tbsp olive oil, plus extra for greasing
15g (½oz) butter
2 large garlic cloves, crushed
1 red onion, halved and sliced
¼ cauliflower, white only, cut into tiny florets
2 young carrots, thinly sliced
115g (4oz) white button, or crimini mushrooms, sliced
2 small courgettes, sliced
salt and freshly ground black pepper
1½ tbsp chopped rosemary
wedge of lemon
4 tbsp tomato purée
4 large tomatoes, sliced
2 tsp dried oregano
125g (4½oz) mozzarella cheese, grated
20g (¾oz) Parmesan cheese, grated

Avocado, baby spinach, and chilli wraps

MAKES 2   **PREPARATION 5 MINS**

Packed with flavour and nutrients, **these wraps make a tasty lunch or snack supper.** Peppery wild rocket or watercress make delicious alternatives to baby spinach.

INGREDIENTS

1 small avocado
1 tsp lemon or lime juice
1 large flour tortilla
2 tbsp mayonnaise
large handful of
   baby spinach
½ red pepper, deseeded
   and cut into thin strips
½ tsp crushed dried chillies
6 slices pickled jalapeño
   chilli pepper
freshly ground black pepper

1 Peel and halve the avocado and remove the stone (see pp324–5). Slice thinly and toss in the lemon or lime juice.

2 Put the tortilla on a board. Spread with the mayonnaise, then add the spinach, avocado, red pepper, chillies, and jalapeño chilli pepper, one after the other. Season with plenty of pepper. Fold in the sides and roll up firmly, then cut in half and serve.

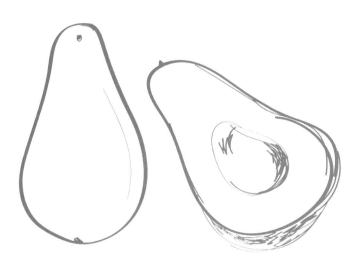

Chilli bean fajitas

MAKES 8   **PREPARATION 20 MINS**   **TO COOK 20 MINS**

Fajitas are perfect for a colourful, informal meal. To turn them into enchiladas, smother with grated cheese in an ovenproof dish and bake in a hot oven until melted.

1 Heat the oil in a large frying pan or wok. Add all the vegetables, cover, and cook for 5–10 minutes until fairly soft, stirring occasionally.

2 Add the garlic and spices and fry for 30 seconds, then stir in the oregano, tomatoes, and tomato purée. Cover and cook, stirring occasionally, for a further 5 minutes until just tender. Add salt and pepper to taste.

3 Put the refried beans in a separate pan and heat through, stirring. Warm the tortillas briefly in the microwave, if liked.

4 Taking each tortilla in turn, spread with a little of the refried beans, then some of the vegetable mixture. Top with 1 tbsp crème fraîche and a little cheese and roll up. Serve immediately with a crisp green salad.

INGREDIENTS

2 tbsp olive oil
1 large onion, halved and sliced
2 red peppers, halved, deseeded, and sliced
2 green peppers, halved, deseeded, and sliced
2 courgettes, sliced
150g (5½oz) green cabbage, shredded
1 large garlic clove, crushed
2 tsp ground cumin
1 tsp crushed dried chillies
1 tsp dried oregano
4 tomatoes, chopped
2 tbsp tomato purée
salt and freshly ground black pepper
435g can refried beans
8 flour or corn tortillas
8 tbsp crème fraîche
115g (4oz) Cheddar cheese, grated
crisp green salad, to serve

Griddled courgette and semi-dried tomato wraps

MAKES 2   **PREPARATION 5 MINS**   **TO COOK 4–6 MINS**

For this recipe, use either bought hummus or make your own (see p313). Slices of aubergine may be substituted for the courgette.

INGREDIENTS

2 courgettes, cut into 5mm
  (¼in) slices lengthways
2 tbsp olive oil
2 large flour tortillas
6 tbsp hummus
8 pieces semi-dried tomatoes
  in oil, drained and
  chopped, oil reserved
handful of rocket
lemon juice
freshly ground black pepper

1 Preheat a griddle pan. Brush the courgette slices with oil, then griddle for 2–3 minutes on each side or until tender and striped brown. Set aside.

2 Put the tortillas on a board and spread with the hummus. Lay the courgette strips on top and scatter with the semi-dried tomatoes.

3 Scatter the rocket on top, drizzle with the tomato oil and a squeeze of lemon juice, then add a good grinding of pepper. Fold in the sides, roll up each tightly, and cut in half.

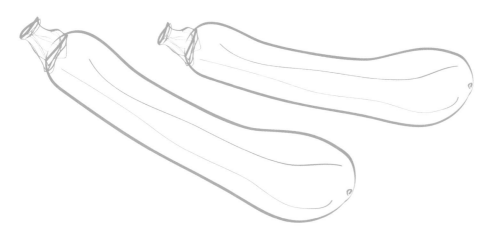

Courgette and pea mini wraps

MAKES 10   **PREPARATION 20 MINS**   **TO COOK 5 MINS**

Pea shoots – the first tendrils of the young plants – can be enjoyed raw. Combine them with **fresh baby peas and raw courgettes in this vibrant, healthy dish.**

INGREDIENTS

250g (9oz) courgettes, grated
handful of baby
   spinach leaves
grated zest and juice of
   1½ lemons
125g (4½oz) young
   peas, shelled
25g (scant 1oz) toasted
   pine nuts
salt and freshly ground
   black pepper
1–2 tbsp mayonnaise, plus
   extra for spreading
5 flour tortillas, halved
handful of pea shoots

1 In a large bowl, mix together the courgettes, spinach, lemon zest and juice, peas, and pine nuts. Season with salt and pepper, then moisten with a little mayonnaise.

2 Heat a dry frying pan over a high heat. Add the tortilla halves, 2 at a time, and toast for about 15 seconds on each side. Set aside the tortilla halves under a clean tea towel to keep warm.

3 Lay one of the tortilla halves flat on a chopping board and spread lightly with a scraping of mayonnaise. Take some of the courgette filling and place in the centre. Arrange some of the pea shoots on top, so that they stick out at one end, then gently roll up the mini wrap. Repeat this process until 10 wraps have been made.

4 To serve, arrange the mini wraps on individual serving plates, allowing 2 per person.

Rainbow pepper Mexican tacos

SERVES 4   PREPARATION **10 MINS**   TO COOK **10 MINS**

These easy-to-make tacos are delicious with a dollop of guacamole instead of the soured cream. The filling tastes equally good in crispy corn tacos.

1 Heat the oil in a wok or large frying pan and sauté the onions and peppers, stirring, for 6–8 minutes until soft. Stir in the garlic and sweetcorn and cook, stirring, for a further 1–2 minutes.

2 Add all of the spices and fry for 30 seconds, stirring. Remove the wok or frying pan from the heat and stir in the lime juice and chopped coriander. Season with salt and pepper to taste.

3 Divide the filling between the tortillas, add a spoonful of soured cream to each, and roll up. Serve immediately while still hot.

INGREDIENTS

2 tbsp sunflower oil
2 red onions, sliced
1 red pepper, deseeded
   and cut into thin strips
1 green pepper, deseeded
   and cut into thin strips
1 yellow pepper, deseeded
   and cut into thin strips
1 orange pepper, deseeded
   and cut into thin strips
1 garlic clove, crushed
115g (4oz) baby sweetcorn,
   halved lengthways
1 tsp ground cumin
1 tsp ground coriander
1 tsp paprika
½ tsp crushed dried chillies
juice of 1 lime
handful of chopped coriander
salt and freshly ground
   black pepper
8 flour tortillas
8 tbsp soured cream

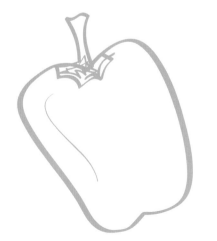

Maki sushi wraps

MAKES 24   **PREPARATION 40 MINS**   **TO COOK 20 MINS, PLUS STANDING AND COOLING**

Sushi is fun to make. Vary the fillings with strips of pepper or batonettes of courgette. Choose sweet, pink pickled ginger rather than the salty biscuit-coloured type.

INGREDIENTS

225g (8oz) sushi rice
4 tbsp rice vinegar
2 tsp caster sugar
2 tsp sesame oil
½ tsp salt
4 nori sheets (dried seaweed)
wasabi paste, pink pickled
   ginger, and tamari or light
   soy sauce, to serve

For the fillings

1 small avocado
1 tsp rice vinegar
1 tomato, deseeded and
   cut into thin strips
4 strips carrot, pared with
   a potato peeler
1 spring onion, cut into short
   lengths and shredded
5cm (2in) piece cucumber,
   peeled, deseeded and
   cut into batonettes

1 Cook the sushi rice according to the packet instructions. Mix the vinegar, sugar, oil, and salt together and sprinkle over the cooked rice. Cover and leave to stand for 20 minutes.

2 For the fillings, halve, stone, and peel the avocado (see pp324–5). Slice the flesh thinly and toss in the vinegar to prevent browning.

3 Place a nori sheet, shiny side down, with the lines in the nori sheet horizontal to you, on a sushi mat or a square of heavy-duty foil. Spread the surface with a quarter of the sushi rice, leaving a 2cm (¾in) strip of nori uncovered at the edge furthest away from you.

4 Mark a line across the centre of the rice. Lay a line of avocado slices and a line of tomato strips all along it and press gently into the rice. Using the mat or foil to help, start to roll the sushi away from you firmly, checking that the roll is tucking under and making sure the filling does not pop out. Press gently while rolling, but do not squash the filling. Dampen the end strip of nori so that it sticks when it is completely rolled. Wrap in cling film. Make another avocado and tomato wrap the same way.

5 Repeat the process with the remaining rice and nori sheets, using a row of carrot strips topped with a row of shredded spring onion (white and green shreds evenly distributed) and a row of cucumber for the filling in each one. Chill all the wrapped rolls until ready to serve.

6 To serve, remove the cling film and cut each roll into 6 pieces. Place on a serving platter with wasabi paste, pickled ginger, and tamari or light soy sauce to add to the sushi before eating.

Tabbouleh lettuce wraps

MAKES 16   **PREPARATION 30 MINS, PLUS COOLING**

Using lettuce leaves instead of flour tortillas, **these low-calorie wraps make an excellent lunchtime snack** or a refreshing starter.

INGREDIENTS

115g (4oz) bulghur wheat
300ml (10fl oz) boiling
   vegetable stock
1 large garlic clove, crushed
large handful each of
   coriander, mint, and
   parsley, chopped
2 tomatoes, finely chopped
5cm (2in) piece cucumber,
   finely chopped
2 tbsp chopped black olives
1 tbsp lemon juice, plus
   more if needed
2 tbsp olive oil
salt and freshly ground
   black pepper
16 large, soft, round
   lettuce leaves

1 Put the bulghur wheat in a bowl and stir in the boiling stock. Leave to stand for 20–30 minutes until swollen and all the liquid is absorbed. Stir in the garlic and herbs and leave to cool.

2 When nearly ready to serve, mix in the tomatoes, cucumber, and olives and add the lemon juice and oil. Season with salt and pepper and add more lemon juice, if liked.

3 Divide the mixture equally among the lettuce leaves on serving platters. Roll up each wrap like a tortilla and serve.

Spicy potato and mango chutney chapatti wraps

MAKES 8   PREPARATION **10 MINS**   TO COOK **20 MINS**

If you need to make only one wrap at a time, store the filling in the refrigerator to use over the next few days – it is just as good served cold.

1 Boil the potatoes in lightly salted water for about 10 minutes until just tender but still holding their shape. Drain.

2 Heat the oil in the rinsed-out pan and fry the spices over a medium heat, stirring, for 30 seconds. Stir in the tomatoes and sugar and fry for 2–3 minutes.

3 Add the potatoes, then stir and turn gently until they are coated in the tomatoes. Sprinkle with a little salt. Cook for 5 minutes, stirring occasionally, until the juice has been absorbed. Add the coriander, then stir and turn one more time. Crush the potatoes with the back of a spoon to break them up. Set aside until just warm.

4 Lay the chapattis on a board and spread the mango chutney down the centre. Top with the crushed potatoes and sprinkle with shredded lettuce. Roll up tightly and cut into halves to serve.

INGREDIENTS

3 potatoes (approx. 350g/12oz), peeled and cut into walnut-sized pieces
salt
1½ tbsp sunflower oil
1 tsp crushed dried chillies
½ tsp ground cumin
½ tsp ground coriander
¼ tsp ground turmeric
2 large tomatoes, chopped
generous pinch of caster sugar
1 tbsp chopped coriander
4 chapattis
4 tbsp mango chutney
4 handfuls shredded iceberg lettuce

Four ways with
Tomatoes

Tomato soup ▶

TAKES 1 hr 15 mins **SERVES** 4

Heat 1 tbsp **olive oil** in a large saucepan over a medium-low heat. Add 1 chopped **onion**, 1 sliced **garlic clove**, and 2 sliced **celery** sticks, then fry, stirring, until soft, but not coloured. Add 1 sliced **carrot**, 1 chopped **potato**, and stir for 1 minute. Add two 400g cans **chopped tomatoes** with their juice, 750ml (1¼ pints) **vegetable stock**, 1 **bay leaf**, and 1 tsp **sugar**. Add **salt** and freshly ground **black pepper**, bring to a boil, reduce the heat, cover, and simmer for 45 minutes. Remove from the heat and allow to cool slightly, then process in a blender or food processor until smooth. Taste and adjust the seasoning, then reheat and serve.

◀ Baked stuffed tomatoes

TAKES 1 hr, plus standing **SERVES** 4

Cut 4 large ripe **beef tomatoes** in half horizontally. Scoop out the insides and discard. Sprinkle the tomatoes with **salt** and drain upside down for 30 minutes. Preheat the oven to 220°C (425°F/Gas 7). Heat 1 tbsp **olive oil** in a pan, then add 2 finely chopped **anchovies** and 1 crushed **garlic clove**. Cook for 30 seconds. Stir in 4 tbsp fresh **breadcrumbs** and cook for 2 minutes. Mix 4 tbsp **mascarpone** cheese, 125g (4½oz) **ricotta** cheese, and 2 tbsp finely chopped **basil leaves**. Season with freshly ground **black pepper**. Fill each tomato with the cheeses and top with the breadcrumb mixture. Bake for 15–20 minutes.

For salads, choose classic globe tomatoes, cherry tomatoes, or the Brandywine beef variety (for slicing). For sauces, soups, grilling, and roasting, **plum and beef tomatoes have the best flavour.**

Tomato, red onion, and mozzarella salad ▶

TAKES 10 mins **SERVES** 4

Put 8 ripe **plum tomatoes**, sliced, 6 **cherry tomatoes**, halved, 1 small **red onion**, peeled and sliced, and a small handful of torn **basil leaves** in a large bowl. Drizzle over plenty of **extra virgin olive oil**, season well with **salt** and freshly ground **black pepper**, and toss. Arrange 2 handfuls of **wild rocket leaves** on a plate, drizzle over a little oil and some **balsamic vinegar**, and season. Spoon over the tomato and basil mixture. Add 2 balls of **mozzarella**, torn. Scatter some basil leaves over and drizzle with a little oil and balsamic vinegar. Serve immediately.

◀ Chunky tomato sauce

TAKES 35 mins **MAKES** 600ml (1 pint)

Heat 4 tbsp **sunflower oil** in a large saucepan over a medium heat. Add 1 chopped **onion** and 1 chopped **garlic clove**. Fry, stirring occasionally, for 5–8 minutes, or until soft and golden. Stir in 4 tbsp **tomato purée**, two 400g cans **chopped tomatoes** with their juice, 4 torn **basil leaves**, and **salt** and freshly ground **black pepper** to taste. Lower the heat and simmer, uncovered, for 20 minutes, or until the sauce has thickened. Stir in a few more torn basil leaves just before serving.

Vietnamese vegetable and beansprout summer rolls

MAKES 8   **PREPARATION 50 MINS**

These colourful rolls make a **healthy, tasty light lunch or supper, or serve one each as a starter.** Ideally, use a lettuce with small round leaves, or halve larger ones.

INGREDIENTS

85g (3oz) fresh rice vermicelli

1 tbsp light soy sauce

1 tsp grated fresh root ginger

1 tsp light brown soft sugar
  or palm sugar

8 small soft, round, green
  lettuce leaves, thick stalk
  ends cut off

handful of beansprouts

5cm (2in) piece cucumber,
  peeled, deseeded, and cut
  in julienne strips

2 spring onions, cut into short
  lengths and shredded

½ carrot, pared with a potato
  peeler into thin ribbons

8 red radishes, sliced

a few sprigs of coriander,
  leaves picked

8 large (22cm/8½in) rice-
  paper wrappers

1 Soak the vermicelli in boiling water for 5 minutes. Drain, rinse with cold water, and dry on kitchen paper.

2 Mix the soy sauce, ginger, and sugar together until well-blended. Add the noodles and toss until completely coated and all the liquid has been absorbed.

3 Arrange all the vegetables and the coriander in neat piles for easy access. Place a large plate on the work surface and have a large shallow dish of warm water to one side, ready to soak the rice wrappers.

4 Put a wrapper into the water and soak for 5 seconds. Remove and lay on the plate. Put a lettuce leaf, bright green side down, on the edge of the rice paper nearest to you. Put an eighth of the noodles alongside it, then add a few beansprouts, strips of cucumber, shreds of spring onion, and a carrot ribbon.

5 Fold the edge of the wrapper nearest to you (with the filling on) up over the filling to make the beginnings of the roll. Lay a row of radish slices, well tucked in, along the line where the rolled bit meets the unrolled bit of wrapper. Lay 3 or 4 coriander leaves alongside.

6 Now fold in the sides of the rice wrapper, then roll it up into a tight cylinder and place, radish-side up, on a serving plate. Cover with a clean, damp cloth while making the remainder, then cover with cling film and keep covered, at room temperature, until ready to serve. These are best eaten within a couple of hours.

Sage and onion quesadillas

MAKES 2   **PREPARATION 5 MINS**   TO COOK **5 MINS**

Sage, onion, and cheese is the perfect combination for a simple quesadilla filling. Ready-grated Cheddar cheese is convenient and often no more expensive than a block.

1 Heat a large non-stick frying pan and place a tortilla in it. Scatter half the onion over it, followed by half the cheese and half the sage.

2 Cover with the second tortilla and press down well with a fish slice. Cook for 2–3 minutes over a medium heat until the base is crisp and brown and the cheese is beginning to melt, pressing down all the time.

3 Carefully flip over the tortilla sandwich and cook the other side for about 2 minutes, pressing down again until the cheese has melted and the base is crisp and brown. Slide the quesadilla out of the pan and cut in quarters. Keep warm while you cook the second tortilla in the same way.

INGREDIENTS

4 flour tortillas
1 small onion, halved
   and thinly sliced
100g (3½oz) Cheddar
   cheese, grated
12 sage leaves, chopped,
   or 1 tsp dried sage

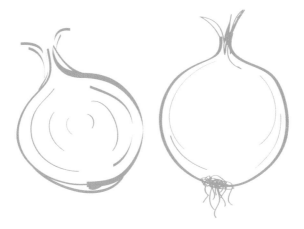

Roasted aubergine, feta, and tomato quesadillas

MAKES 2   **PREPARATION 10 MINS**   TO COOK **40–50 MINS, PLUS COOLING**

The aubergine may be roasted in advance, perhaps when the oven is already on, and used in the next day or two, or frozen. Alternatively, use a jar of roasted aubergine.

INGREDIENTS

1 small aubergine, approx.
  275g (9½oz)
1 small garlic clove, crushed
1 tbsp olive oil
squeeze of lemon juice
salt and freshly ground
  black pepper
4 large flour tortillas
1 tomato, chopped
100g (3½oz) feta
  cheese, crumbled
½ tsp dried oregano

1 Preheat the oven to 200°C (400°F/Gas 6). Roast the aubergine whole for 30–40 minutes, turning occasionally until soft. Place in a plastic bag and leave to cool.

2 Remove the stalk, peel off the skin, and chop the flesh. Place in a bowl and add the garlic, oil, lemon juice, and some salt and pepper. Mash well.

3 Heat a large non-stick frying pan and place a tortilla on it. Spread with half of the aubergine mixture, then scatter over the chopped tomato and half the crumbled feta. Sprinkle with half the oregano.

4 Cover with a second tortilla and cook over a medium heat, pressing down well with a fish slice, for 2–3 minutes until crisp and brown underneath. Carefully invert onto a plate, then slide back into the pan and cook the other side for 2–3 minutes, still pressing down, until crisp and brown underneath.

5 Slide out onto a plate and keep warm while cooking the remaining quesadilla in the same way. Cut them in quarters and serve.

Pizzas, wraps, and quesadillas

Sweetcorn, Cheddar cheese, and chilli sauce quesadillas

MAKES 4   **PREPARATION 5 MINS**   TO COOK **20 MINS**

An easy and nutritious snack, these quesadillas are packed with flavour. **Make sure the sweetcorn is drained and dried thoroughly,** or the mixture will be too wet.

1 Drain the can of sweetcorn with peppers and dry on kitchen paper, then tip into a bowl. Mix the cheese and mayonnaise into the sweetcorn and peppers.

2 Put 2 tortillas on a board and spread each with 1 tbsp sweet chilli sauce. Heat a large frying pan and add 1 tsp oil. Put one of the sauce-topped tortillas in the pan, sauce-side up. Spread with half the corn mixture and top with the second tortilla. Press down with a fish slice. Cook over a medium heat for 2 minutes until sizzling and golden underneath. Invert onto a plate.

3 Slide the quesadilla back into the pan, browned-side up. Press down again and cook for a further 2 minutes, or until the cheese has melted and everything is brown and sizzling. Slide out of the pan and keep warm while cooking the remaining quesadillas. It is best to cut them in quarters when they have cooled slightly as corn tortillas are quite soft.

INGREDIENTS

200g can sweetcorn
  with peppers
4 large handfuls of grated
  mature Cheddar cheese
4 tbsp mayonnaise
8 tbsp sweet chilli sauce
8 corn tortillas
4 tsp sunflower oil

Guacamole and Cheddar quesadillas

MAKES 2   **PREPARATION 5 MINS**   TO COOK **5 MINS**

The Mexican tomato, onion, and coriander salsa on pp310–11 is excellent with these quesadillas. **Make sure the avocados are ripe** or they may taste bitter.

INGREDIENTS

2 avocados
2 tsp lime juice
1 tsp crushed dried
  chillies, or to taste
2 thin spring onions,
  finely chopped
5cm (2in) piece cucumber,
  finely chopped
2 tomatoes, deseeded and
  finely chopped
salt and freshly ground
  black pepper
4 flour tortillas
2 large handfuls of grated
  Cheddar cheese
2 tbsp chopped coriander
a few drops of Worcestershire
  sauce or mushroom ketchup

1 For the guacamole, halve, stone, and peel the avocados (see pp324–5). Put the flesh in a bowl and mash well with the lime juice, then mix in the chillies, spring onions, cucumber, and tomatoes. Add salt and pepper to taste.

2 Heat a large non-stick frying pan. Put one tortilla on a board and spread with half the guacamole. Place in the frying pan and scatter over half the cheese and then half the coriander. Add a few drops of Worcestershire sauce and top with a second tortilla. Press down well with a fish slice.

3 Cook for 2–3 minutes over a medium heat until the base is crisp and brown and the cheese is beginning to melt, pressing down constantly. Invert the tortilla onto a plate, then slide back into the pan and cook the other side for about 2 minutes, pressing down again, until the cheese has melted and the base is crisp and brown. Tip out onto a plate and cut into quarters. Keep warm while making the second quesadilla in the same way.

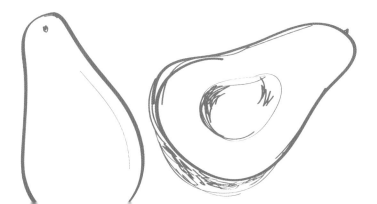

Rocket, pear, blue cheese, and walnut quesadillas

MAKES 2   **PREPARATION 10 MINS**   TO COOK **10 MINS**

Peppery rocket, sweet pears, tangy blue cheese, and earthy walnuts – a great combination for a sophisticated quesadilla. Chop the nuts finely for the best flavour.

INGREDIENTS

45g (1½oz) soft blue cheese, such as St Agur or cambazola, cut into small pieces

30g (1oz) Emmental cheese, grated

20g (¾oz) walnuts, finely chopped

2 tbsp crème fraîche

4 large flour tortillas

1 not-too-ripe pear, peeled, cored, and thinly sliced

2 handfuls of rocket

1 Mash the cheeses with the walnuts and crème fraîche. Spread half over 1 tortilla. Top with half the pear and rocket, then top with a second tortilla. Press down well.

2 Heat a large non-stick frying pan and cook the quesadilla over a medium heat, pressing down well with a fish slice, for 2–3 minutes until crisp and golden underneath. Carefully turn over and fry the other side for a further 2 minutes, pressing down again, until the cheese has melted and the base is crisp.

3 Slide out of the pan and cut in quarters. Set aside to cool slightly while you cook the second quesadilla in the same way.

Cream cheese and roasted pepper quesadillas

MAKES 2   **PREPARATION 20 MINS, PLUS COOLING**   TO COOK **20 MINS**

A drained pimiento from a can or jar can be used for these delicious quesadillas, but **a freshly roasted pepper will always give the tastiest result**.

1 Cut the pepper into thin slices. Mix the cheese with the basil and pine nuts and add a good grinding of pepper.

2 Heat 1 tsp oil in a frying pan. Add 1 corn tortilla, then spread with the cheese mixture and top with the pepper slices. Place another tortilla on top and press down well with a fish slice. Fry the quesadilla for 2–3 minutes until golden underneath, then slide out onto a plate.

3 Heat the remaining oil in the pan. Invert the plate over the pan so the tortilla is cooked-side up. Fry the other side for about 2 minutes until golden and hot through, pressing down all the time. Slide out of the pan and keep warm while making the second quesadilla. These are softer than flour tortilla quesadillas, so leave to cool slightly before cutting into quarters.

INGREDIENTS

1 small red pepper, roasted, peeled, and deseeded (see p326)
75g (2½oz) cream cheese
2 tbsp chopped basil
2 tbsp pine nuts
freshly ground black pepper
2 tsp olive oil
4 corn tortillas

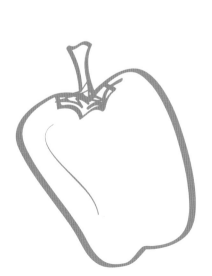

Tortillas, frittatas, and omelettes

Spanish tortilla

SERVES 4   **PREPARATION 10 MINS**   TO COOK **45 MINS**

A delicious choice for a light meal with a crisp salad, this tortilla is also great cut into cubes and served as tapas with drinks, Spanish-style.

INGREDIENTS

300ml (10fl oz) olive oil, plus
   1 tbsp for frying
5 potatoes, peeled and sliced,
   approx. 5mm (¼in) thick
3 onions, quartered and sliced
sea salt and freshly ground
   black pepper
5 eggs, beaten

1 Put the oil in a deep-sided ovenproof frying pan (preferably non-stick), add the potatoes, and simmer gently for about 15 minutes, or until soft. Remove the potatoes with a slotted spoon and put them in a large bowl to cool.

2 Tip most of the oil out of the pan and add the onions and a pinch of salt. Cook over a low heat until soft and beginning to caramelize. Add to the potatoes and leave to cool.

3 Pour the eggs into the cooled potato and onion mixture, season with salt and pepper, and combine gently so that all the potatoes are coated.

4 Heat 1 tbsp oil in the pan until hot, then carefully slide the egg mixture in, spreading it evenly so it covers the base of the pan. Reduce the heat to medium-low and cook for 6–10 minutes, or until almost set. Invert onto a plate and return to the pan to cook the other side. Alternatively, preheat the grill and put the pan under the grill for a few minutes to brown and set the top. Remove from the pan, leave to cool and set, then cut into wedges. Serve warm or cold.

Aubergine and potato tortillas

SERVES 4   **PREPARATION 5 MINS**   TO COOK **15 MINS**

Aubergines soak up a lot of oil, but **blanching them along with the potatoes, as below, will reduce the calorie count.** Alternatively, simply fry them for about 5 minutes.

1 Bring a pan of water to a boil, drop in the aubergine and potato slices, and blanch for 2–3 minutes until tender. Drain thoroughly and dry on kitchen paper.

2 Heat the oil in a large non-stick frying pan. Add the onion and garlic and fry over a medium heat for 2 minutes. Add the potato and aubergine and season with salt and pepper and rosemary. Toss gently until thoroughly combined and heated through.

3 Add the beaten eggs. Cook gently, lifting and stirring at first, until the egg has almost set – this should take 4–5 minutes. Loosen the edge, invert onto a plate, slide back into the pan, and cook for a few minutes to brown the other side. Alternatively, preheat the grill and put the pan under the grill for a few minutes to brown and set the top. Slide out onto a plate and serve, cut into wedges.

INGREDIENTS

1 small aubergine,
  thinly sliced
1 large potato, scrubbed,
  halved lengthways, and
  thinly sliced
2 tbsp olive oil
1 onion, chopped
1 garlic clove, crushed
salt and freshly ground
  black pepper
1 tbsp chopped rosemary
6 eggs, beaten

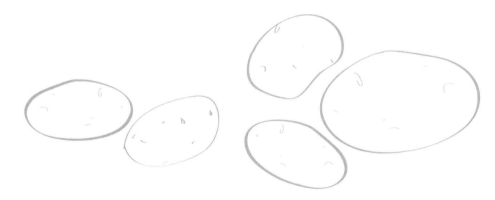

Sweet potato and leek tortilla with fresh tomato sauce

SERVES 4   PREPARATION **15 MINS**   TO COOK **15 MINS**

Tortillas always contain potato, which differentiates them from frittatas. These **use sweet potatoes as they go so well with leeks**, but ordinary potatoes can be substituted.

INGREDIENTS

1 small sweet potato (approx. 450g/1lb), peeled, halved lengthways, and thinly sliced crossways
30g (1oz) butter
2 tbsp olive oil
2 leeks, thinly sliced
2 tbsp chopped thyme, plus extra to garnish
6 large eggs, beaten

For the tomato sauce

1 tbsp olive oil
1 garlic clove, crushed
2 beef tomatoes, skinned and chopped
1 tbsp tomato purée
generous pinch of caster sugar
½ tsp ground cinnamon
salt and freshly ground black pepper

1 First, make the tomato sauce. Heat the oil in a saucepan, add the garlic and tomatoes, and fry, stirring, for 2 minutes until the juices are running. Stir in the tomato purée, sugar, cinnamon, and a little salt and pepper. Cover and simmer gently for 5 minutes. Remove the lid and boil rapidly for about 3 minutes until thick and pulpy, stirring constantly. Remove from the heat, then reheat when ready to serve.

2 Bring a pan of water to a boil, drop in the slices of sweet potato, and cook for 4–5 minutes until they are just tender but still holding their shape. Drain thoroughly.

3 Heat the butter and oil in a large non-stick frying pan. Add the leeks and fry over a medium heat for 2 minutes. Add the sweet potatoes, thyme, and salt and pepper. Toss gently until thoroughly combined. Add the beaten eggs and cook gently for 4–5 minutes, lifting and stirring at first, until the egg has almost set.

4 Meanwhile, preheat the grill. Put the frying pan under the grill for a few minutes to brown and set the top of the tortilla. Slide out onto a plate and garnish with a few thyme leaves. Cut into wedges and serve with the tomato sauce.

Tortillas, frittatas, and omelettes
French bean, garlic, and tomato omelette

SERVES 4 **PREPARATION 10 MINS** TO COOK **20 MINS**

Packed with fresh vegetables, these omelettes are a healthy choice. If the beans are chopped before cooking, the mixture makes a delicious sauce for long pasta, too.

INGREDIENTS

225g (8oz) thin French beans,
  topped and tailed
2 tbsp olive oil
2 tomatoes, roughly chopped
4 tbsp dry white wine or cider
1 tsp tomato purée
1 large garlic clove,
  finely chopped
pinch of caster sugar
salt and freshly ground
  black pepper
1 tbsp chopped parsley
1 tbsp chopped basil
8 eggs
a little butter

1 Blanch the beans in boiling water for 3 minutes, then drain. Heat the oil in a saucepan. Add the tomatoes and cook gently, stirring, for 2 minutes until they start to soften. Add the wine, tomato purée, garlic, sugar, and salt and pepper. Bring to a boil. Add the beans, reduce the heat, and simmer gently for 5 minutes, stirring occasionally, until the beans are just tender and bathed in a thick sauce. Add the parsley and basil, taste, and season again. Cover with a lid and keep warm.

2 Beat 2 eggs at a time with a little salt and pepper. Add a dash of cold water. Heat a little butter in an omelette pan until it foams, then pour in the eggs. Cook over a medium heat, lifting and stirring until the base is set and golden, and the eggs are almost firm but still slightly creamy.

3 Spoon a quarter of the tomato and bean mixture over one half of the omelette. Tilt the pan over a warmed plate. Flip the other side of the omelette over the beans, then slide out onto the plate. Keep the omelette warm while you quickly make the others in the same way.

Piperade

SERVES 4   **PREPARATION 5 MINS**   TO COOK **20 MINS**

This savoury scrambled egg dish is from the Basque region of southwest France, where it is served as either a main course or a side dish.

1 Heat the oil in a large frying pan and fry the onion over a gentle heat until softened. Add the garlic and peppers and fry for 5 minutes, stirring occasionally.

2 Add the tomatoes and simmer for 2–3 minutes, or until any liquid has evaporated.

3 Pour the eggs into the pan and scramble, stirring frequently until creamy and the eggs are just set. Take care not to let the mixture boil or it will curdle. Season with salt and pepper, sprinkle with parsley, and serve.

INGREDIENTS

2 tbsp olive oil
1 large onion, finely sliced
   or chopped
2 garlic cloves, crushed
1 red pepper, deseeded
   and chopped
1 green pepper, deseeded
   and chopped
4 tomatoes, chopped
8 eggs, beaten
salt and freshly ground
   black pepper
2 tbsp chopped parsley,
   to garnish

Four ways with
Courgettes

Courgettes stuffed with sultanas, red onion, and pine nuts ▶

TAKES 30 mins **SERVES** 4

Preheat the oven to 200°C (400°F/Gas 6). Halve 8 **courgettes** lengthways. Scoop out the flesh, chop, and set aside. Heat 1 tbsp **olive oil** in a frying pan over a low heat. Add 1 finely chopped **red onion** and a pinch of **salt**. Sweat for 5 minutes until soft, then stir in the courgette flesh and a pinch of **chilli flakes**. Cook for 2 more minutes. Stir in a small handful each of toasted **pine nuts** and **sultanas**. Remove from the heat. Spoon the mixture into the shells. Top with 75g (2½oz) crumbled **feta cheese**. Roast in the oven for 10–15 minutes. Drizzle with olive oil and serve.

◀ Moroccan couscous salad

TAKES 10 mins **SERVES** 4

Put 250g (9oz) **couscous** in a large bowl with just enough hot **vegetable stock** to cover. Seal with cling film and leave for 5 minutes, then fluff up with a fork. Chop 2 **courgettes**. Heat a little **olive oil** in a frying pan and cook the courgettes until golden. Add to the couscous with a good pinch of **paprika**, the juice of 2 **lemons**, and a handful each of finely chopped fresh **flat-leaf parsley** and chopped **olives**. Season well with **salt** and freshly ground **black pepper** and stir to combine.

Courgettes cook quickly and **can be steamed, boiled, sautéed, or baked**. Just top and tail, then slice, cut in batons, or chop. Cook baby ones whole, or stuff larger ones. The flowers are also delicious stuffed and fried.

Grated courgettes with goat's cheese omelette ▶

TAKES 15 mins **SERVES** 1

Put 3 lightly beaten **eggs** and 1 small grated **courgette** in a jug. Season with **sea salt** and freshly ground **black pepper**. Melt a knob of **butter** in a non-stick frying pan over a medium-high heat until foaming, then pour in the egg mixture, swirling it around to cover the base. When it begins to cook around the edges, scatter over 50g (1¾oz) crumbled **soft goat's cheese** evenly. Cook until the centre is almost cooked, but still a little wet. Remove from the heat and leave for 2 minutes to set. Sprinkle a little pepper over, carefully slide out of the pan, and serve.

◀ Courgette fritters with dill tzatziki

TAKES 30 mins, plus draining **SERVES** 4

Grate 200g (7oz) **courgettes**, sprinkle with 1 tsp **salt**, and drain in a sieve for 1 hour. Rinse and squeeze dry. Whisk together 100g (3½oz) **ricotta cheese**, 1 **egg**, and 2 tbsp **plain flour**. Add 2 crushed **garlic cloves** and a small handful each of chopped **basil** and **flat-leaf parsley**. Season well with **salt** and freshly ground **black pepper**. Mix in the courgettes. Fry tablespoons of the batter in **olive oil** for 2–3 minutes on each side. Drain. Serve with tzatziki made with 1 crushed **garlic clove**, 2 tbsp chopped **dill**, 200g (7oz) **Greek-style yogurt**, a squeeze of **lemon juice**, and salt and pepper.

Minted new potato, pea, and lettuce tortilla

SERVES 4   **PREPARATION** **15 MINS**   TO COOK **18 MINS**

This fresh, summery tortilla is **delicious eaten cold with salad as a picnic lunch**. You can also tuck it into soft bread rolls for lunch on the go, adding some salad, too.

INGREDIENTS

350g (12oz) small new
   potatoes, scrubbed
   and sliced
salt and freshly ground
   black pepper
115g (4oz) shelled fresh
   or frozen peas
large knob of butter
1 tbsp sunflower oil
4 spring onions, chopped
1 Little Gem lettuce, shredded
1 tbsp chopped mint
1 tbsp chopped parsley
6 eggs, beaten

1 Cook the potatoes in salted boiling water for 3 minutes. Add the peas and cook for a further 4 minutes until both are tender. Drain, rinse with cold water, and drain again.

2 Heat the butter and oil in a large frying pan. Add the spring onions and fry, stirring, for 2 minutes over a medium heat. Add the lettuce and fry for another minute until the lettuce is wilted and the onions are soft, but not brown. Add the potatoes and peas and fry, stirring, for 1 minute. Sprinkle with the mint and parsley and add some salt and pepper.

3 Pour in the eggs and cook, lifting and stirring at first, for 4–5 minutes until the mixture has almost set. Invert on a plate, slide back into the pan, and cook the other side for 2 minutes until brown. Alternatively, preheat the grill and put the pan under the grill for a few minutes to brown and set the top. Slide out onto a plate and serve, cut into wedges.

Mixed mushroom and garlic omelettes

MAKES 4   **PREPARATION 5 MINS**   TO COOK **20 MINS**

This is a delicious way to serve wild mushrooms. As many of the wild varieties are now cultivated, you may be able to find them in the shops all year round.

1 Melt the butter in a saucepan with the oil. Add the shallot and garlic and fry, stirring, for 2 minutes to soften. Add the mushrooms and cook, stirring, for 3–4 minutes until soft.

2 Add the wine and boil until the liquid has almost disappeared, stirring all the time. Stir in the cream and boil for 1 minute. Season the mixture with salt and pepper and stir in the parsley. Keep hot.

3 Beat 2 eggs with a little salt and pepper. Add a dash of cold water. Heat a little butter in an omelette pan until it foams, then pour in the eggs. Cook over a medium heat, lifting and stirring, for 1–2 minutes until the base is set and golden and the eggs are almost firm, but still slightly creamy.

4 Spoon a quarter of the mushroom mixture over one half of the omelette. Tilt the pan over a warmed plate. Flip the other side of the omelette over the mushrooms, then slide out onto a plate. Keep warm while quickly making 3 more omelettes in the same way.

INGREDIENTS

knob of butter, plus
  extra for frying
1 tbsp olive oil
1 shallot, finely chopped
2 garlic cloves, chopped
350g (12oz) mixed wild
  mushrooms, cut into
  pieces if large
4 tbsp dry white wine
4 tbsp double cream
salt and freshly ground
  black pepper
1 tbsp chopped parsley
8 eggs

Cheese soufflé omelette with sweetcorn and pepper

MAKES 1   **PREPARATION 15 MINS**   TO COOK **6 MINS**

If making more than one omelette, **serve each as it is ready** as their lovely texture is rapidly lost as they cool. Serve with crusty bread and a green salad.

INGREDIENTS

2 eggs, separated
knob of butter

For the sauce
knob of butter
handful of fresh or thawed
   frozen sweetcorn kernels
½ small red pepper, deseeded
   and finely chopped
2 tsp cornflour
7 tbsp milk
2 tsp snipped chives,
   plus a few extra
   to garnish
20g (¾oz) Gruyère
   cheese, grated
20g (¾oz) Cheddar
   cheese, grated
pinch of cayenne pepper
salt and freshly ground
   black pepper

1 To make the sauce, heat the butter in a saucepan. Add the corn and red pepper, stir, then cover and cook very gently for 5 minutes or until tender. Stir in the cornflour, followed by the milk. Bring to a boil and cook for 2 minutes, stirring all the time, until thick. Stir in the chives, cheeses, cayenne, and salt and pepper to taste.

2 Beat the egg yolks with 2 tbsp water and add salt and pepper. Whisk the egg whites until stiff and fold into the yolks with a metal spoon.

3 Preheat the grill. Heat a knob of butter in an omelette pan, add the egg mixture, and gently spread it out. Cook over a medium heat for about 3 minutes until golden underneath. Immediately place the pan under the grill and cook for 2–3 minutes until risen and golden on top. Meanwhile, reheat the sauce, stirring.

4 Slide the omelette out onto a plate. Quickly spread one half with the cheese and corn sauce (don't worry if it oozes over the edge). Flip the uncovered side over the top to fold the omelette in half, and garnish with a few snipped chives. Serve immediately.

Asparagus and spring onion soufflé omelette

SERVES 2   **PREPARATION 10 MINS**   TO COOK **14 MINS**

To **make individual omelettes** instead, simply use an omelette pan, cook half the egg mixture and use half the vegetables, then repeat with the remaining ingredients.

INGREDIENTS

115g (4oz) thin asparagus
  spears, trimmed if necessary
4 thick spring onions
1 tbsp olive oil
4 large eggs, separated
salt and freshly ground
  black pepper
1 tbsp chopped thyme
knob of butter

1 Steam the asparagus spears or boil in water for 3–4 minutes until tender. Drain thoroughly and set aside.

2 Trim off most of the green part of the spring onions so they are the same length as the asparagus. Cut in halves lengthways. Heat the oil in a non-stick frying pan and sauté the onions over a medium heat for 4–5 minutes until they are soft and lightly golden. Remove with a slotted spoon and add to the asparagus. Mix together gently.

3 Beat the egg yolks with a pinch of salt and some pepper, thyme, and 4 tbsp water. Whisk the egg whites until stiff and fold into the yolk mixture.

4 Reheat the frying pan and melt the butter, swirling it around the pan. Add the egg mixture, then spread it out and cook over a medium heat for 2 minutes until golden underneath. Slide out of the pan onto a plate.

5 Lay the asparagus and spring onions in the pan. Invert the plate with the omelette over the pan so the uncooked side of the omelette sits on top of the vegetables. Cook for a further 2 minutes until just firm, then tip out onto a plate, vegetable-side up. Cut the omelette in half and serve immediately.

Vegetable egg foo yung

SERVES 4   **PREPARATION 10 MINS, PLUS SOAKING**   TO COOK **10 MINS**

Beansprouts are key to achieving the desired flavour, but any of the other **vegetables can be substituted as long as they are cut thinly** so they cook in 2–3 minutes.

1 If using dried mushrooms, soak them in hot water for 30 minutes, then drain before use.

2 Heat 2 tbsp oil in a wok or large frying pan. Stir-fry the mushrooms and other vegetables for 2–3 minutes until they are softened, but still have some texture. Tip into a bowl, mix in the beaten eggs, and add the soy sauce, ginger, and five-spice powder.

3 Heat ½ tbsp of the remaining oil in an omelette pan. Add a quarter of the mixture and spread out evenly. Fry for 1–2 minutes until almost set, lifting the edges and tilting the pan so the runny egg flows underneath.

4 Carefully fold the omelette in half and slide it out onto a warmed plate. Keep it warm while cooking the remaining omelettes in the same way. Serve warm with sweet chilli sauce or soy sauce to drizzle over, if required.

INGREDIENTS

2 heaped tbsp dried sliced shiitake mushrooms, or 4 fresh mushrooms, sliced

4 tbsp sunflower oil

1 carrot, cut into thin batonettes

5cm (2in) piece cucumber, deseeded and cut into thin batonettes

85g (3oz) cooked fresh peas or frozen (thawed)

4 small handfuls of beansprouts

2 spring onions, chopped

2 heads pak choi, shredded

8 eggs, beaten

1 tbsp soy sauce

1 tsp grated fresh root ginger

½ tsp Chinese five-spice powder

sweet chilli sauce or extra soy sauce, to serve (optional)

Butternut squash, spinach, and goat's cheese frittata

SERVES 4 **PREPARATION 10 MINS** TO COOK **20 MINS**

This fresh-tasting frittata is equally good with chopped Swiss chard or pak choi instead of the spinach. Cottage cheese can replace the soft goat's cheese, too.

INGREDIENTS

1 small butternut squash
 (approx. 500g/1lb 2oz),
 peeled, halved, deseeded,
 and diced
2 tbsp olive oil
knob of butter
1 small onion, chopped
200g (7oz) spinach
125g (4½oz) soft
 goat's cheese
4 pieces of semi-dried
 tomatoes in oil, drained
 and cut into small pieces
2 tbsp grated
 Parmesan cheese
grated nutmeg
2 tbsp chopped tarragon
6 eggs, beaten
salt and freshly ground
 black pepper

1 Blanch the squash in boiling water for 2–4 minutes to soften slightly. Drain thoroughly.

2 Heat the oil and butter in a large non-stick frying pan. Add the onion and fry, stirring, for 3 minutes until softened and lightly golden. Add the squash and fry, stirring, for 2 minutes until tender, but still holding its shape.

3 Scatter the spinach into the pan and cook, stirring, for 2 minutes to wilt. Boil rapidly for 1–2 minutes to drive off any liquid, stirring gently and spreading the spinach evenly into the squash. Add small spoonfuls or pieces of the goat's cheese and semi-dried tomatoes. Sprinkle with Parmesan, dust with nutmeg, and scatter the tarragon over.

4 Season the beaten eggs with a little salt and plenty of pepper. Pour into the pan and cook, lifting and stirring, until beginning to set. Cover the pan and cook gently for about 5 minutes until the eggs are almost set and the base is golden.

5 Meanwhile, preheat the grill. When the eggs are nearly set, put the pan under the grill for about 3 minutes to finish setting – the frittata should only just be starting to brown so that all the colours remain vibrant. Remove from the grill and leave to cool for at least 5 minutes. Serve warm or cold, cut into wedges.

Spiced crushed carrot, pine nut, and cottage cheese frittata

SERVES 4   **PREPARATION 5 MINS**   TO COOK **20 MINS**

The sweet carrots and pine nuts perfectly complement the creamy, soft cottage cheese in this dish, which draws its inspiration from the Middle East.

INGREDIENTS

400g (14oz) baby Chantenay carrots, topped and tailed
salt and freshly ground black pepper
2 tbsp olive oil, plus extra for drizzling
2 tbsp pine nuts
1 tbsp black mustard seeds
2 tsp cumin seeds
6 eggs
1 tbsp chopped thyme
150g (5½oz) cottage or ricotta cheese
2 tbsp chopped coriander

1 Halve any fat carrots lengthways so that they cook evenly, then boil the carrots in lightly salted water or steam for about 10 minutes until tender. Drain well, then roughly crush with a potato masher until well broken up, but not mushy. Set aside.

2 Heat half the oil in a frying pan. Add the pine nuts, mustard, and cumin and fry, stirring, for about 1 minute until the mustard seeds begin to pop and the pine nuts are golden. Add to the carrots and mix well. Season with plenty of pepper.

3 Preheat the grill. Beat the eggs in a bowl with the thyme and a little salt and pepper. Heat the remaining oil in the frying pan. Add the crushed carrot mixture and spread out. Dot with small spoonfuls of cheese. Pour the eggs over and sprinkle with the coriander. Cook over a gentle heat for 4–5 minutes, lifting and stirring the mixture gently at first and tilting the pan to allow the uncooked egg to run underneath until the frittata is almost set and the base is golden.

4 When the frittata is almost set, place the pan under the hot grill for a few minutes to brown and cook the top. Cut into wedges and serve warm.

Tortillas, frittatas, and omelettes

Swiss chard, beetroot, and goat's cheese frittata

SERVES 4   PREPARATION **10 MINS**   TO COOK **20 MINS**

When Swiss chard isn't available, use spinach instead. If you have a **larger disc of goat's cheese, dice it rather** than cutting it into slices.

1 Wash the Swiss chard, but don't dry it. Shred the leaves and chop the stalks.

2 Heat the oil and butter in a large non-stick frying pan. Add the onion and fry, stirring, for 3 minutes until soft. Add the chard and stir-fry for about 5 minutes until wilted and the stalks are tender, adding a splash of water if necessary – this should all be evaporated when the vegetables are tender. Spread the mixture out in the pan and scatter the beetroot over.

3 Preheat the grill. Season the eggs with a little salt and pepper and pour into the pan. Scatter the cheese slices and then the dill over the eggs. Cook over a gentle heat for 4–5 minutes, lifting and stirring the mixture gently at first and tilting the pan to allow the uncooked egg to run underneath the omelette.

4 When the base is golden and set but the top is still creamy, put the pan under the hot grill for a few minutes to brown and set the top. Cut into wedges and serve warm.

INGREDIENTS

200g (7oz) Swiss chard (preferably red-stalked)
2 tbsp olive oil
knob of butter
1 small onion, chopped
2 cooked beetroots, diced
6 eggs, beaten
salt and freshly ground black pepper
100g (3½oz) narrow-cylinder goat's cheese, thinly sliced
2 tbsp chopped dill

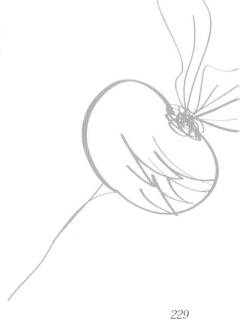

Tarts, pies, and parcels

Tarts, pies, and parcels
Caramelized shallot tart

SERVES 4–6   **PREPARATION 20 MINS, PLUS CHILLING**   TO COOK **45 MINS**

The allium family is indispensable to most cooks, yet onions and shallots rarely take centre stage. **This simple recipe gives shallots a starring role.**

INGREDIENTS

175g (6oz) plain flour
pinch of salt
115g (4oz) butter
2 tbsp olive oil
400g (14oz) shallots, peeled
   and split in half lengthways
2 tbsp balsamic vinegar
a few sprigs of thyme
green salad, to serve

1 For the pastry, combine the flour, salt, and 85g (3oz) butter in a food processor, and mix to form fine breadcrumbs. With the motor running, add cold water, a tbsp at a time, until the pastry starts to stick together. Form the pastry into a ball, wrap it in cling film, and leave it in the refrigerator to chill for 30 minutes. Alternatively, use 250g (9oz) ready-made shortcrust pastry.

2 Preheat the oven to 200°C (400°F/Gas 6). In a 23–25cm (9–10in) ovenproof frying pan, melt the remaining butter with the oil. Put the shallots in, cut-side down, and cook very gently for 10 minutes, or until they are browned. Turn over and cook for another 5 minutes. Add the vinegar and 2 tbsp water, then remove from the heat. Tuck the thyme sprigs between the shallots.

3 Roll out the pastry to a circle a little larger than the frying pan. Lay the pastry over the shallots, trim, and tuck it in. Transfer the pan to the oven and cook for 30 minutes until the pastry is golden brown.

4 Remove the pan from the oven and bang gently to loosen the shallots. Run a knife around the edges of the pastry, then put a large plate over the pan and quickly turn it over. Serve warm with a green salad.

Roasted squash and Gorgonzola tart

SERVES 4–6   **PREPARATION 25 MINS, PLUS CHILLING**   TO COOK **1 HR 30 MINS**

Make this wonderful tart in the early autumn when spinach and squash are readily available. You can use chard in place of the spinach.

1 Preheat the oven to 180°C (350°F/Gas 4). Roll out the pastry on a lightly floured surface, to a thickness of about 3mm (⅛in) in a circle a little larger than a 20cm (8in) loose-bottomed tart tin. Line the tart tin with the pastry. Chill for 30 minutes.

2 Put the squash slices in a roasting tin and brush with oil. Bake for 30 minutes, or until tender. Meanwhile, place the spinach and a little oil in a saucepan and cook over a medium heat for 4 minutes until wilted. Drain and leave to cool. Whisk the eggs, egg yolk, cream, Parmesan, and nutmeg together, and season with salt and pepper.

3 Line the pastry case with greaseproof paper and fill with baking beans. Bake blind for 15 minutes. Remove the beans and paper and bake for another 10 minutes.

4 Squeeze the spinach dry and spread it across the bottom of the tart case, then add the squash and Gorgonzola. Pour the egg mixture over and bake for 30–40 minutes, or until the filling is set. Remove from the oven and let it sit for 10 minutes before serving.

INGREDIENTS

250g (9oz) ready-made
  shortcrust pastry
plain flour, for dusting
450g (1lb) squash, peeled,
  halved, deseeded, and
  thickly sliced
1–2 tbsp olive oil
400g (14oz) spinach
2 large eggs
1 egg yolk
300ml (10fl oz) double cream
50g (1¾oz) Parmesan
  cheese, grated
pinch of grated nutmeg
salt and freshly ground
  black pepper
115g (4oz) Gorgonzola
  cheese, crumbled

233

Stuffed portobello mushroom en croûte

SERVES 4   PREPARATION **30 MINS**   TO COOK **45 MINS**

Chestnuts make a hearty, flavoursome filling for mushrooms. These pies are delicious served with new potatoes and a selection of baby vegetables.

INGREDIENTS

1 tbsp olive oil
knob of butter
1 onion, finely chopped
1 celery stick, finely chopped
240g can cooked chestnuts
2 tbsp chopped
   flat-leaf parsley
2 tbsp chopped thyme
1 tsp grated lemon zest
2 tbsp mushroom ketchup
   or Worcestershire sauce
60g (2oz) wholemeal
   breadcrumbs
salt and freshly ground
   black pepper
2 small eggs
4 large portobello mushrooms,
   peeled and stalks reserved
450g packet puff pastry
sprigs of parsley, to garnish

For the sauce

2 tbsp sunflower oil
175g (6oz) chestnut
   mushrooms, finely chopped
1 garlic clove, crushed
150ml (5fl oz) dry cider
200ml (7fl oz) double cream
2 tsp chopped thyme

1 Heat the oil and butter in a saucepan. Add the onion and celery and fry, stirring, for 3 minutes until softened and lightly golden. Remove from the heat, add the chestnuts, and mash with a fork. Work in the herbs, lemon zest, ketchup, breadcrumbs, and salt and pepper. Beat one of the eggs and stir into the mixture. Press into the mushrooms.

2 Preheat the oven to 200°C (400°F/Gas 6). Cut the pastry into quarters and cut a third off each. Roll out the thirds to rounds about 2cm (¾in) larger in diameter than the mushrooms. Line a baking sheet with baking parchment, lay the rounds on it, and place a stuffed mushroom in the centre of each. Beat the second egg and brush the edges with it.

3 Roll out the remaining pastry to rounds about 8cm (3in) larger than the mushrooms. Place the pastry over and press the edges to seal. Knock up and flute the edges with the back of a knife, then brush all over with beaten egg. Make a hole in the centre of each to allow steam to escape. Make leaves out of pastry trimmings, if liked, and arrange on top. Brush with the remaining egg. Bake in the oven for 40 minutes, or until puffy and golden and the mushrooms are cooked through.

4 Meanwhile, make the sauce. Heat the sunflower oil in a saucepan and add the chestnut mushrooms, finely chopped portobello mushroom stalks, and garlic. Cook, stirring, over a medium heat for about 3 minutes until tender and the liquid has evaporated.

5 Add the cider and boil for 2 minutes until reduced by half. Stir in the cream, thyme, and 6 tbsp water. Simmer for 3 minutes until reduced and thickened, stirring. Season with salt and pepper. Transfer the pies to plates, garnish with parsley, and serve with the sauce.

Asparagus cream cheese quiche

SERVES 4–6   **PREPARATION 20 MINS, PLUS CHILLING**   TO COOK **45 MINS**

Griddling the asparagus enhances its flavour and keeps the colour beautifully green. The cream cheese in the quiche adds a velvety texture and extra goodness.

INGREDIENTS

175g (6oz) plain flour
pinch of salt
85g (3oz) cold butter, diced
175g (6oz) green
   asparagus spears
a little olive oil
115g (4oz) cream cheese
2 tsp chopped thyme
freshly ground black pepper
85g (3oz) mature Cheddar
   cheese, grated
2 eggs
150ml (5fl oz) single cream

1 Sift the flour and salt into a bowl. Add the butter and rub in with the fingertips until the mixture resembles fine breadcrumbs. Mix with 2 tbsp cold water to form a firm dough. Knead gently on a lightly floured surface. Roll out and use to line a 20cm (8in) flan ring set on a baking sheet. Chill for 30 minutes.

2 Preheat the oven to 200°C (400°F/Gas 6). Line the pastry case with greaseproof paper and fill with baking beans. Bake for 10 minutes. Remove the paper and baking beans, then bake for a further 5 minutes to dry out. Remove from the oven and lower the oven temperature to 180°C (350°F/Gas 4).

3 Toss the asparagus spears in a little oil and cook on a hot griddle pan for 2 minutes on each side until bright green and just tender.

4 Spread the cream cheese over the bottom of the pastry case and sprinkle with thyme, some pepper, and the cheese. Trim the asparagus to fit the flan, as necessary. Scatter the trimmings over the cheese and lay the asparagus attractively on top.

5 Beat the eggs and cream together with a little salt and pepper and pour into the flan. Bake in the oven for about 30 minutes until golden and set. Serve warm or cold.

Swiss chard and cheese tart

SERVES 6   **PREPARATION 15 MINS**   TO COOK **1 HR 20 MINS, PLUS COOLING**

Traditional Swiss chard with **succulent, thick white stems is best for this dish**. When it is not in season, spinach makes an ideal alternative.

1 Preheat the oven to 200°C (400°F/Gas 6). Roll out the pastry on a floured surface, into a circle large enough to fit a loose-bottomed 23cm (9in) tart tin. Trim away any excess. Line the pastry shell with greaseproof paper and fill with baking beans. Bake in the oven for 15–20 minutes until the edges are golden. Remove the beans and paper and brush the bottom of the shell with a little of the egg wash. Return to the oven for 5 minutes to crisp up, then set aside. Reduce the oven temperature to 180°C (350°F/Gas 4).

2 For the filling, heat the oil in a pan over a low heat. Add the onion and a pinch of salt and sweat for 5 minutes until soft. Add the garlic and rosemary and cook for a few seconds, then add the chard. Stir for 5 minutes until it wilts.

3 Spoon the onion and chard mixture into the pastry shell. Sprinkle the Gruyère over and scatter evenly with feta. Season well with salt and pepper. Mix together the cream and the 2 eggs until well combined and carefully pour over the tart filling. Bake in the oven for 30–40 minutes until set and golden. Leave to cool for 10 minutes before releasing from the tin. Serve warm or at room temperature.

INGREDIENTS

350g (12oz) ready-made
  shortcrust pastry
plain flour, for dusting
2 eggs, plus 1 lightly beaten,
  for egg wash
1 tbsp extra virgin olive oil
1 onion, finely chopped
salt and freshly ground
  black pepper
2 garlic cloves, finely chopped
a few sprigs of rosemary,
  leaves picked and
  finely chopped
250g (9oz) Swiss
  chard, chopped
125g (4½oz) Gruyère
  cheese, grated
125g (4½oz) feta cheese, diced
200ml (7fl oz) double cream or
  whipping cream

Fennel and Gruyère tart

SERVES 6   **PREPARATION 20 MINS, PLUS CHILLING**   TO COOK **45 MINS**

The light aniseed flavour of the fennel and the sweet tanginess of the Gruyère are a winning combination in this dish – an ideal choice for a summertime lunch.

INGREDIENTS

3 tbsp olive oil
1 onion, sliced
1 large fennel bulb, trimmed,
  quartered, and sliced
salt and freshly ground
  black pepper
½ tsp grated nutmeg
4 eggs
300ml (10fl oz) double cream
350g (12oz) ready-made
  shortcrust pastry
plain flour, for dusting
100g (3½oz) Gruyère
  cheese, grated
salad leaves, to serve

1 Preheat the oven to 200°C (400°F/Gas 6). For the filling, heat the oil in a frying pan, add the onion, and fry on a medium heat for 2–3 minutes. Add the fennel and sauté for 6–8 minutes, stirring occasionally, until golden. Season with salt and pepper and nutmeg and set aside. Beat the eggs and cream together in a jug.

2 Roll out the pastry on a lightly floured surface to a thickness of 5mm (¼in). Lift it over a 23cm (9in) round, 3cm (1¼in) deep, fluted tart tin and press into the base and sides. Trim the edges. Prick the base with a fork, line with greaseproof paper, fill with baking beans, and bake for 15–20 minutes. Remove the beans and paper, then return to the oven for another 5 minutes to crisp up.

3 Scatter the onions and fennel over the base and sprinkle with the cheese. Pour the egg and cream mixture into the pastry case. Return the tart to the oven. Reduce the temperature to 180°C (350°F/Gas 4) and bake for 20–25 minutes, or until the filling is set and golden brown. Serve warm or cold with salad leaves.

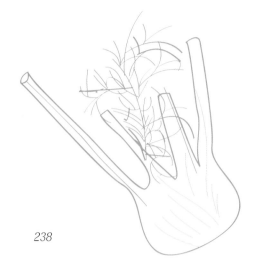

Red pepper and chilli tart

SERVES 4–6   **PREPARATION 25–30 MINS**   TO COOK **1 HR 30 MINS**

These hot flavours are tempered with mild sheep's cheese. If preferred, swap the cheese for another favourite such as Brie, feta, or a blue cheese.

1 Preheat the oven to 200°C (400°F/Gas 6). For the filling, sit the peppers and chillies on a baking sheet and coat with half the oil. Cook in the oven for 30–40 minutes until the skins begin to char. Transfer the peppers to a plastic bag to cool. Chop and deseed the chillies. When the peppers are cool, remove and discard the skins and seeds, roughly chop the flesh, and add to the chillies.

2 Carefully roll out the pastry on a lightly floured surface to a thickness of 5mm (¼in). Lift it over a 20cm (8in) round, loose-bottomed tart tin and press into the base and sides. Prick the base with a fork, line with greaseproof paper, fill with baking beans, and bake for 15–20 minutes. Remove the beans and paper and return to the oven for another 5 minutes to crisp up. Reduce the oven temperature to 180°C (350°F/Gas 4).

3 Heat the remaining oil in a frying pan, add the onion, and cook for 6–8 minutes on a medium-low heat until softened. Season with salt and pepper, then stir through half the thyme. Leave to cool a little, then transfer to the pastry case. Add the peppers and chillies, spreading them out evenly, and scatter the cheese so it covers all the tart. Mix together the cream and egg, and season with salt and pepper. Add the remaining thyme and the garlic and stir well. Pour the mixture over the tart evenly, place the tin on a baking sheet, and bake for 20–25 minutes, or until the top is set and golden. Remove and leave to cool before releasing from the tin.

INGREDIENTS

3 red peppers
2 red chillies
2 tbsp olive oil
250g (9oz) ready-made
  shortcrust pastry
plain flour, for dusting
1 red onion, finely chopped
salt and freshly ground
  black pepper
leaves from a few sprigs
  of thyme
150g (5½oz) soft sheep's
  cheese, crumbled
150ml (5fl oz) double cream
2 eggs
2 garlic cloves, crushed

Leek, sage, walnut, and tomato tartlets

SERVES 4   **PREPARATION 30 MINS, PLUS CHILLING**   **TO COOK 15 MINS**

Serve these pretty tartlets with new potatoes and a crisp green salad. The crispy sage leaves add an extra dimension, but can be omitted if preferred.

INGREDIENTS

500g pack puff pastry,
  thawed if frozen
60g (2oz) butter
4 leeks, cut into thick slices
12 cherry tomatoes, halved
60g (2oz) walnut pieces,
  roughly chopped
1 tbsp chopped sage, plus
  a small handful of sage
  leaves, to garnish
salt and freshly ground
  black pepper
2 eggs, beaten
4 tbsp mayonnaise
sunflower oil, for frying

1 Cut the puff pastry into quarters and roll out to rectangles of about 15 × 18cm (6 × 7in). Place on 2 baking sheets lined with baking parchment. Score a line about 2cm (¾in) from each edge of the rectangles, taking care not to cut right through the pastry. This will form the rims of the tartlets. Chill for at least 30 minutes.

2 Meanwhile, make the filling. Melt the butter in a saucepan. Add the leeks and cook gently, stirring, for 2 minutes to soften slightly, but not brown. Reduce the heat, cover, and cook gently for 4 minutes until the leeks are soft, but still bright green and holding their shape. Tip into a bowl and set aside to cool, then add the tomatoes, walnuts, sage, and salt and pepper.

3 Preheat the oven to 200°C (400°F/Gas 6). Brush a little of the beaten egg around the rims of each tartlet. Beat the remainder with the mayonnaise and stir into the leek mixture. Spoon into the centres of the tartlets, leaving the rims free and making sure each tartlet gets a good mixture of leeks, walnuts, and tomatoes. Bake in the oven for about 20 minutes until the centres are set and the edges puffy and golden.

4 Meanwhile, heat about 1cm (½in) oil until hot, but not smoking. Put the sage leaves in a slotted spoon and lower into the hot oil. Cook for a few seconds, just until they stop sizzling and are bright green. Remove immediately and drain on kitchen paper. Scatter a few crispy leaves over each tartlet before serving.

Wild mushroom and Taleggio tart

SERVES 6   PREPARATION **20 MINS**   TO COOK **50 MINS**

This is an earthy, robust tart that is excellent for entertaining, served with roasted new potatoes and a lightly dressed watercress and orange salad.

INGREDIENTS

350g (12oz) ready-made
  shortcrust pastry
plain flour, for dusting
2 tbsp olive oil
150g (5½oz) mixed wild or
  exotic mushrooms, larger
  ones sliced
150g (5½oz) chestnut
  mushrooms, roughly
  chopped
25g (scant 1oz) dried porcini
  mushrooms, soaked
  in boiling water for
  30 minutes and drained
3 garlic cloves, finely chopped
50g (1¾oz) hazelnuts, toasted
  and roughly chopped
salt and freshly ground
  black pepper
handful of flat-leaf parsley,
  finely chopped
3 tbsp double cream
1 egg, lightly beaten
200g (7oz) Taleggio
  cheese, sliced
pinch of sweet paprika

1 Preheat the oven to 200°C (400°F/Gas 6). Roll out the pastry on a lightly floured surface to a thickness of 5mm (¼in). Use it to line a 35 × 12cm (14 × 5in) rectangular, 2.5cm (1in) deep, loose-bottomed tart tin. Trim to neaten. Prick the base with a fork and line with greaseproof paper. Fill with baking beans and bake in the oven for 15 minutes, or until the edges start turning golden. Remove the beans and paper and return to the oven for 5 minutes to crisp up. Reduce the oven temperature to 180°C (350°F/Gas 4).

2 Meanwhile, for the filling, heat the oil in a large frying pan. Add all the mushrooms and cook on a medium-high heat for 10 minutes. Stir through the garlic and nuts and season with salt and pepper.

3 Transfer the mixture to a large bowl and toss with the parsley, cream, and egg. Spoon the mixture into the tart case and top with the cheese. Sprinkle with paprika and bake for 15–20 minutes until golden and set. Remove and leave for at least 10 minutes before releasing from the tin.

Sweetcorn and jalapeño tart

SERVES 4   **PREPARATION 20 MINS**   TO COOK **45 MINS–1 HR**

The **mix of sweet and hot flavours** in this colourful tart is characteristic of the American Southwest. Pair it with a tomato and avocado salad.

1 Preheat the oven to 200°C (400°F/Gas 6). Roll out the pastry on a lightly floured surface to a thickness of 5mm (¼in). Line an 18cm (7in) round, loose-bottomed, straight-sided tart tin with the pastry. Trim to neaten. Prick the base with a fork and line with greaseproof paper, then fill with baking beans and bake for 15 minutes. Remove the beans and paper and return to the oven for a further 5 minutes to crisp up. Reduce the oven temperature to 180°C (350°F/Gas 4).

2 Meanwhile, for the filling, heat the oil in a large pan, add the spring onions, and cook on a low heat for 2 minutes. Stir in the cayenne or paprika, if using, and add the red pepper. Cook for a further 5 minutes, add the sweetcorn, and season with salt and pepper. Remove from the heat and leave to cool.

3 Stir in the cream and egg to coat the onions and pepper. Spoon the mixture into the pastry case and top with the jalapeños and cheese. Bake for 20–30 minutes or until set and golden. Remove and leave to cool for 10 minutes, then slice and serve with a tomato and avocado salad.

INGREDIENTS

175g (6oz) ready-made shortcrust pastry
plain flour, for dusting
2 tbsp olive oil
bunch of spring onions, finely chopped
pinch of cayenne pepper or sweet paprika (optional)
1 large red pepper, halved, deseeded, and finely chopped
400g can sweetcorn, drained
salt and freshly ground black pepper
150ml (5fl oz) double cream
1 egg, beaten
1–2 tbsp sliced green jalapeño chillies, from a jar
60g (2oz) Monterey Jack or Cheddar cheese, sliced or grated
tomato and avocado salad, to serve

Cheese and asparagus turnovers

MAKES 9   **PREPARATION 20 MINS**   TO COOK **20–25 MINS**

These flaky, crumbly parcels are perfect for a light lunch or picnic on a sunny summer's day. Using ready-made pastry makes the preparation quick and easy.

INGREDIENTS

salt and freshly ground
  black pepper
100g (3½oz) asparagus spears,
  cut into 1cm (½in) strips
50g (1¾oz) mature Cheddar
  cheese, grated
3 tbsp snipped chives
500g ready-made puff pastry
plain flour, for dusting
1 egg, beaten, to glaze
sweet paprika, for dusting
salad leaves, to serve

1 Bring a small pan of salted water to a boil and blanch the asparagus spears for 2 minutes. Drain and refresh in cold water. Drain again and cool. Mix the asparagus with the cheese, chives, and plenty of pepper. Set aside.

2 Carefully roll out the pastry on a lightly floured surface to form a 30cm (12in) square, 5mm (¼in) in thickness. Trim the edges, then cut out 9 equal squares. Brush the edges of each square with water. Divide the asparagus filling between the squares, heaping it over one diagonal half of each. Fold the pastry over the filling and pinch the edges together to seal. Use a knife to flute and crimp the edges together.

3 Place the triangles well apart on a large, lightly greased baking sheet. Make a steam hole in the top of each, then glaze with beaten egg and dust with paprika. Bake for 20–25 minutes, or until golden and risen. Serve warm or cold with salad leaves.

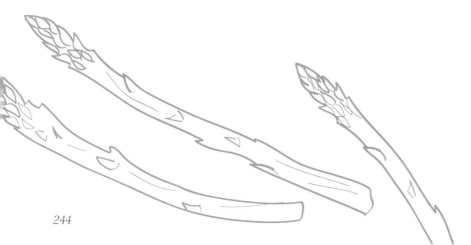

Spanakopita

SERVES 6   PREPARATION **20 MINS**   TO COOK **1 HR**

This is a **classic pie, filled with spinach, feta, and a hint of nutmeg**. Brushing the filo with butter between layers gives a really crisp, golden finish when baked.

1 Preheat the oven to 200°C (400°F/Gas 6). Heat the oil in a large frying pan, add the onion, and cook for 2–3 minutes. Season with salt and pepper. In a separate large pan, cook the spinach in 4 batches of 250g (9oz) each on a low heat for 4–5 minutes until it wilts. Remove and set aside.

2 In a bowl, stir together the feta, nutmeg, and dill, and season with more pepper. Add the eggs and combine. Squeeze any excess water from the spinach, then add this and the onion to the feta mixture and mix.

3 Brush a 1.4 litre (2¹/₂ pint) shallow rectangular dish with a little of the butter. Line with 1 sheet of filo and brush again. Lay the second sheet at right-angles to the first and brush again with butter. Repeat with a third sheet at right-angles again.

4 Fill the dish with the spinach mixture. Fold the edges of the filo over the top. Lay one of the remaining sheets of filo on top of the dish, folding the edges underneath so it fits the top of the dish. Brush with butter and lay another sheet on top folded the same way, then the final sheet. Brush the top with any remaining butter. Place the pie on a baking sheet.

5 Bake in the oven for about 20–25 minutes or until crisp and golden brown. Remove from the oven and leave to cool for 5–10 minutes before serving with a tomato salad.

INGREDIENTS

1 tbsp olive oil
½ onion, very finely chopped
salt and freshly ground
   black pepper
1kg (2¼lb) spinach
250g (9oz) feta cheese,
   crumbled
pinch of grated nutmeg
handful of dill, finely chopped
3 eggs
30g (1oz) butter, melted
6 sheets filo pastry
tomato salad, to serve

Four ways with
Peppers

Red pepper salad ▶

TAKES 35 mins **SERVES** 4

Heat 3 tbsp **olive oil** in a large frying pan. Add
6 **red peppers**, deseeded and cut into large strips,
and 2 finely chopped **garlic cloves**. Fry over a low
heat for 5 minutes, stirring, then add 250g (9oz)
ripe **tomatoes**, skinned, deseeded, and chopped.
Increase the heat, bring to simmering point, then
reduce to low, cover, and cook for 12–15 minutes.
Stir in 2 tbsp chopped **parsley**, season with **salt**
and freshly ground **black pepper**, and cook for
2 minutes. Transfer the peppers to a serving dish.
Add 1 tbsp **sherry vinegar** to the pan, increase
the heat, and simmer for 5–7 minutes. Pour the
sauce over the peppers and allow to cool.

◀ Pasta with roasted peppers

TAKES 35 mins **SERVES** 4

Roast and skin 6 **red peppers** (see p326) and
cut into strips. Melt a knob of **butter** with
3 tbsp **olive oil** in a frying pan and gently fry
2 chopped **garlic cloves** together with 1 **red
chilli** and 1 **green chilli**, deseeded and chopped,
for 2 minutes to soften, but not brown. Add a
generous pinch of **dried oregano** and 1 tbsp
thyme leaves. Cook 350g (12oz) **dried penne**
according to the packet instructions. Drain,
reserving a little of the cooking water. Return to
the pan, add the pepper mixture, and toss gently
with 25g (scant 1oz) grated **Pecorino cheese**.
Serve drizzled with **chilli oil**.

Peppers become sweeter as they ripen from green, through yellow and orange, to red. If you **buy them when glossy and firm**, they will store in the fridge for up to 2 weeks, but use them within 24 hours once cut.

Roasted mixed pepper bruschetta ▶

TAKES 1 hr **SERVES** 4

Remove the seeds from 1 **red pepper** and 1 **yellow pepper**. Then slice the flesh into strips and add to a frying pan with a little **olive oil**. Season with **salt** and freshly ground **black pepper**. Cook until the peppers begin to soften. Increase the heat, add a drop of **balsamic vinegar**, and cook for a couple more minutes. Toast 4 **ciabatta** slices. Peel and cut 1 **garlic clove** in half. Rub the cut side over each slice. Spoon the pepper mixture onto the bread slices and serve hot, garnished with a scattering of **basil** leaves.

◀ Red pepper and walnut dip

TAKES 50 mins **SERVES** 8

Heat 90ml (3fl oz) **olive oil** in a heavy-based frying pan over a low heat. Add 1 sliced **onion**, then sweat gently for 5 minutes until soft and translucent. Tip in 4 **red peppers**, deseeded and sliced, and cook for about 30 minutes until soft, stirring regularly. Stir in 2 crushed **garlic cloves** and cook for a further 30 seconds, or until the garlic has turned white. Transfer the pepper mixture to a blender or food processor. Add 125g (4½oz) toasted and chopped **walnuts** and grated zest and juice of 1 **lemon**, then blend to a chunky purée. Serve with bread or crudités, such as carrot or cucumber batons, for dipping.

Tarts, pies, and parcels
Creamy broccoli and blue cheese puffs

SERVES 4   **PREPARATION 20 MINS**   **TO COOK 35 MINS**

Broccoli and blue cheese are perfect partners in these tasty, simple-to-make pies, but goat's cheese or even Cheddar make an equally good match.

INGREDIENTS

175g (6oz) broccoli, cut into tiny florets

375g (13oz) sheet ready-rolled puff pastry (approx. 23 × 40cm/9 × 16in)

100g (3½oz) creamy blue cheese, crumbled

6 tbsp crème fraîche, plus extra for glazing

salt and freshly ground black pepper

1 Cook the broccoli in lightly salted boiling water for 2 minutes until almost tender. Drain, rinse with cold water, and drain again. Preheat the oven to 220°C (425°F/Gas 7).

2 Cut the pastry in quarters. Pile the broccoli at one end of each oblong, leaving a border. Add some cheese and crème fraîche. Season with pepper and a few grains of salt (the cheese is quite strong).

3 Brush the pastry edges with water. Fold over the uncovered halves of the pastry, press the edges together to seal, and transfer to a dampened baking sheet. Make a few slashes in the tops and glaze with crème fraîche. Bake for 30 minutes until puffy, crisp, and golden.

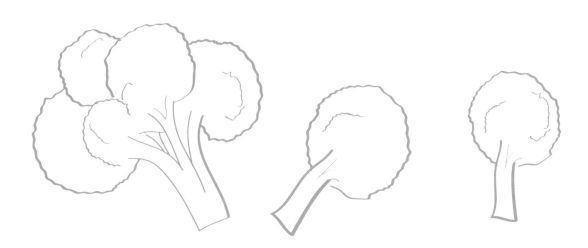

Artichoke, black olive, tomato, and feta tart

SERVES 4–6   **PREPARATION 15 MINS**   TO COOK **1 HR**

This tart is bursting with the wonderful flavours of the Mediterranean. If fresh thyme isn't available, a couple of pinches of dried oregano will work equally well.

1 Preheat the oven to 200°C (400°F/Gas 6). Roll out the pastry on a lightly floured work suface and use to line a 35 × 12cm (13 × 5in) loose-bottomed, fluted tart tin. Trim away the excess, line the pastry shell with greaseproof paper, and fill with ceramic baking beans. Bake in the oven for 15–20 minutes until the edges are golden. Remove the beans and paper, brush the bottom of the shell with a little of the egg wash, and return to the oven for 5 minutes to crisp up. Remove and set aside. Reduce the oven temperature to 180°C (350°F/Gas 4).

2 Heat the oil in a pan over a low heat. Add the onion and sweat gently for about 5 minutes until soft and translucent. Add the garlic and cook for a few seconds more. Spoon the onion mixture evenly over the bottom of the tart shell. Arrange the artichokes down the centre with tomatoes and olives alternately along either side, then sprinkle with the feta and thyme leaves.

3 Mix together the cream and 2 eggs and season well with salt and pepper. Carefully pour over the tart filling. Bake in the oven for 25–35 minutes until set, puffed, and golden. Leave to cool for about 10 minutes before releasing from the tin. Serve warm or at room temperature, with a rocket and tomato salad.

INGREDIENTS

250g (9oz) ready-made
   shortcrust pastry
plain flour, for dusting
2 eggs, plus 1 lightly beaten
   for egg wash
1 tbsp olive oil
1 onion, finely chopped
2 garlic cloves,
   finely chopped
400g can artichoke
   hearts, drained
6 semi-dried tomato pieces
12 pitted black olives
175g (6oz) feta cheese, diced
a few sprigs of thyme,
   leaves picked
200ml (7fl oz) double cream
salt and freshly ground
   black pepper
rocket and tomato salad,
   to serve

Wild mushroom and hollandaise tartlets

SERVES 6   **PREPARATION 35 MINS, PLUS COOLING**   TO COOK **10 MINS**

Halved **English muffins, hollowed out and baked with butter until golden**, make a delicious alternative to pastry for these tartlet cases.

INGREDIENTS

3 English muffins
45g (1½oz) butter, melted
30g (1oz) unsalted butter
1 small onion, chopped
400g (14oz) field or open cup
   mushrooms, sliced
15g (½oz) dried wild
   mushrooms, soaked in
   boiling water for 30 minutes,
   drained, and chopped
2 tbsp chopped tarragon
juice of ½ lemon
salt and freshly ground
   black pepper
175g (6oz) mascarpone cheese
a few chive stalks, to garnish

For the hollandaise

3 eggs
1½ tbsp lemon juice
175g (6oz) butter, melted
pinch of cayenne pepper

1 Preheat the oven to 190°C (375°F/Gas 5). Scoop out most of the soft filling from the muffins, leaving a 5mm (¼in) border all around. Brush all over with melted butter. Place on a baking sheet and bake in the oven for 15 minutes until golden, but not too crisp. Remove from the oven and set aside.

2 For the filling, melt the unsalted butter in a frying pan and cook the onion and field mushrooms over a medium heat. Add the dried mushrooms. Once all the mushrooms are soft, increase the heat and boil until the liquid has evaporated. Add the tarragon and lemon juice and season with salt and pepper. Remove from the heat, cool, then put in the food processor with the mascarpone cheese and purée until fairly smooth. Adjust the seasoning.

3 To make the hollandaise, whisk the eggs with the lemon juice in a small pan. Gradually whisk in the melted butter. Cook over a very gentle heat, whisking all the time until thick – do not boil or it will curdle. Remove from the heat and season to taste with salt and pepper, and a pinch of cayenne pepper.

4 Spoon the mixture into the muffin tartlets and pour the hollandaise over. Bake for 10 minutes to glaze the tops. Serve hot, garnished with chive stalks.

Tomato and onion tart

SERVES 4–6   **PREPARATION 25 MINS**   **TO COOK 25 MINS**

Adding cinnamon to the wholemeal pastry adds a **lovely depth of flavour to this simple, rustic tart**. Use good-quality, ripe tomatoes for the best result.

1 Preheat the oven to 200°C (400°F/Gas 6). Mix the flour, salt, and cinnamon together. Rub in the butter until the mixture resembles breadcrumbs, then mix with enough cold water to form a firm dough. Knead gently on a lightly floured surface. Roll out and use to line a 23cm (9in) shallow flan dish or tin. Line with greaseproof paper, fill with baking beans, and bake in the oven for 10 minutes. Remove the paper and beans and cook for a further 5 minutes to dry out.

2 Meanwhile, fry the onions gently in the oil, stirring, for 5 minutes until soft but not brown. Add the garlic, tomatoes, tomato purée, and sugar, and season with some salt and pepper. Simmer gently, stirring occasionally, for 10 minutes until pulpy. Stir in the parsley, taste, and season again, if necessary.

3 Spoon into the flan case and spread out. Top with the olives and bake for 10 minutes. Serve warm or cold.

INGREDIENTS

175g (6oz) wholemeal flour
pinch of salt
1 tsp ground cinnamon
100g (3½oz) butter, diced
2 Spanish onions,
    roughly chopped
3 tbsp olive oil
1 garlic clove, crushed
450g (1lb) tomatoes, skinned
    and chopped
1 tbsp tomato purée
½ tsp caster sugar
salt and freshly ground
    black pepper
2 tbsp chopped parsley
a few black olives

Courgette, broad bean, and fresh pea quiches

SERVES 6 **PREPARATION 15 MINS, PLUS CHILLING** **TO COOK 30 MINS**

Yellow courgettes have a slightly sweeter flavour than green ones and go particularly well with peas. They also add colour to this fresh-tasting quiche.

INGREDIENTS

200g (7oz) plain flour, plus extra for dusting
100g (3½oz) unsalted butter, plus extra for greasing
1 egg yolk
45g (1½oz) Parmesan cheese, grated
salt and freshly ground black pepper
a little milk
675g (1½lb) broad beans in the pod, or 225g (8oz) frozen
200g (7oz) courgettes, preferably yellow, cut into 1cm (½in) cubes
400g (14oz) fresh peas (125g/4½oz podded weight)
6 egg yolks
150ml (5fl oz) double cream
1 tbsp chopped mint
salt and freshly ground black pepper

1 Preheat the oven to 180°C (350°F/Gas 4). In a food processor, pulse the flour for 1 minute, then add the butter in small knobs. Once incorporated, add the egg yolk, Parmesan, and some salt and pepper to season. Tip out onto the work surface and bring the pastry together with a little milk. Wrap in cling film and rest in the refrigerator for at least 30 minutes until needed.

2 Bring a saucepan of salted water to a boil and drop in the broad beans. Blanch them for 3–4 minutes, then drain under cold running water and pop them out of their skins.

3 Take 6 mini tart tins, 10cm (4in) in diameter and 5cm (2in) deep, and grease with butter, then dust with flour. Roll out the pastry on a lightly floured surface and use to line the tins. Chill for 10 minutes, then bake the pastry cases for 8 minutes. Cool and fill with the beans, courgettes, and peas.

4 Mix together the egg yolks and cream, then add the mint and some salt and pepper. Pour over the tarts, right up to the top, and bake for about 25 minutes until the custard has just set. Let them stand for 5 minutes before serving with a few dressed mixed leaves.

Celeriac and pecan soufflé pie

SERVES 4   PREPARATION **40 MINS, PLUS CHILLING**   TO COOK **50 MINS**

This light-textured pie is **equally good made with parsnips or sweet potatoes instead of celeriac**. Try walnuts or hazelnuts instead of pecans, too.

1 Mix the flour and salt in a bowl. Add the caraway seeds. Rub in the butter until the mixture resembles breadcrumbs. Stir in the cheese. Mix 3 tbsp cold water with the egg yolk and stir into the flour mixture to form a firm dough, adding more water if necessary. Knead gently on a lightly floured surface, then wrap and chill for at least 30 minutes.

2 Meanwhile, cook the celeriac in salted boiling water until tender. Drain and return to the pan. Dry out briefly over a gentle heat. Mash with the butter and milk. Beat in the pecans, egg yolks, and chives. Season well with pepper.

3 Preheat the oven to 200°C (400°F/Gas 6). Roll out the dough and use it to line a 20cm (8in) flan tin. Line with greaseproof paper and fill with baking beans. Bake blind in the oven for 10 minutes, then remove the paper and beans. Bake for a further 5 minutes and remove from the oven.

4 Whisk the 3 egg whites until stiff. Mix 1 tbsp of the whites into the celeriac mixture. Fold in the remainder with a metal spoon. Spoon into the pastry case and bake for 25 minutes until risen, just set, and golden. Serve straightaway.

INGREDIENTS

175g (6oz) wholemeal or
    spelt flour
generous pinch of salt
1 tbsp caraway seeds
75g (2½oz) butter, chilled
    and diced
85g (3oz) mature Cheddar
    cheese, grated
1 egg, separated
plain flour, for dusting
1 celeriac, approx. 450g (1lb),
    peeled and cut into chunks
60g (2oz) butter
4 tbsp milk
60g (2oz) pecan nuts, chopped
2 eggs, separated
2 tbsp snipped chives
freshly ground black pepper

Mediterranean vegetable and feta filo pie

SERVES 4   **PREPARATION 35 MINS**   **TO COOK 25 MINS**

This pie is delicious hot or cold. **Brush the layers of filo with olive oil instead of butter if preferred** – although the butter gives a crisper finish to the dish.

INGREDIENTS

2 tbsp olive oil
1 red onion, chopped
1 garlic clove, crushed
1 red pepper, deseeded
   and cut into small chunks
1 green pepper, deseeded
   and cut into small chunks
1 aubergine, halved
   lengthways and sliced
1 large courgette, sliced
4 tomatoes, chopped
1 tsp dried oregano
small handful of pitted black
   olives, halved
salt and freshly ground
   black pepper
50g (1¾oz) butter, melted
6 sheets filo pastry
200g (7oz) feta cheese, diced
green salad, to serve

1 Heat the oil in a large saucepan. Add the onion and garlic along with the vegetables and fry, stirring, for about 3 minutes until slightly softened. Cover, reduce the heat, and cook gently for 20 minutes, stirring occasionally.

2 Stir in the oregano, olives, and a little salt and pepper (the cheese and olives will be salty when added). Set aside to cool.

3 Preheat the oven to 200°C (400°F/Gas 6). Brush a 1.4 litre (2½ pint) shallow rectangular dish with a little of the butter. Line with a sheet of filo and brush again. Lay a second sheet at right-angles to the first and brush again with butter. Repeat with a third sheet at right-angles again.

4 Fill the dish with the vegetable mixture and scatter the cheese over, pressing it into the surface. Fold the edges of the filo over the top. Lay one of the remaining sheets of filo on top of the dish, folding the edges underneath so it fits the top of the dish. Brush with butter and lay another sheet on top folded the same way, then the final sheet. Brush the top with any remaining butter. Place the pie on a baking sheet.

5 Bake in the oven for about 20–25 minutes, or until crisp and golden brown. Remove from the oven and leave to cool for 5–10 minutes before serving with a green salad.

Limoges potato and onion pie

SERVES 6–8   **PREPARATION 35 MINS**   TO COOK **1 HR 15 MINS**

Flavoured with herbs, **this substantial pie makes full use of earthy new potatoes**. When wild garlic is in season, stir in a few chopped leaves instead of the garlic cloves.

INGREDIENTS

1kg (2¼lb) new potatoes,
   scrubbed and sliced
salt and freshly ground
   black pepper
60g (2oz) butter
3 onions, halved and
   thinly sliced
2 garlic cloves, chopped
500g (1lb 2oz) puff pastry,
   thawed if frozen
2 tbsp snipped chives
2 tbsp chopped parsley
2 tbsp chopped mint
2 eggs
300ml (10fl oz) single cream
pickles and green salad,
   to serve

1 Boil the potatoes in salted water for about 5 minutes until tender, but still holding their shape. Drain well and leave to cool.

2 Melt the butter in the rinsed-out saucepan. Fry the onions and garlic gently for 5 minutes, stirring, until soft and browning slightly. Set aside.

3 Preheat the oven to 220°C (425°F/Gas 7). Cut the pastry in half, roll out one half, and use to line a deep pie dish, 25cm (10in) in diameter.

4 Layer the potatoes, onions, and garlic, seasoning each layer with salt and pepper and sprinkling with herbs. Repeat 3 times to make 4 layers. Whisk the eggs and cream together with a little salt and pepper. Pour all over the filling and allow it to soak down into the pie. Reserve the dregs of the egg and cream mixture for glazing the pie.

5 Roll out the remaining pastry and use as a lid, pressing it down all around, then trim off excess pastry and crimp the edges together between the finger and thumb to seal and decorate.

6 Brush the top with the dregs of the eggs and cream mixture to glaze. Make leaves out of the pastry trimmings and arrange on the pie. Brush again. Make a hole in the centre to allow steam to escape.

7 Place the pie on a baking sheet and bake in the oven for 30 minutes until puffy and golden. Cover the pie loosely with foil to prevent over-browning and cook for a further 30–35 minutes until the custard is set and the pie is well risen and crisp. Cool for a few minutes to allow the flavours to develop before serving the pie with pickles and a green salad.

Root vegetable and fennel pasties with seed pastry

MAKES 4   **PREPARATION 30 MINS, PLUS CHILLING**   TO COOK **45–50 MINS**

These well-flavoured pasties are **delicious served hot with cauliflower or broccoli in cheese sauce** or cold with pickles and salad.

1 Mix the flours together in a bowl with a pinch of salt. Add the butter and rub in with the fingertips until the mixture resembles fine breadcrumbs. Stir in the fennel seeds, then mix with about 4 tbsp cold water to form a soft but not sticky dough. Wrap in cling film and leave to rest in the refrigerator for 30 minutes.

2 In a large bowl, mix the vegetables together with the thyme, and a little salt and plenty of pepper.

3 Preheat the oven to 190°C (375°F/Gas 5). Knead the dough gently on a lightly floured surface and cut into quarters. Roll out each quarter to rounds, about 18cm (7in) in diameter. Spread the centre of each round with 1 tbsp cream cheese and pile the vegetables on top. Brush the edges with a little beaten egg.

4 Working with one pasty at a time, spoon ½ tbsp stock over to moisten, then draw the dough up over the filling and press together to seal. Flute between your finger and thumb to give an attractive edge, then transfer to a non-stick baking sheet. Repeat with the remaining pasties.

5 Brush the pasties with beaten egg to glaze, then bake in the oven for 45–50 minutes until the pasties are golden brown and the vegetables are tender. Cover loosely with foil after 30 minutes if over-browning. Serve hot or cold.

INGREDIENTS

175g (6oz) wholemeal flour
175g (6oz) plain flour,
   plus extra for dusting
salt and freshly ground
   black pepper
175g (6oz) butter, cut
   into small pieces
1 tbsp fennel seeds

For the filling
1 small onion, chopped
1 carrot, cut into small cubes
1 small potato, peeled and cut
   into small cubes
1 small turnip, cut into
   small cubes
1 fennel bulb, chopped
2 tbsp chopped thyme
4 tbsp cream cheese
1 small egg, beaten
2–3 tbsp vegetable stock

Tarts, pies, and parcels
Vegetable samosas

SERVES 4   PREPARATION **45 MINS, PLUS RESTING AND COOLING**   TO COOK **35–40 MINS**

Serve these Indian pastries hot or cold. In India they would be fried in ghee, a clarified butter that can be heated to a high temperature, but oil works equally well.

INGREDIENTS

350g (12oz) plain flour, plus
  extra for dusting
salt and freshly ground
  black pepper
9 tbsp sunflower oil or ghee,
  plus extra for frying
450g (1lb) potatoes, scrubbed
225g (8oz) cauliflower,
  chopped into small pieces
175g (6oz) peas, thawed
  if frozen
2 shallots, sliced
2 tbsp curry paste
2 tbsp chopped coriander
1 tbsp lemon juice

1 To make the pastry, sift the flour into a bowl with ½ tsp salt. Stir in 6 tbsp oil or ghee and gradually add 120ml (4fl oz) warm water, mixing to make a dough. Knead the dough on a floured surface until smooth. Wrap in cling film and leave to rest for at least 30 minutes.

2 To make the filling, cook the potatoes in a saucepan of boiling water until tender. Drain and cool, then peel and chop into small pieces. Blanch the cauliflower florets in a pan of boiling water for 2–3 minutes, or until just tender, then drain. If using fresh peas, blanch them with the cauliflower.

3 Heat the remaining oil in a large frying pan and fry the shallots for 3–4 minutes, stirring frequently, until soft. Add the potatoes, cauliflower, peas, curry paste, coriander, and lemon juice and cook over a low heat for 2–3 minutes, stirring occasionally. Set aside to cool.

4 Divide the dough into 8 equal pieces. Roll them out so each forms an 18cm (7in) round. Cut each round in half and shape into a cone, dampening the edges to seal. Spoon a little of the filling into each cone, dampen the top edge of the dough, and press down over the filling to enclose it. Repeat with the rest of the dough and filling.

5 Heat oil for deep-frying to 180°C (350°F), or until a cube of day-old bread browns in 30 seconds. Fry the samosas in batches for 3–4 minutes, or until golden brown on both sides. Drain on kitchen paper and serve hot or cold.

Sweetcorn and pepper empanadas

MAKES 24   **PREPARATION 45 MINS, PLUS CHILLING**   **TO COOK 40–50 MINS**

These Spanish pastries make versatile snacks. For a main meal, make fewer, larger pies, using a tea plate as a guide to cut out the dough. The baking time is the same.

1 To make the pastry, sift the flour into a large mixing bowl with ½ tsp salt. Add the butter and rub in with your fingertips until it resembles fine breadcrumbs. Add the beaten eggs with 4–6 tbsp water and combine to form a dough. Cover with cling film and chill for 30 minutes.

2 Heat the oil in a frying pan, add the onion, and fry for 3 minutes until softened. Add the green pepper and fry for a further 3 minutes, stirring frequently. Add the tomatoes, tomato purée, and paprika. Season with salt and pepper, partially cover and simmer, stirring occasionally, for 5 minutes until pulpy. Stir in the chopped egg and parsley.

3 Preheat the oven to 190°C (375°F/Gas 5). Roll out the pastry to a thickness of 3mm (⅛in). Cut out 24 rounds with a 9cm (3½ in) round pastry cutter. Put a heaped tsp of the mixture on each, then brush the edges with water, fold over, and pinch together.

4 Place the empanadas on an oiled baking tray and brush with some beaten egg. Bake for 25–30 minutes, or until golden brown, and serve warm.

INGREDIENTS

450g (1lb) plain flour, plus
  extra for dusting
salt and freshly ground
  black pepper
85g (3oz) butter, diced
2 eggs, beaten, plus extra
  to glaze
1 tbsp olive oil
1 onion, finely chopped
1 green pepper, deseeded
  and finely chopped
2 tomatoes, chopped
2 tsp tomato purée
1 tsp sweet paprika
2 hard-boiled eggs, chopped
2 tbsp finely chopped parsley

Grills and bakes

Shiitake mushroom and water chestnut teriyaki

SERVES 4   PREPARATION **10 MINS**   TO COOK **20–25 MINS**

A simple Japanese-style grill, this is **great with a salad of beansprouts** tossed with some chopped spring onion in a dash of soy sauce, rice vinegar, and sesame oil.

INGREDIENTS

6 tbsp tamari (or light soy sauce), plus extra to serve

2 tbsp lime juice

2 tsp grated fresh root ginger

2 garlic cloves, crushed

1 fat red chilli, deseeded and chopped

3 tbsp clear honey

1 tsp sunflower oil

300g (10oz) shiitake mushrooms, halved if large

250g can water chestnuts, drained

2 red onions, quartered and separated into slices

udon noodles, tossed in sesame oil, and beansprout salad, to serve

torn coriander or flat-leaf parsley leaves, to garnish

1 Put all the ingredients except the mushrooms, water chestnuts, and onions in a saucepan. Stir well, bring to a boil, and continue to boil for 2–3 minutes until syrupy. Remove from the heat and stir in the vegetables until well coated.

2 Preheat the grill. Spread the coated vegetables on a large baking tray lined with oiled foil. Grill about 5cm (2in) from the heat source for 15–20 minutes, turning once or twice, until richly browned and glazed.

3 Serve spooned onto noodles, sprinkled with torn coriander or flat-leaf parsley leaves, with a beansprout salad and extra tamari to sprinkle over.

Grills and bakes
Aubergine koftas with tzatziki

MAKES 8   **PREPARATION** **20 MINS**   TO COOK **6–8 MINS**

These kebabs make a delicious main meal served as below or in **pitta breads with a salad**. Put 8 wooden skewers in cold water to soak before preparing the dish.

1 Preheat a griddle pan. Brush the aubergine slices with oil and griddle in two batches for 2–3 minutes on each side until tender and striped brown. Finely chop in a food processor or by hand. Tip into a bowl and mix in all the remaining kebab ingredients. Season with ½ tsp salt and a little pepper. Using your hands, squeeze the mixture well to mix thoroughly.

2 Divide into 8 equal pieces and shape each into a cylinder around a soaked wooden skewer, making them about a third of the length of the skewers.

3 Brush with oil and place on the grill rack. Grill about 5cm (2in) from the heat source for about 8 minutes, turning once until golden and cooked through.

4 Meanwhile, mix the tzatziki ingredients together, season with salt and pepper, and chill until ready to serve.

5 Serve the koftas, garnished with lemon wedges, with the tzatziki, couscous, and a mixed salad.

INGREDIENTS

1 large aubergine, sliced
2–3 tbsp olive oil for brushing
115g (4oz) breadcrumbs
2 large garlic cloves, crushed
1 small onion, grated
2 tsp ground cumin
1 tsp ground coriander
1 tsp dried mint
2 tbsp chopped coriander
½ tsp salt
freshly ground black pepper
1 egg, beaten
lemon wedges, to garnish
couscous and mixed salad,
   to serve

For the tzatziki
150g (5½oz) Greek-style
   yogurt
1 garlic clove, crushed
5cm (2in) piece cucumber,
   peeled and grated
2 tsp dried mint

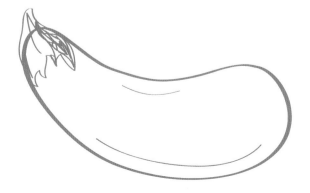

Grilled marinated halloumi on seeded vegetable ribbons

SERVES 4   PREPARATION **20 MINS, PLUS MARINATING**   TO COOK **6 MINS**

Salty halloumi, fragrant with herbs and garlic, marries beautifully with sweet-tasting vegetables here. Take care not to overcook the veg – it should retain some bite.

INGREDIENTS

1 lime
8 tbsp olive oil
1 tsp crushed dried chillies
1 tsp dried oregano
½ tsp dried mint
1 garlic clove, crushed
salt and freshly ground
  black pepper
250g (9oz) block halloumi
  cheese, cut into 8 slices
Mediterranean flatbreads
  (khobez), and a dish each
  of olives and pickled
  chillies, to serve

For the vegetable ribbons

2 thin parsnips, peeled
  but left whole
2 large carrots, peeled
  but left whole
2 courgettes, trimmed
  but left whole
1 tbsp sesame oil
2 tbsp black onion seeds
2 tbsp sesame seeds

1 Put 8 wooden skewers in cold water to soak. Finely grate the zest of the lime into a shallow dish. Squeeze the juice into a separate dish. Whisk 6 tbsp olive oil into the zest with half the lime juice, chillies, herbs, garlic, and plenty of pepper. Add the cheese slices, turn to coat completely, and leave to marinate for several hours or overnight, turning once or twice.

2 Pare the vegetables with a potato peeler, holding them firmly at each side and turning at intervals to shave them all around. There will be a central piece you cannot pare, which can be set aside to use for soup.

3 Heat the remaining olive oil in a large frying pan or wok. Add all the vegetables and stir-fry for 2 minutes until beginning to soften. Cover and cook for a further 2 minutes until tender, but still with a little crunch. Add the sesame oil, remaining lime juice, onion seeds, and sesame seeds, and toss well. Season lightly with salt and pepper. Remove from the heat.

4 Preheat an oiled, flat griddle pan or grill rack. Remove the cheese from the marinade and thread a piece on each of the soaked wooden skewers. Griddle for 1 minute on each side, pressing down with a fish slice, until charred brown in places. Place on a plate and drizzle the remaining marinade over.

5 Toss the ribbons over a high heat once more to heat through. Serve the vegetable ribbons with the cheese sticks, Mediterranean flatbreads, olives, and pickled chillies.

Grilled stuffed romano peppers with chilli and cheese

SERVES 4   **PREPARATION 15 MINS**   TO COOK **20 MINS**

When available, baby romano peppers stuffed like this make a great starter (use 8 and halve the filling). The large peppers are enough for a light main meal.

INGREDIENTS

4 large romano peppers
250g (9oz) medium-fat
  soft cheese
175g (6oz) mature Cheddar
  cheese, grated
60g (2oz) fresh breadcrumbs
1–2 green chillies,
  finely chopped
2 tbsp chopped parsley, plus
  extra to garnish
2 tbsp chopped coriander
salt and freshly ground
  black pepper
olive oil
crusty bread and mixed
  salad, to serve

1 Preheat the grill. Cut the stalk ends off the peppers and discard. Split them down one side and carefully remove any remaining seeds and pith, taking care not to break the peppers.

2 Mix the cheeses with the breadcrumbs, chillies, herbs, and salt and pepper to taste. Divide the cheese mixture among the peppers, spreading it evenly inside them.

3 Place the peppers on oiled foil in the grill pan. Brush with oil. Grill for 8–10 minutes on each side until the cheese is melting and bubbling and the peppers are soft, but not blackened.

4 Carefully transfer to plates (including any lovely gooey bits that have oozed out). Drizzle with a little more oil and sprinkle with a little parsley to garnish. Serve immediately with plenty of crusty bread and a mixed salad.

Grills and bakes

Grilled avocado with semi-dried tomato dressing

SERVES 4   PREPARATION **10 MINS**   TO COOK **8 MINS**

Cooked avocados are delicious, as long as they are ripe – under-ripe ones will taste bitter. Ricotta cheese can be substituted for cottage cheese in this recipe.

1 Halve the avocados and remove the stones. Brush the cut surfaces and the skin with olive oil.

2 For the dressing, whisk the olive oil with 2 tbsp tomato oil, white balsamic condiment, garlic, and some salt and pepper, then stir in the semi-dried tomatoes and basil. Set aside.

3 Preheat a griddle pan. Mix the cheese with the olives and set aside. Place the avocados cut-side down on the griddle and cook for 3 minutes until striped brown, pressing down gently with a fish slice for even cooking of the cut side. Turn the avocados over and cook for a further 2–3 minutes until hot through. It does not matter if the skins burn a little, but take care not to overcook the avocados as they will become unpleasantly mushy.

4 Place the avocado halves on serving plates and spoon the cool cheese into the centres. Spoon the dressing over and serve with walnut or multigrain bread and a watercress and orange salad.

INGREDIENTS

4 large or 8 small
   ripe avocados
2 tbsp olive oil, plus
   extra for brushing
6 semi-dried tomatoes in oil,
   drained and chopped,
   oil reserved
1 tbsp white
   balsamic condiment
1 small garlic clove, crushed
salt and freshly ground
   black pepper
2 tbsp chopped basil
250g (9oz) plain cottage
   cheese, or flavoured
   with chives
2 tbsp black olives, chopped
walnut or multigrain bread
   and watercress and orange
   salad, to serve

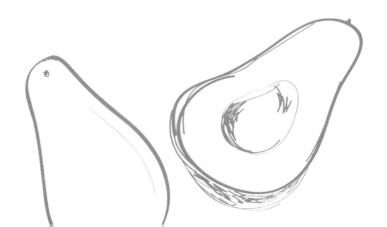

Mixed vegetable cottage pie with swede crust

SERVES 4   **PREPARATION 30 MINS**   TO COOK **40 MINS**

This rich, intensely flavoured variation on a family favourite will please even the most dedicated meat-eater. Parsnips may be substituted for the swede in the topping.

INGREDIENTS

1 tbsp sunflower oil

1 onion, finely chopped

115g (4oz) white
mushrooms, sliced

2 carrots, grated

2 turnips, grated

60g (2oz) shelled fresh
or thawed frozen peas

2 × 400g cans borlotti beans,
rinsed and drained

450ml (15fl oz) vegetable stock

1 tbsp soy sauce

1 tbsp mushroom ketchup
or Worcestershire sauce

1 tsp dried mixed herbs

salt and freshly ground
black pepper

4 tbsp plain flour

1 small swede, cut into
small chunks

450g (1lb) potatoes, peeled
and cut into small chunks

knob of butter

4 tbsp milk

grated nutmeg

60g (2oz) strong Cheddar
cheese, grated

shredded greens, to serve

1 Heat the oil in a large saucepan. Add the onion and fry, stirring, for 3 minutes until lightly golden. Add the mushrooms, carrots, turnips, peas, and borlotti beans. Stir in the stock, soy sauce, mushroom ketchup, herbs, and salt and pepper to taste. Bring to a boil, reduce the heat, cover, and simmer gently for 10 minutes until the vegetables are tender. Blend the flour with 4 tbsp water. Stir into the pan and cook, stirring, for 2 minutes to thicken.

2 While the other vegetables are simmering, cook the swede and potato in salted boiling water for 15 minutes or until tender. Drain and return to the pan over a low heat to dry out slightly. Mash with the butter, milk, a generous grating of nutmeg, and a generous grinding of pepper. Beat well with a wooden spoon until smooth.

3 Preheat the oven to 190°C (375°F/Gas 5). Spoon the mixture into a 1.7 litre (3 pint) ovenproof dish or 4 individual dishes. Top with the swede mash and fluff up with a fork. Sprinkle the cheese over and bake in the oven for about 40 minutes until golden. Serve hot with some shredded greens.

Baked ricotta with roasted courgettes and tomatoes

SERVES 4   **PREPARATION 5 MINS**   TO COOK **35 MINS**

Using the ripest tomatoes and the best olive oil, **this dish captures the flavours of the Mediterranean**. Serve with freshly baked bread and a green salad.

INGREDIENTS

4 tbsp olive oil, plus extra
    for drizzling and greasing
2 courgettes, sliced
1 garlic clove, finely chopped
salt and freshly ground
    black pepper
2 tsp chopped rosemary
12 cherry tomatoes, halved
250g (9oz) ricotta
    cheese, drained
2 tbsp grated
    Parmesan cheese
ciabatta and crisp green
    salad, to serve

1 Preheat the oven to 220°C (425°F/Gas 7). Lightly oil 2 small roasting tins. Put the courgette slices in one, toss with 2 tbsp oil, and sprinkle with the garlic, some salt and pepper, and the rosemary. Roast for 10 minutes. Carefully turn over the slices.

2 Arrange the tomatoes in the second baking tin. Drizzle with the remaining oil and season with salt and pepper. Bake with the courgettes for a further 10 minutes until the tomatoes have softened and started to collapse and the courgettes are tender and lightly golden. Remove from the oven.

3 Spoon half the ricotta into a lightly oiled 600ml (1 pint) gratin dish and roughly spread it out. Arrange the courgette slices on top, then the tomatoes. Spoon the remaining ricotta on top and roughly spread out – it won't cover the vegetables completely.

4 Sprinkle with Parmesan, drizzle with a little extra oil, and add a good grinding of pepper. Bake for 15 minutes until lightly golden on top. Serve hot with ciabatta and a crisp green salad.

Grills and bakes
Kohlrabi and potato gratin

SERVES 4–6 **PREPARATION 15–20 MINS** TO COOK **1 HR 30 MINS**

This dish is **enlivened with the addition of finely sliced kohlrabi** – a brassica that has the taste and crunch of a broccoli stem or cabbage heart and is also good raw.

1 Preheat the oven to 180°C (350°F/Gas 4) and grease a 20cm (8in) ovenproof gratin dish with butter.

2 Slice the potatoes and kohlrabi quarters into even rounds, 3mm (⅛in) thick, using a mandolin or a food processor fitted with a fine slicing blade. Rinse the slices in cold water, drain, and pat dry with kitchen paper or a clean tea towel.

3 Arrange the potatoes and kohlrabi in layers in the prepared dish. Season with salt and pepper.

4 Bring the cream to a boil in a saucepan with the garlic and nutmeg, then pour the cream over the potatoes. Dot the top with a few knobs of butter.

5 Cover with foil and place in the oven for about 1–1½ hours, or until the vegetables are tender. During the last 10 minutes of cooking, remove the foil and increase the heat to get a fine golden crust on the top. Serve hot, straight from the oven.

INGREDIENTS

45g (1½oz) butter, softened, plus extra for greasing
450g (1lb) even-sized waxy potatoes, peeled
450g (1lb) kohlrabi, peeled, trimmed, and quartered
sea salt and freshly ground black pepper
600ml (1 pint) double cream
1 garlic clove, cut in half
pinch of ground nutmeg

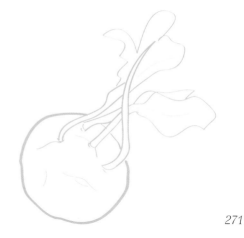

Tomato and courgette gougère

SERVES 4   **PREPARATION 35 MINS**   TO COOK **1 HR**

This gougère is **crisp and golden on the outside and soft, light, and cheesy inside**. For a short cut, use a 400g can of chopped tomatoes and omit the tomato purée.

INGREDIENTS

2 tbsp olive oil
1 onion, chopped
1 leek, sliced
2 large courgettes, sliced
1 garlic clove, crushed
2 beef tomatoes,
  skinned and chopped
1 tbsp tomato purée
1 tsp dried basil
generous pinch of
  caster sugar
salt and freshly ground
  black pepper
2 tbsp grated
  Parmesan cheese
a few torn basil leaves,
  to garnish

For the cheese choux

150g (5½oz) plain flour
115g (4oz) butter
4 eggs, beaten
115g (4oz) Cheddar
  cheese, grated

1 Heat the oil in a saucepan. Add the onion, leek, courgettes, and garlic and fry, stirring, for 2 minutes to soften slightly. Add the tomatoes, cook for 1 minute, stirring, then reduce the heat, cover, and cook gently for 10 minutes.

2 Remove the lid, stir in the tomato purée, basil, and sugar, and boil rapidly for about 5 minutes, stirring frequently, until the vegetables are bathed in a light tomato sauce. Season with salt and pepper to taste and set aside.

3 Preheat the oven to 200°C (400°F/Gas 6). To make the cheese choux, sift the flour and ¾ tsp salt into a bowl. Put 300ml (10fl oz) water in a saucepan and add the butter. Over a low heat, stir until the butter melts. Bring to a boil, then reduce the heat, add the flour in one go, and beat with a wooden spoon until the mixture forms a soft ball and leaves the sides of the pan clean.

4 Remove from the heat, leave to cool slightly, then gradually beat in the eggs, a little at a time, until smooth and glossy, but the mixture still holds its shape. Beat in the Cheddar cheese.

5 Lightly grease a large, shallow 1.4 litre (2½ pint) ovenproof dish. Spoon the cheese choux all around the edge and the vegetable mixture in the centre. Sprinkle the choux with the Parmesan. Bake in the oven for 30 minutes, then cover loosely with foil and bake for a further 30 minutes until the pastry is risen, crisp, and golden brown. Serve hot, garnished with a little torn basil.

Mushroom pot with feta and herb topping

SERVES 4   PREPARATION **15 MINS**   TO COOK **50 MINS**

This is a hearty stew made with **meaty mushrooms for a rich depth of flavour**. Try baking individual portions if you have some mini ovenproof casserole dishes.

1 Heat the oil in a large flameproof casserole or lidded ovenproof pan, add the onion, and cook for 2--3 minutes on a low heat. Stir in the garlic, oregano, paprika, lemon zest, and some salt and pepper, and cook for a further 1–2 minutes.

2 Add the green peppers and cook on a low heat for 5 minutes, or until beginning to soften, then add the mushrooms and cook for a further 5 minutes. Increase the heat, add the wine, and bubble for 1 minute. Add the stock and bring to a boil. Partially cover and cook on a low-medium heat for 20 minutes; it should begin to thicken slightly. If it is too thin, uncover, increase the heat a little, and cook for a further 3–4 minutes.

3 Preheat the oven to 180°C (350°F/Gas 4). To make the topping, mix together the feta, eggs, half the parsley, and a little salt and pepper; you may not need much salt as feta is already salty. Pour this over the mushroom mixture and bake in the oven for 15–20 minutes until the egg has set and the top is golden. Remove and sprinkle with the remaining parsley to serve.

INGREDIENTS

2 tbsp olive oil
1 red onion, finely chopped
2 garlic cloves, finely chopped
2 tsp dried oregano
1 tsp paprika
grated zest of ½ lemon
salt and freshly ground
    black pepper
2 green peppers, halved,
    deseeded, and sliced
200g (7oz) chestnut
    mushrooms, quartered
200g (7oz) baby
    button mushrooms
1 small glass dry white wine
450ml (15fl oz) hot
    vegetable stock

For the topping
150g (5½oz) feta
    cheese, crumbled
2 eggs
handful of flat-leaf
    parsley, finely chopped

Watercress and beetroot roulade with smooth cheese sauce

SERVES 4   **PREPARATION 30 MINS**   **TO COOK 18 MINS**

This light and luscious roulade is also **delicious served cold with dill-flavoured mayonnaise**. For an alternative filling, the chunky tomato sauce on p201 is ideal.

INGREDIENTS

1 bunch watercress, finely chopped

2 tbsp chopped parsley

2 tbsp grated Parmesan cheese, plus extra for dusting

4 eggs, separated

For the cheese sauce

2 tbsp plain flour

300ml (10fl oz) milk

15g (½oz) butter

½ tsp English mustard

60g (2oz) Cheddar cheese, grated

salt and freshly ground black pepper

For the filling

100g (3½oz) crème fraîche

1 spring onion, finely chopped

2 cooked beetroot (approx. 125g/4½oz), finely chopped

1 tbsp chopped dill, plus extra to garnish (optional)

squeeze of lemon juice

grated nutmeg

1 First, make the sauce. Put the flour in a small saucepan. Whisk in the milk, then add the butter. Bring to a boil and cook for 2 minutes, whisking constantly, until thickened. Stir in the mustard and Cheddar cheese until melted and add salt and pepper to taste. Cover with a circle of damp greaseproof or baking parchment to prevent a skin forming and keep warm.

2 To make the filling, mix the ingredients together in a small saucepan with a generous grating of nutmeg and a little salt and pepper. Heat through, stirring gently. Keep warm.

3 Preheat the oven to 200°C (400°F/Gas 6). Grease an 18 × 28cm (7 × 11in) Swiss roll tin and line with baking parchment.

4 Put the watercress in a bowl, then add the parsley and Parmesan. Beat in the egg yolks and some salt and pepper. Whisk the egg whites until stiff and fold into the watercress mix with a metal spoon. Transfer to the prepared tin and smooth the surface. Bake in the oven for about 8 minutes until risen and just firm to the touch.

5 Place a clean sheet of baking parchment on a clean tea towel on the work surface. Dust the parchment with a little grated Parmesan. Turn out the roulade onto the prepared paper, then loosen the cooking paper and remove gently.

6 Quickly spread the roulade with the beetroot filling, leaving a small border all around. Roll up, using the parchment to help. Transfer to a serving plate and garnish with some chopped dill, if using. Cut in slices and serve with the cheese sauce.

Butternut squash tagine

SERVES 4   **PREPARATION 20 MINS**   **TO COOK 1 HR**

Most squashes ripen once the summer draws to a close and autumnal fare takes over. **This spicy tagine uses the best of early-autumn produce.**

INGREDIENTS

4 tbsp olive oil

2 red onions, finely chopped

1 large red pepper, deseeded and diced

4 garlic cloves, chopped

1 thumb-sized piece fresh root ginger, finely chopped

1 tsp chilli powder

1 tsp ground cinnamon

2 tsp smoked paprika

2 tsp ground coriander

1 tbsp ground cumin

2 × 400g cans chopped tomatoes

600ml (1 pint) vegetable stock

2 tbsp clear honey

salt and freshly ground black pepper

400g (14oz) butternut squash, peeled, halved, deseeded, and diced

2 × 400g cans chickpeas, drained and rinsed

100g (3½oz) dried apricots, chopped

bunch of coriander leaves, chopped

couscous, to serve

1 Pour the oil into a large saucepan. Add the onions, red pepper, garlic, and ginger, and fry over a low heat for 2 minutes until softened, but not brown.

2 Add the chilli, cinnamon, paprika, coriander, and cumin. Continue to cook for a further 2 minutes over a low heat to release the flavour of the spices. Add the tomatoes, stock, and honey, and season with salt and pepper. Bring the sauce to a boil and turn down the heat. Simmer slowly, uncovered, for 30 minutes.

3 Add the butternut squash, chickpeas, and apricots and continue to cook for 10–15 minutes until the squash is soft, but not falling apart. Add more water if it is beginning to look a little dry. Season again and stir in the chopped coriander. Serve with couscous.

Stuffed butternut squash

SERVES 4   PREPARATION **15 MINS**   TO COOK **1 HR 15 MINS**

This is a vibrantly coloured dish that would work just as well with pumpkin. Use Cheddar, Parmesan, or goat's cheese instead of the Gruyère, if preferred.

1 Preheat the oven to 190°C (375°F/Gas 5). Brush 2 baking sheets with oil. With a sharp knife, score a crisscross pattern on the flesh of each butternut squash half and brush with oil. Sit the squash on the greased baking sheets, flesh-side down, and roast for about 1 hour until the flesh begins to soften. Now scoop out most of the flesh, leaving a thin layer still attached to the skins, and reserve the hollowed squash halves.

2 Place the flesh in a bowl and mash with a fork. Add the hazelnuts, cranberries, parsley, chilli flakes, and salt and pepper to the mashed squash and mix well. Divide the mixture between the squash halves.

3 Sprinkle the cheese over and return the squash halves to the oven. Bake for a further 10–15 minutes until the cheese is bubbling. Serve the squash with a lightly dressed wild rocket salad.

INGREDIENTS

1 tbsp olive oil, plus extra
  for greasing
2 butternut squash (approx.
  675g/1½lb each), halved
  lengthways and deseeded
100g (3½oz) hazelnuts, toasted
  and roughly chopped
75g (2½oz) dried cranberries,
  roughly chopped
small handful of flat-leaf
  parsley, finely chopped
pinch of dried chilli flakes
salt and freshly ground
  black pepper
225g (8oz) Gruyère
  cheese, grated
wild rocket salad, to serve

Grills and bakes
Squash and cider cobbler

SERVES 6   **PREPARATION 20 MINS**   TO COOK **1 HR**

Here, autumn vegetables are **simmered in cider and topped with a herby scone**. Try brushing the potatoes with oil and sprinkling with caraway seeds before baking.

INGREDIENTS

1 butternut squash, peeled, halved, deseeded, and cut into bite-sized cubes

2 tbsp olive oil

pinch of grated nutmeg

a few sage leaves, roughly chopped

salt and freshly ground black pepper

1 onion, finely chopped

2 garlic cloves, finely chopped

2 leeks, sliced

400g can chopped tomatoes

300ml (10fl oz) dry cider

400ml (14fl oz) vegetable stock

225g (8oz) self-raising flour

100g (3½oz) butter, chilled and diced

a few sprigs of rosemary, finely chopped

5 tbsp buttermilk

200g (7oz) Savoy cabbage, cored and roughly chopped

jacket potatoes, to serve (optional)

1 Preheat the oven to 200°C (400°F/Gas 6). Put the squash in a roasting tin, add half the oil, and toss to coat thoroughly. Add the nutmeg and sage, season well with salt and pepper, and toss again. Roast for 15 minutes, then remove and set aside.

2 Heat the remaining oil in a large flameproof casserole or lidded ovenproof pan, add the onion, and cook for 2–3 minutes. Season, stir in the garlic and leeks, and cook on a low heat for 2 minutes more. Add the tomatoes and cider, then 400ml (14fl oz) stock, or enough to cover the vegetables. Bring to a boil, reduce to a simmer, and stir in the squash. Simmer gently for 5–10 minutes.

3 For the cobbler topping, place the flour and a pinch of salt in a bowl. Add the butter and rub it in with the fingertips until it resembles breadcrumbs. Stir in the rosemary and add the buttermilk, a little at a time, until it forms a soft dough. Alternatively, make the topping in a food processor, adding the buttermilk a little at a time and pulsing until the dough forms.

4 Stir the cabbage into the simmering vegetables, then tear off large lumps of the dough, flatten slightly, and place on top of the vegetables. Bake in the oven for 25–30 minutes, or until golden and bubbling. Cover loosely with foil if it starts to brown too much. Serve alone or with jacket potatoes.

Stuffed mushrooms with spinach, pine nuts, and halloumi

SERVES 4   **PREPARATION 10 MINS**   TO COOK **20 MINS**

Open-cup mushrooms make great bases for fillings.
Serve one as a starter or two for a main course, and substitute crumbled feta for the halloumi, if you prefer.

1 Shake off excess water from the spinach, then cook in a pan with no extra water, stirring, for 2–3 minutes until wilted. Drain thoroughly in a colander, squeeze out as much moisture as possible, then chop or snip with scissors.

2 Preheat the oven to 190°C (375°F/Gas 5). Remove the stalks from the mushrooms and chop the stalks finely. Place the mushrooms in an oiled baking tin and add 6 tbsp water to the tin.

3 Heat the oil in a large frying pan and fry the onion and mushroom stalks over a medium heat for 2–3 minutes, stirring, until softened. Add the garlic, pine nuts, cinnamon, herbs, and spinach. Season with salt and pepper to taste.

4 Spoon the mixture into the mushrooms and top with a slice of halloumi. Drizzle with a little extra oil and bake for about 20 minutes until the mushrooms are tender and the cheese is lightly golden. Place on serving plates with the mushroom juices spooned over and sprigs of parsley as a garnish. Serve with crusty bread and a mixed salad.

INGREDIENTS

200g (7oz) spinach, well washed
8 open-cup mushrooms, peeled if necessary
2 tbsp olive oil, plus extra for drizzling
1 onion, finely chopped
2 garlic cloves, crushed
60g (2oz) pine nuts
1 tsp ground cinnamon
1 tsp dried oregano
3 tbsp chopped flat-leaf parsley, plus sprigs, to garnish
salt and freshly ground black pepper
250g block halloumi, cut into 8 slices
crusty bread and mixed salad, to serve

Four ways with
Aubergines

Aubergine and goat's cheese crostini ▶

TAKES 30 mins   **SERVES** 4

Preheat the oven to 180°C (350°F/Gas 4). Brush 12 slices of **French bread** on both sides with **olive oil**. Toast for 10 minutes. Halve 1 **garlic clove** and rub the cut side over each slice. Slice 1 **aubergine** into 5mm (¼in) thick rounds, brush each side with oil, and griddle both sides until cooked. Quarter the aubergine slices and place in a bowl. Add 1 tbsp olive oil, 2 tbsp chopped **mint**, and 1 tbsp **balsamic vinegar**. Toss and season with **salt** and freshly ground **black pepper**. Spread the crostini with 60g (2oz) **soft goat's cheese**, top with aubergine, and serve.

◀ Steamed aubergine salad

TAKES 35 mins   **SERVES** 6

Cut 2 medium peeled **aubergines** into 2cm (¾in) cubes and steam, covered, for 10 minutes. When cool, squeeze gently to extract as much water as possible. In a bowl, combine 60g (2oz) crumbled **soft goat's cheese**, 2 ripe **tomatoes**, deseeded and diced, 1 small finely diced **red onion**, a handful of finely chopped **flat-leaf parsley**, 60g (2oz) lightly toasted and roughly chopped **walnuts**, and 1 tbsp lightly toasted **sesame seeds**. For the dressing, whisk together 1 crushed **garlic clove**, 4 tbsp **walnut oil**, and the juice of 1 **lemon**. Drizzle over the salad, season with **salt** and freshly ground **black pepper**, and toss to mix.

The aubergines most commonly available are the deep purple variety – but you may also find **the prettily mottled Rosa Bianca**, the round Prosperosa, which is ideal for stuffing, or **crispy-textured East Asian varieties**.

Tomato and aubergine confit ▶

TAKES 15 mins, plus standing **SERVES** 6

Heat 2 tbsp **olive oil** and 5 tbsp **sunflower oil** in a large frying pan over a medium-high heat until the oil begins to smoke. Add 300g (10oz) **aubergines**, cut into 7.5cm (3in) batons, and fry, stirring often, for 3 minutes, or until golden brown. Drain. Add 4 tbsp **garlic-infused oil** to the pan, then add 125g (4½oz) **cherry tomatoes**, halved. Cook for 2 minutes, or until softened. Place the batons in a bowl. Add 10 torn **basil leaves** and the tomatoes and mix gently. Cover and leave to infuse for up to 1 hour in a warm place. Season with **salt** and freshly ground **black pepper**. Serve warm.

◀ Grilled aubergines with pomegranate vinaigrette

TAKES 20 mins **SERVES** 6

To make the vinaigrette, whisk together 6 tbsp **olive oil**, 3 tbsp **pomegranate syrup**, and 3 tbsp chopped **coriander**, and season with **salt** and freshly ground **black pepper**. Set aside. Preheat a griddle pan over a high heat. Cut 3 large **aubergines** into 1cm (½in) thick slices. Brush both sides of the aubergine slices with olive oil, season, then griddle both sides until tender. Layer the aubergines and 2 very finely sliced **shallots** in a serving dish and pour over the vinaigrette. Scatter with **pomegranate seeds** and serve.

Potatoes Dauphinoise with Emmental

SERVES 4–6 **PREPARATION 25 MINS** TO COOK **45 MINS**

This fantastically hearty supper dish is a twist on the classic Dauphinoise recipe, with **the Emmental lifting the humble potato to a higher level**.

INGREDIENTS

1.5kg (3lb 3oz) potatoes,
  peeled and thinly sliced
300ml (10fl oz) whole milk
300ml (10fl oz) double cream
150g (5½oz) Emmental
  cheese, sliced
2 garlic cloves, crushed
salt and freshly ground
  black pepper
green beans or a salad,
  to serve

1 Preheat the oven to 200°C (400°F/Gas 6). In a large pan, simmer the potatoes in the milk and cream for 10–15 minutes, then remove with a slotted spoon. Reserve the milk and cream mixture.

2 Layer the potatoes and cheese in a large gratin dish, sprinkling the garlic over the cheese and seasoning with salt and pepper. Pour the milk and cream over, cover with foil, and cook in the oven for 45 minutes. Remove the foil for the last 15 minutes of cooking time to brown the top. Serve with green beans or a salad.

Grills and bakes
Gratin of Swiss chard with beans

SERVES 4–6   **PREPARATION 10 MINS, PLUS SOAKING**   TO COOK **1 HR 20 MINS**

This rich, warming dish uses only the dark green leaves of the chard, but **cut the stems into lengths, steam them for a few minutes,** and serve alongside.

1 Preheat the oven to 200°C (400°F/Gas 6). Drain the soaked beans, put them in a large pan of water, and bring to a boil. Turn down to a strong simmer and skim off any foam that has collected on the surface. Continue to cook for around 40 minutes, or until soft.

2 In a large, deep-sided pan, heat the oil, add the garlic and chard, and cook, stirring, for about 1 minute until the chard has collapsed but is still al dente.

3 Add the cooked beans to the chard. Mix well, stir in the cream, and season with paprika and salt and pepper.

4 Tip everything into a 1.5 litre (2¾ pint) gratin dish and top with breadcrumbs made by whizzing up the white bread, Parmesan, and basil in a food processor. Cook at the top of the oven for about 30 minutes until golden brown. Leave the gratin to rest for 10 minutes before serving.

INGREDIENTS

400g (14oz) dried haricot
   or cannellini beans,
   soaked overnight
2 tbsp olive oil
4 garlic cloves, crushed
400g (14oz) Swiss chard,
   destalked and
   finely shredded
600ml (1 pint) double cream
1 tsp smoked paprika
salt and freshly ground
   black pepper
100g (3½oz) white bread
60g (2oz) Parmesan
   cheese, grated
8 basil leaves

Lentil, mushroom, and egg loaf with celeriac remoulade

SERVES 8   **PREPARATION** **30 MINS**   TO COOK **1 HR**

This loaf is **best made the day before eating** so that it has time to cool properly and firm up. Serve with baby plum tomatoes and jacket potatoes.

INGREDIENTS

4 savoy cabbage leaves
2 tbsp olive oil, plus extra
  for greasing
knob of butter
2 shallots, finely chopped
115g (4oz) crimini
  mushrooms, sliced
2 × 410g cans green lentils,
  rinsed and drained
115g (4oz) fresh breadcrumbs
2 tbsp chopped thyme
2 tbsp chopped parsley
1 tbsp mushroom ketchup
  or Worcestershire sauce
1 tsp ground coriander
salt and freshly ground
  black pepper
1 egg, beaten
3 hard-boiled eggs, shelled

For the remoulade
4 tbsp mayonnaise
4 tbsp crème fraîche
2 tsp grated horseradish or
  hot horseradish relish
2 tsp white balsamic condiment
1 small celeriac

1 Cut the thick central stalks out of 4 large outer leaves from the cabbage. Blanch the leaves in boiling water for 2 minutes, then drain, rinse with cold water, and drain again. Dry on kitchen paper. Oil a 900g (2lb) loaf tin. Line with overlapping cabbage leaves, outer sides against the tin and stalk ends upwards, allowing enough to hang over the top edge all around to form a wrap for the loaf.

2 Heat the oil and butter in a large pan. Add the shallots and fry, stirring, for 2 minutes. Add the mushrooms and fry for 2 minutes, stirring. Remove from the heat. Add the lentils, breadcrumbs, herbs, ketchup, coriander, and salt and pepper. Mix with the beaten egg.

3 Preheat the oven to 190°C (375°F/Gas 5). Spoon half the lentil mixture into the tin and press down. Lay the boiled eggs down the centre, end-to-end, and press gently into the mixture. Top with the remaining mixture, pressing gently. Fold the overhanging leaves over.

4 Cover the tin with oiled foil, twisting it under the rim to secure. Bake in the oven for 1 hour until just firm. Remove from the oven and leave to cool, then weigh down with cans of food and chill to firm.

5 An hour before serving, make the remoulade. Blend the mayonnaise, crème fraîche, horseradish, and balsamic condiment in a bowl. Peel the celeriac, slice thinly, and cut into thin matchsticks, or shred in a food processor. Place immediately in the dressing and toss well. Season with salt and pepper. Cover the bowl with cling film and chill.

6 Turn the loaf out onto a serving dish. Serve sliced with the remoulade. Any leftovers are delicious with pickles and crusty bread for another meal.

Courgette and carrot pavé

SERVES 4   **PREPARATION 15 MINS**   TO COOK **40 MINS**

This baked slab, or pavé, of lightly spiced vegetables is delicious hot or cold. It can also be served in little squares as bite-sized snacks or canapés.

1 Preheat the oven to 190°C (375°F/Gas 5). Mix all the ingredients except the sesame seeds in a bowl until thoroughly blended.

2 Transfer to an oiled 18 × 28cm (7 × 11in) shallow baking tin. Sprinkle liberally with the sesame seeds. Bake in the oven for 40 minutes until golden and firm to the touch.

3 Cool for 5 minutes, then cut into quarters. Place each pavé on a serving plate. Garnish with sprigs of parsley and drizzle the plates with a splash of sesame oil. Serve with new potatoes and a mixed salad.

INGREDIENTS

1 large onion, finely chopped
2 large courgettes, grated
2 large carrots, grated
115g (4oz) Cheddar
   cheese, grated
115g (4oz) plain flour
1 tsp ground cumin
1 tsp dried mixed herbs
1 tsp crushed dried chillies
salt and freshly ground
   black pepper
6 tbsp sunflower oil
5 eggs, beaten
2 tbsp sesame oil, plus
   extra for drizzling
3–4 tbsp sesame seeds
a few sprigs of parsley,
   to garnish
new potatoes and mixed
   salad, to serve

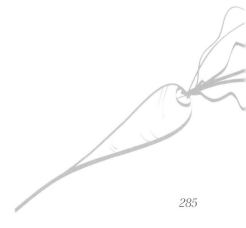

Potato and mixed nut moussaka

SERVES 4–6   **PREPARATION 45 MINS**   **TO COOK 45 MINS**

A simple, rustic dish, this is delicious served with a Greek-style salad, topped with cubes of feta cheese, and drizzled with olive oil and red wine vinegar.

INGREDIENTS

675g(1½lb) potatoes, scrubbed and cut into 5mm (¼in) slices

2 tbsp olive oil, plus extra for greasing

1 large onion, chopped

2 garlic cloves, crushed

2 courgettes, sliced

1 green pepper, deseeded and chopped

400g can chopped tomatoes

400g can cannellini beans, rinsed and drained

115g (4oz) chopped mixed nuts

2 tbsp tomato purée

2 tsp dried oregano

1 tsp ground cinnamon

3 tbsp sliced black olives

salt and freshly ground black pepper

400g (14oz) crème fraîche

2 eggs

50g (1¾oz) Parmesan cheese, grated

1 Cook the potatoes in boiling water for about 5 minutes, or until tender, but still holding their shape. Drain, rinse with cold water, and drain again.

2 Heat the oil in a large saucepan and add the onion, garlic, courgettes, and green pepper. Fry, stirring, for 5 minutes, turning the vegetables over as they soften slightly. Add the tomatoes, beans, nuts, tomato purée, 1 tsp oregano, cinnamon, olives, and plenty of pepper. Bring to a boil, reduce the heat, and simmer for about 15 minutes until the vegetables are tender and the sauce is thick, stirring occasionally.

3 Preheat the oven to 180°C (350°F/Gas 4). Put half the vegetable mixture into a lightly oiled 2 litre (3½ pint) rectangular ovenproof dish and spread it out. Top with a layer of half the potatoes. Repeat the layers with the remaining vegetable mixture and potatoes.

4 Beat the crème fraîche with the eggs, remaining oregano, Parmesan, and some salt and pepper. Spread over the top of the potatoes. Bake in the oven for about 45 minutes until the top is golden and set. Leave to cool for a while to intensify the flavours, and serve warm.

Curried leek, celeriac, and soya bean loaf

SERVES 8   **PREPARATION 25 MINS**   TO COOK **1 HR 30 MINS**

Dried natural breadcrumbs are available in tubs, or **bake stale bread in a low oven** until straw-coloured and crisp, then crush and store in an airtight container.

INGREDIENTS

2 tbsp sunflower oil, plus extra for greasing
3 tbsp dried breadcrumbs
knob of butter
2 leeks, thinly sliced
1 small celeriac (approx. 350g/12oz), peeled and grated
1 potato, grated
2 tbsp Madras curry paste
2 × 400g cans soya beans, rinsed and drained
60g (2oz) fresh breadcrumbs
2 tbsp mango chutney
2 eggs, beaten
salt and freshly ground black pepper
baby potatoes roasted in their skins and mixed salad, to serve

For the curried mayonnaise

8 tbsp mayonnaise
1 tbsp curry paste
1 tbsp smooth mango chutney
squeeze of lemon juice

1 Preheat the oven to 190°C (375°F/Gas 5). Grease a 900g (2lb) loaf tin and coat completely with dried breadcrumbs.

2 Heat the oil and butter in a large saucepan and fry the leeks, stirring, for 2 minutes to soften. Stir in the celeriac and potato and cook for 1 minute, stirring – add a splash of water if the potato starts to stick. Cover the pan, reduce the heat, and cook gently for 10 minutes until soft, but not brown, stirring occasionally.

3 Add the curry paste and cook, stirring, for 30 seconds. Remove from the heat. Mash the soya beans and add with the remaining ingredients, seasoning well with salt and pepper.

4 Press the mixture into the prepared tin. Cover with oiled foil, twisting and folding under the rim to secure, then bake in the oven for 1½ hours until firm to the touch. Remove from the oven and leave to rest for 10 minutes.

5 Meanwhile, mix the ingredients for the mayonnaise together, seasoning with salt and pepper to taste.

6 Turn the loaf out onto a serving plate and serve sliced warm or cold with the curried mayonnaise, baby potatoes roasted in their skins, and a mixed salad.

Red lentil and mixed root crumble with soured cream and chives

SERVES 4   **PREPARATION 45 MINS**   TO COOK **45 MINS**

To make full use of the oven, **thread small potatoes on metal skewers** to bake with the crumble – the metal skewers will speed up the cooking time of the potatoes.

1 Heat the oil and butter in a flameproof casserole and fry the grated vegetables, stirring, for 2 minutes. Add the lentils and stock and bring to a boil. Reduce the heat, cover, and simmer gently for 25 minutes until the lentils and vegetables are cooked and most of the liquid has been absorbed. Add the vinegar, tarragon, parsley, and salt and pepper to taste and simmer for a further 5 minutes, stirring occasionally.

2 Meanwhile, preheat the oven to 190°C (375°F/Gas 5). To make the crumble, mix the oats and flour together in a bowl with a generous pinch of salt. Rub in the butter until the mixture resembles breadcrumbs. Stir in the cheeses and the caraway seeds.

3 Sprinkle the crumble over the vegetables and press down gently. Bake in the oven for about 45 minutes until the top is golden-brown.

4 Meanwhile, blend the soured cream with the chives in a small bowl, season with salt and pepper, and chill until ready to serve. When the crumble is cooked, serve hot with the chilled soured cream and chives, jacket potatoes, and a green salad.

INGREDIENTS

2 tbsp sunflower oil
knob of butter
1 red onion, grated
2 large beetroots, grated
2 large carrots, grated
1 turnip, grated
115g (4oz) red lentils
750ml (1¼ pints)
   vegetable stock
1 tbsp red wine vinegar
1 tbsp chopped tarragon
1 tbsp chopped parsley
salt and freshly ground
   black pepper
150g (5½oz) soured cream
2 tbsp snipped chives
jacket potatoes and green
   salad, to serve

For the crumble

115g (4oz) rolled oats
60g (2oz) plain flour
85g (3oz) butter, cut into
   small pieces
85g (3oz) red Leicester
   cheese, grated
30g (1oz) Parmesan
   cheese, grated
1 tbsp caraway seeds

Grills and bakes
Carrot, onion, and Stilton hot dogs

MAKES 12   **PREPARATION 20 MINS, PLUS CHILLING**   TO COOK **5 MINS**

These hot dogs can be made in advance and kept in the refrigerator for several days before cooking. They are equally good with Cheddar cheese instead of Stilton.

INGREDIENTS

knob of butter
1 onion, finely chopped
4 carrots, grated
350g (12oz) rolled oats
100g (3½oz) plain flour,
  plus extra for dusting
175g (6oz) crumbled
  Stilton cheese (or similar
  crumbly blue cheese)
2 tbsp tomato purée
1 tbsp soy sauce
2 tbsp mushroom ketchup
  or Worcestershire sauce
1 tsp dried mixed herbs
2 tbsp chopped parsley
2 large eggs, beaten
salt and freshly ground
  black pepper
sunflower oil, for frying
hot dog finger rolls,
  American mild mustard,
  and a salad, to serve

For the garnish
knob of butter
4 large onions, halved
  and thinly sliced
4 ripe tomatoes, deseeded
  and chopped

1 Heat the butter in a saucepan. Add the onion and carrots and fry gently for 2 minutes, stirring. Remove from the heat and transfer to a food processor. Add the remaining ingredients and plenty of salt and pepper, then blend well. Chill the mixture for about 30 minutes, if necessary, to firm before shaping.

2 With floured hands, shape the mixture into 12 long sausages (like slightly fat hot dogs). Chill for at least 30 minutes to firm.

3 Meanwhile, make the garnish. Melt the butter in the same saucepan, add the onions, and fry, stirring, for 2 minutes. Reduce the heat, cover, and cook gently for 10 minutes until soft and lightly golden, stirring occasionally. Stir in the tomatoes and cook for 1 minute. Season to taste.

4 Shallow-fry the sausages in a little hot oil for about 5 minutes, turning occasionally, until golden brown. Drain on kitchen paper.

5 Place the sausages in the split finger rolls and add the onion and tomato garnish and a squeeze of American mustard. Serve with a salad on the side.

Grills and bakes
Mixed vegetable satay

SERVES 4   **PREPARATION 25 MINS**   TO COOK **10 MINS**

This recipe is **also good with cooked waxy new potatoes,** mixed with pieces of blanched courgettes and shiitake mushrooms. Soak 12 wooden skewers beforehand.

INGREDIENTS

3 large carrots, cut into
   bite-sized chunks
2 parsnips, cut into
   bite-sized chunks
1 small swede, cut into
   bite-sized chunks
1 large turnip, cut into
   bite-sized chunks
salt
75g (2½oz) butter
2 tbsp clear honey
½ tsp chilli powder
squeeze of lemon juice
lime wedges, to garnish
plain boiled rice and green
   salad, to serve

For the sauce
2 spring onions,
   finely chopped
8 tbsp crunchy peanut butter
1 tbsp clear honey
2 tbsp soy sauce
2 tsp crushed dried chillies

1 Cook the vegetables in lightly salted boiling water for about 5 minutes until just tender, but still with a little texture. Drain, rinse with cold water, and drain again. Thread the vegetables onto 12 soaked wooden skewers, alternating them. Lay on the grill rack.

2 Preheat the grill. Melt the butter and honey together and mix with the chilli powder, lemon juice, and a generous pinch of salt. Brush over the kebabs. Grill, turning once, for 8–10 minutes until lightly golden, brushing with the remaining butter and honey mixture during cooking.

3 Put all the sauce ingredients with 200ml (7fl oz) water in a small saucepan and heat, stirring, until the peanut butter has melted. Bring to a boil and simmer for 1 minute until the mixture forms a thick sauce. Spoon into individual small bowls for dipping (or trickle over for serving).

4 Lay the kebabs on a bed of boiled rice and garnish with lime wedges. Serve with a green salad and with the sauce alongside or spooned over.

Cajun stuffed potatoes with crushed avocado

SERVES 4   **PREPARATION 15 MINS**   **TO COOK 2 HRS 15 MINS**

For a substantial meal, **use very large baking potatoes**. To reduce baking time by about half, microwave the potatoes first for 15 minutes until almost tender.

1 Preheat the oven to 200°C (400°F/Gas 6). Prick the potatoes all over with a fork, coat in oil, then cover all over in the spice blend and place on a baking sheet. Bake in the oven for 2 hours until the skins are really crisp and the potatoes feel soft when squeezed.

2 Meanwhile, if using corn cobs, remove the kernels (see p321). Melt half the butter in a saucepan, add the spring onions, chilli, and red pepper and cook, stirring, for 2 minutes. Add the corn, cumin, and oregano. Reduce the heat, cover, and cook gently for 5 minutes. Set aside.

3 Put the avocado flesh into a bowl. Crush well with the chillies and lime juice, leaving some texture, and season with salt and pepper to taste. Chill until ready to serve.

4 When the potatoes are cooked, remove them from the oven. Once they are cool enough to handle, cut in half and scoop out most of the soft potato into a large bowl, leaving a small wall of potato to keep the shells firm. Pop the shells back into the oven to dry out a little while finishing the filling.

5 Mash the potato with the remaining butter, then work in the corn filling, coriander, and cheese. Season with salt and pepper to taste. Pile into the potato skins and return to the oven for 10–15 minutes until hot through and browning on top. Serve with a dollop of the crushed avocado on top and a green salad.

INGREDIENTS

4 large baking
    potatoes, scrubbed
2 tbsp olive oil
2 tbsp Cajun spice blend
2 corn cobs (or 225–300g/
    8–10oz sweetcorn kernels)
60g (2oz) butter
2 spring onions, chopped
1 fat green chilli, deseeded
    and chopped
1 red pepper, deseeded,
    cut into thin strips,
    and chopped
1 tsp ground cumin
1 tsp dried oregano
2 tbsp chopped coriander
2 large handfuls of grated
    mature Cheddar cheese
green salad, to serve

For the crushed avocado

2 ripe avocados, stoned and
    peeled (see pp324–5)
1 tsp crushed dried chillies
1 tbsp lime juice
salt and freshly ground
    black pepper

Pestos, pickles, salsas, and dips

Classic basil pesto

MAKES 1 SMALL JAR (approx. 175g/6oz)   **PREPARATION 10 MINS**

Toss spoonfuls of this classic green pesto with freshly cooked spaghetti, or **mix it with extra virgin olive oil and a splash of vinegar or lemon juice for dressing salads**.

INGREDIENTS

30g (1oz) basil
2 garlic cloves, lightly crushed
30g (1oz) pine nuts
salt and freshly ground
   black pepper
30g (1oz) Parmesan
   cheese, grated
5 tbsp extra virgin olive oil

1 Pick the leaves off the thicker stalks in the basil and discard the stalks. Place the leaves in a food processor with the garlic, pine nuts, salt and pepper, cheese, and 1 tbsp oil. Whizz until the pesto is well-blended, stopping and scraping down the sides as necessary. With the machine running, trickle in 3 tbsp of the remaining oil until you have a glistening paste.

2 Alternatively, pound the herbs and garlic in a mortar with a pestle. Gradually add the nuts, crushing them to a paste with the herbs. Add salt and pepper, then work in a little of the cheese and a little of the oil. Continue until both are used up, except for 1 tbsp oil, and the paste is glistening.

3 Spoon into a clean, sterilized jar and top with the remaining oil to prevent air getting in. Screw the lid on and store in the refrigerator. Use within 2 weeks.

Pea, mint, and pistachio pesto

MAKES 1 JAR (approx. 350g/12oz)   **PREPARATION 25 MINS**

This pesto is **great with pasta, but is also delicious spread on crostini or chicory spears** as an appetizer, or beaten with some crème fraîche as a dip.

1 Put the pistachios in a bowl, cover with boiling water, and leave to stand for 5 minutes. Drain, then rub off the skins with a new disposable kitchen cloth.

2 Meanwhile, boil the peas in a little salted water for 5 minutes until tender. Drain, rinse with cold water, and drain again.

3 Place the mint leaves in a food processor with the pistachios, peas, spring onions, garlic, nutmeg, pepper, Parmesan, and 2 tbsp oil. Whizz until well-blended, stopping and scraping down the sides as necessary. With the machine running, trickle in 3 tbsp oil until you have a glistening paste. Taste and adjust the seasoning, if needed.

4 Alternatively, pound the herbs, spring onions, and garlic in a mortar with a pestle. Gradually add the peas and nuts, crushing them to a paste with the herbs. Add the seasoning, then work in a little of the cheese and a little of the oil. Continue until both are used up, except for 1 tbsp oil, and the paste is glistening.

5 Spoon into a clean, sterilized jar and top with the remaining oil to prevent air getting in. Screw the lid on and store in the refrigerator. Use within 2 weeks.

INGREDIENTS

30g (1oz) shelled
   pistachio nuts
115g (4oz) shelled fresh
   or frozen peas
salt and freshly ground
   black pepper
20g (¾oz) mint, leaves picked
2 spring onions, chopped
1 garlic clove, crushed
generous pinch of
   grated nutmeg
30g (1oz) Parmesan
   cheese, grated
6 tbsp extra virgin olive oil

Roasted red pepper, almond, and chilli pesto

MAKES 1 SMALL JAR (approx. 175g/6oz) **PREPARATION 10 MINS**

As well as stirring it through pasta, **try spreading this zingy pesto on bruschetta** and topping it with tomatoes and basil. It also works well on pizza bases.

INGREDIENTS

1 red pepper, roasted (see p326), deseeded and roughly chopped
4 semi-dried tomatoes in oil, drained
1–2 fat red chillies, deseeded and roughly chopped
2 garlic cloves, lightly crushed
30g (1oz) ground almonds
30g (1oz) grated Parmesan cheese
2 tbsp tomato oil from the jar
salt and freshly ground black pepper
4 tbsp extra virgin olive oil

1 Place the red pepper in a food processor with the semi-dried tomatoes, chillies, garlic, almonds, cheese, tomato oil, and a generous sprinkling of salt and pepper. Run the machine until well blended, stopping and scraping down the sides as necessary. With the machine running, trickle in 2 tbsp olive oil until you have a glistening paste.

2 Alternatively, put the red pepper, tomatoes, chillies, and garlic in a mortar and pound with a pestle. Gradually add the almonds and salt and pepper. Work in a little of the cheese, then add a little each of the tomato oil and olive oil. Continue until the cheese, tomato oil, and 2 tbsp olive oil are used up and you have a glistening paste.

3 Spoon into a clean, sterilized jar, top with the remaining olive oil to prevent air getting in, screw the lid on, and store in the refrigerator. Use within 2 weeks.

Lemon, carrot, and leek marmalade

MAKES 1 JAR (approx. 300g/10oz)   **PREPARATION 10 MINS**   TO COOK **20 MINS**

The sharp fruitiness of the lemon combined with the sweetness of the carrots and the mild onion tang of the leeks makes this **a great relish to serve with cheese**.

INGREDIENTS

1 lemon, scrubbed
1 star anise
1 leek, white part only, thinly sliced
1 carrot, grated
2 dessert apples
5 tbsp caster sugar
1 tbsp cider or white wine vinegar

1 Quarter the lemon lengthways and remove the pips. Place the quarter, rind-side up, on a chopping board and cut crossways into thin slices. Put in a medium pan with 150ml (5fl oz) water and the star anise. Bring to a boil, cover, reduce the heat, and simmer for about 15 minutes, or until the lemon is really soft (once you add the sugar it won't soften any more).

2 Add the leek and carrot, stir well, then cover and simmer for a further 5 minutes. There should be about 2 tbsp liquid left. If more, boil rapidly to reduce; if less, add a little more water.

3 Meanwhile, peel, core, and quarter the apples. Chop the flesh and add to the lemon mixture with the sugar and cider or vinegar. Stir gently until the sugar dissolves, then boil for 2 minutes, stirring, until everything is tender, but still with a little texture.

4 Leave to cool, then spoon the mixture into a clean, sterilized jar with a non-metallic vinegar-proof lid. For added flavour, leave the star anise in the marmalade, but remove it before screwing the lid on, if preferred. This is not a relish with store-cupboard longevity, but it can be kept in the refrigerator for a few weeks.

Kimchi

MAKES 1 LARGE JAR (approx. 500g/1lb 2oz)   **PREPARATION** **10 MINS, PLUS MARINATING**

This fermented pickle is delicious served with cheese or hard-boiled eggs, or simply with fresh crusty bread. It will improve in the refrigerator – keep for up to a week.

1 Separate the Chinese leaf chunks into individual leaves and place in a large colander on the draining board. Add the salt, toss well, and leave to stand for 2 hours. Rinse thoroughly under cold water, tossing to remove the salt. Drain and dry on kitchen paper. Place in a large plastic container with a sealable lid.

2 Meanwhile, toast the seeds in a dry frying pan, stirring until fragrant and lightly golden. Tip immediately out of the pan into a bowl to prevent further cooking. When cold, add to the Chinese leaves. Add the sliced shallot and herbs.

3 Blend the remaining ingredients together and add to the vegetable mixture. Toss well. Cover and leave to marinate in the refrigerator for at least 24 hours before serving.

INGREDIENTS

small head Chinese leaves, cut into small chunks
1 tbsp salt
1 tbsp black onion seeds
1 tbsp sesame seeds
1 tbsp cumin seeds
1 shallot, halved and thinly sliced
2 tbsp chopped coriander
1 tbsp chopped parsley
2 tbsp sambal oelek chilli paste
4 tbsp rice vinegar
1 tbsp lime juice
1 tbsp toasted sesame oil

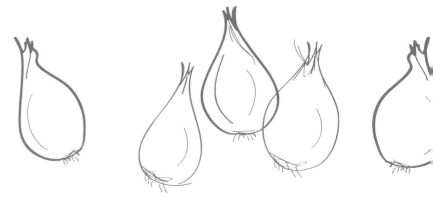

Four ways with
Onions

Onion confit ▶

TAKES 50 mins **MAKES** 750g (1lb 10oz)

Melt 30g (1oz) **butter** in a heavy-based saucepan. Peel and finely slice 900g (2lb) **onions** and add to the melted butter. Stir and cook for about 5 minutes, or until soft and translucent. Now add 100g (3½oz) **demerara sugar**, 3 tbsp **sherry vinegar**, 1½ tbsp **crème de cassis** (optional), and 2 tsp **salt**. Stir the ingredients well and simmer, uncovered, for 30–40 minutes, stirring occasionally so that the confit does not stick to the pan or burn. To serve, try the confit spread on bruschetta with grilled **goat's cheese**, or in wraps with grated **Cheddar cheese** and some salad.

◀ Onion bhajis

TAKES 30 mins **SERVES** 4

Mix together 225g (8oz) chopped **onions**, 115g (4oz) **besan** (gram flour), 2 tsp **cumin seeds**, ½ tsp **turmeric**, 1 tsp ground **coriander**, and 1 **green** or **red chilli**, deseeded and very finely chopped. Add about 8 tbsp cold water to bind the mixture to a thick batter. Heat **sunflower oil** in a deep-fat fryer to 190°C (375°F). When hot, place spoonfuls of the mixture, roughly the size of golf balls, into the oil. Fry, turning occasionally, until golden all over. Remove the bhajis using a slotted spoon and drain. Return them to the pan and quickly fry a second time until crisp and golden brown all over. Drain and serve hot.

Most main-course dishes include onions, but **here they are the star ingredient**. Choose spring onions for salads and stir-fries, brown or white onions for general use, red ones for a sweeter flavour, and **shallots for a milder taste**.

Onion and almond soup ▶

TAKES 1 hr 10 mins **SERVES** 4

Add 100g (3½oz) **almonds** to boiling water, cover, and soak for 15 minutes. Slip off the skins. Whizz in a blender with 100ml (3½oz) hot **vegetable stock**. Fry ¼ tsp **nigella seeds** in 60g (2oz) **butter** for 1 minute. Add 4 diced **onions** and 1 chopped **red chilli**, cover, and cook for 25 minutes. Uncover and when the onions are golden, add 1 tsp **muscovado sugar**. Cook until it catches on the bottom. Add 2 tbsp **balsamic vinegar** and cook until sticky. Add 600ml (1 pint) stock and the almond paste; simmer for 20 minutes. Whizz in a blender. Return to the pan, add 120ml (4fl oz) **single cream**, and season. Reheat, garnish with fried sliced onion, and serve.

◀ Onion tart

TAKES 1 hr 10 mins **SERVES** 6

Preheat the oven to 200°C (400°F/Gas 6). Heat 1 tbsp **olive oil** in a non-stick frying pan, add 4 sliced **onions**, sweat gently for 15 minutes, remove from the heat, and stir in 1 tbsp **plain flour**. Add a little of 300ml (10fl oz) **milk** and stir. Return the pan to the heat and slowly stir in the milk. Add 1 tsp mild **paprika** and season with **salt** and freshly ground **black pepper**. Remove from the heat. Roll out 300g (10oz) **shortcrust pastry** and use to line a tart tin. Trim excess pastry and bake blind (see p338). Reduce the oven to 180°C (350°F/Gas 4). Spoon the onion mixture into the shell and top with 1 tsp **paprika**. Bake for 15–20 minutes. Serve.

Indian-spiced vegetable chutney

MAKES 3 JARS (approx. 350g/12oz each)   PREPARATION **30 MINS**   TO COOK **2 HR 15 MINS**

A selection of vegetables simmered in Indian spices and vinegar give this colourful chutney its flavour. Add 1–2 finely chopped green chillies for heat.

INGREDIENTS

900g (2lb) butternut squash, seeds removed, peeled, and cut into bite-sized chunks

2 onions, finely chopped

225g (8oz) cooking apples, peeled, cored, and chopped

3 courgettes, halved lengthways and chopped

50g (1¾oz) ready-to-eat stoned dates, chopped

450ml (15fl oz) cider vinegar

2 tbsp medium or hot curry powder

1 tsp ground cumin

2.5cm (1in) piece fresh root ginger, grated or finely chopped

450g (1lb) granulated or light soft brown sugar

1 Put the squash, onions, cooking apples, courgettes, and dates in a preserving pan or a large, heavy-based, stainless steel saucepan. Pour in the vinegar, add the spices and ginger, and mix well.

2 Bring the mixture to a boil, then reduce the heat and simmer for 40–45 minutes, or until the vegetables are soft, stirring occasionally.

3 Add the sugar, stir until it has dissolved, then continue to cook on a gentle simmer for 1–1½ hours, or until the chutney is thick and the liquid has been absorbed. Stir continuously near the end of the cooking time so that the chutney doesn't catch on the base of the pan.

4 Ladle into warmed sterilized jars with non-metallic vinegar-proof lids, making sure there are no air gaps. Cover each pot with a waxed paper disc, seal, and label.

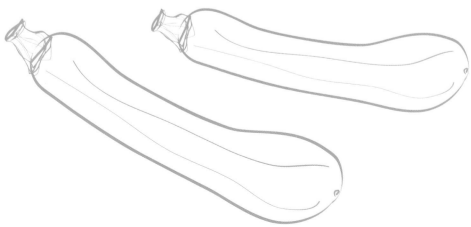

Pestos, pickles, salsas, and dips
Corn relish

MAKES 2 LARGE JARS (approx. 500g/1lb 2oz each)   **PREPARATION 25 MINS**   TO COOK **20 MINS**

Made from diced fruit or vegetables, relish is part-pickle, part-chutney, but cooked for a shorter time than the latter. **It packs a tangy punch of flavour.**

1 Strip the kernels from the cobs using a sharp knife (see p321). Blanch them in a saucepan of boiling water for 2 minutes, then drain well.

2 Put the sweetcorn and the other ingredients in a saucepan, bring to a boil, and stir. Simmer gently, stirring, for 15–20 minutes.

3 Check the seasoning, then spoon into warmed sterilized jars. The relish should be a spoonable consistency and wetter than a chutney.

4 Seal with non-metallic or vinegar-proof lids, leave to cool, and label. Store in a cool, dark place. Once opened, store the jars in the refrigerator.

INGREDIENTS

4 sweetcorn cobs
2 peppers, green or red, deseeded and diced
2 celery sticks, finely sliced
1 red chilli, deseeded and sliced
1 onion, peeled and sliced
450ml (15fl oz) white wine vinegar
225g (8oz) caster sugar
2 tsp sea salt
2 tsp mustard powder
½ tsp ground turmeric

Beetroot relish

MAKES 2 LARGE JARS (approx. 500g/1lb 2oz each)   **TO COOK 2 HRS 15 MINS**

Sweet with a hint of spice, this relish is delicious served with cheese or cold cuts. To save time making the relish, you can cook the beetroots the night before.

INGREDIENTS

1.35kg (3lb) beetroots
1 tsp caster sugar
450g (1lb) shallots,
  finely chopped
600ml (1 pint) cider vinegar
  or white wine vinegar
1 tbsp pickling spices, placed
  in a muslin spice bag
450g (1lb) caster or
  granulated sugar

1 Put the beetroots in a preserving pan or a large, heavy-based, stainless steel saucepan. Pour over enough water to cover them and add the caster sugar. Bring to a boil and simmer for 1 hour, or until the beetroots are soft and cooked. Drain and leave to cool. When cool enough to handle, peel and dice into small, neat pieces.

2 Put the shallots and vinegar in the rinsed preserving pan or saucepan and cook for 10 minutes on a low heat. Add the chopped beetroots and the muslin bag of pickling spices. Give the mixture a stir, add the sugar, and cook gently until the sugar has dissolved. Bring to a boil and cook at a rolling boil for 5 minutes, then reduce the heat to a simmer and cook for about 40 minutes, or until the mixture thickens.

3 Remove the spice bag, then ladle into warmed, sterilized jars with non-metallic vinegar-proof lids, making sure there are no air gaps. Seal, label, and store in a cool, dark place. Allow the flavours to mature for 1 month and refrigerate after opening.

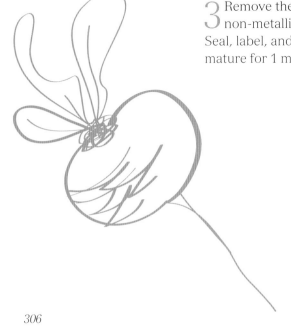

Red onion marmalade

MAKES 2 JARS (approx. 350g/12oz each)   PREPARATION **20 MINS**   TO COOK **1 HR 10 MINS**

This delicious marmalade – made with sweet, sticky onions – has become a modern classic. It is **perfect served with cheese**.

1 Heat the oil in a preserving pan or a large, heavy-based, stainless steel saucepan. Add the onions and a pinch of salt and pepper. Cook over a low-medium heat for about 30 minutes until the onions soften and turn translucent, stirring occasionally so they don't catch and burn. Slow cooking is essential at this point, as this is where the delicious caramel taste is developed.

2 Increase the heat a little, add the wine and vinegars, and stir to combine. Bring to a boil, then reduce the heat. Stir in the sugar and cook on a low heat, stirring occasionally, for 30–40 minutes until most of the liquid has evaporated.

3 Remove the pan from the heat. Taste and adjust the seasoning if necessary (although the flavours will mature with time). Spoon into warmed sterilized jars with non-metallic vinegar-proof lids, making sure there are no air gaps. Cover with waxed paper discs, seal, label, and store in the refrigerator for 1 month to allow the flavours to mature. Keep refrigerated after opening.

INGREDIENTS

2 tbsp olive oil
1kg (2¼lb) red onions, peeled, halved, and sliced
salt and freshly ground black pepper
150ml (5fl oz) red wine
3 tbsp balsamic vinegar
3 tbsp white wine vinegar
6 tbsp light soft brown sugar

Tapenade

MAKES 1 SMALL JAR (approx. 200g/7oz)   **PREPARATION 15 MINS**

This full-flavoured olive spread is popular in the Mediterranean. It is great with crudités, spread on crostini, tossed with pasta, or in dressings.

INGREDIENTS

2 large garlic cloves
250g (9oz) Mediterranean
  black olives, pitted
1½ tbsp capers, drained
  and rinsed
1 tsp thyme leaves
1 tsp chopped rosemary
2 tbsp lemon juice
2 tbsp extra virgin olive oil
1 tsp Dijon mustard
freshly ground black pepper

1 Place the garlic, olives, capers, thyme, and rosemary in a food processor or blender and whizz until smooth. Add the lemon juice, oil, mustard, and pepper to taste, then blend until the paste is thick.

2 Transfer to a bowl and chill until ready to use. Alternatively, spoon into a clean, sterilized jar and store in the refrigerator – it will keep for several weeks.

Avocado salsa

SERVES 4–6   **PREPARATION 15 MINS**

A delicious salsa that **goes brilliantly with spicy foods**, this is also delicious served with grilled halloumi or an omelette – you could even use it as a filling for the latter.

1 Cut the avocado flesh into small cubes and place in a bowl. Add all the remaining ingredients except the crushed chillies and toss gently until well combined, taking care not to crush the avocados.

2 Pile into a serving dish, sprinkle with the crushed chillies, and chill until ready to serve. It is best used within 2 hours or the avocado may discolour.

INGREDIENTS

2 large just-ripe avocados, halved, stoned, and peeled (see pp324–5)
4 spring onions, chopped
1 red pepper, halved, deseeded, and diced
2 tomatoes, deseeded and diced
1 fat red chilli, deseeded and thinly sliced
¼ cucumber, diced
6 radishes, sliced
2 tbsp lime juice
2 tbsp olive oil
salt and freshly ground black pepper
2 tbsp roughly chopped coriander
1 tsp crushed dried chillies, to garnish

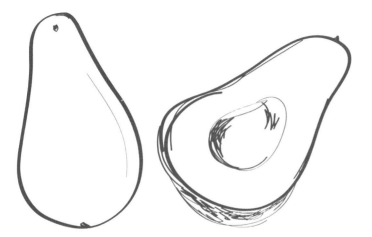

Mexican tomato, onion, and coriander salsa

SERVES 4   **PREPARATION 10 MINS, PLUS CHILLING**

This simple salsa is delicious with fajitas, tacos, and plain quesadillas, or just with corn tortilla chips as a nibble before a meal.

INGREDIENTS

1 large red onion,
   finely chopped
2–3 large tomatoes,
   finely chopped
1 large green chilli, such as
   jalapeño, deseeded and
   finely chopped
large handful of
   coriander, chopped
juice of 1 lime
salt and freshly ground
   black pepper

1 Mix all the vegetables with the coriander in a bowl. Add the lime juice and season with salt and pepper.

2 Cover with cling film and chill for at least 30 minutes to allow the flavours to develop before serving.

Pestos, pickles, salsas, and dips
Yogurt, aubergine, and pine nut dip

SERVES 8–10   **PREPARATION 15 MINS**   **TO COOK 40 MINS**

This dip is also delicious with a pinch of cinnamon added as well as (or instead of) the cumin. It is great served with olives, and pickled chillies, too.

INGREDIENTS

1 large aubergine
1 tbsp olive oil
2–3 tbsp tahini
2 garlic cloves, finely chopped
   or crushed
juice of 1 lemon, plus extra
   if needed
pinch of ground cumin
salt and freshly ground
   black pepper
pitta bread, to serve

1 Preheat the oven to 200°C (400°F/Gas 6). Pierce the aubergine a few times all over with a knife. Next, using your hands, rub the aubergine with oil. Roast in the oven for 30–40 minutes until it begins to char and the flesh is tender.

2 When the aubergine is cool enough to handle, peel off the skin and put the roasted flesh in a blender or food processor. Add the tahini, garlic, lemon juice, and cumin and blend to a purée.

3 Taste and season with salt and pepper, adding more lemon juice if needed. Blend again briefly. Spoon into a bowl or serving dish and serve with pitta bread.

Hummus

SERVES 8–10 **PREPARATION 10 MINS**

Try this nutritious dip spread on spears of chicory, celery sticks, hollowed-out chunks of cucumber or, for a colourful effect, wedges of red pepper.

1 Put all the ingredients except the oil in a blender or food processor. Blend to a smooth purée.

2 With the motor running, gradually add the oil, a little at a time, until the hummus reaches the preferred consistency. Taste and season with salt, adding some more lemon juice if you like. Blend again. Serve as a dip with some warmed pitta bread.

INGREDIENTS

400g can chickpeas, drained and rinsed
2 garlic cloves, crushed
juice of 1 lemon, plus extra if needed
2–3 tbsp tahini
pinch of sweet paprika
salt
2–3 tbsp olive oil
pitta bread, to serve

Techniques

Slice, dice, deseed, peel, pummel, and knead your way to culinary perfection with these essential step-by-step techniques. Find out how to prepare and cook your favourite vegetables, herbs, and spices – as well as base dishes such as risotto rice and pastry.

Techniques
Dicing onions
Slice thickly for large dice and thinly for fine dice.

1 Using a sharp chef's knife, hold the onion firmly in one hand, then cut it in half lengthways. Peel off the skin, but leave the root intact so that the layers are held together.

2 Lay one half on a chopping board, cut-side down. Make a few slices into the onion horizontally, making sure that you cut up to, but not through, the root.

3 Hold the onion firmly, then, with the tip of the knife, slice down vertically, cutting close to the root. Repeat, slicing at regular intervals.

4 Cut across the slices for even dice. Use the root to hold the onion steady; discard this part when the rest of the onion has been diced.

Washing and slicing leeks

Leeks are related to onions, but have a much milder flavour.

1 Trim off the root and some of the dark leaf top. Cut in half lengthways. Spread the layers apart and rinse well to remove any soil, then pat dry.

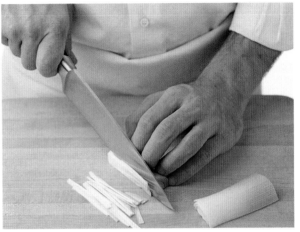

2 Lay the halved leek, flat-side down, on the chopping board and slice it into thick or thin strips, according to the recipe.

Peeling and chopping or crushing garlic

Garlic needs to be chopped or crushed to release all of its flavour.

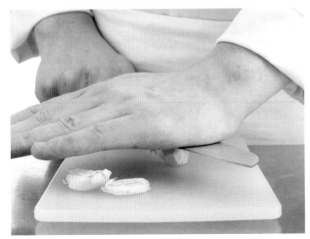

1 Place the garlic clove on a chopping board. Push down with the flat side of a large knife; this makes it easier to peel. Cut off the ends.

2 Slice lengthways, then cut across into tiny chunks. Collect them into a pile and finely chop again or crush with the flat of the knife.

Peeling and deseeding tomatoes

Choose firm tomatoes; vine-ripened ones have the best flavour.

1 Hold the tomato steady and use a sharp knife to score an "X" through the skin at the base. Immerse completely in boiling water for about 20 seconds, or until the skin splits.

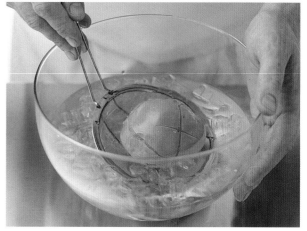

2 Using a slotted spoon, carefully remove the tomato from the boiling water and immediately plunge it into a bowl of iced water to cool it.

3 When the tomato is cool enough to handle, use a paring knife to peel off the skin, starting at the base where the "X" was made.

4 Slice the tomato in half, then gently squeeze the seeds out and discard. Place the seedless tomato on a board, hold firmly, and slice into strips.

Peeling raw beetroot and cutting into batonettes

Raw beetroot can also be very thinly sliced or grated.

1 Hold the beetroot firmly in one hand and peel the skin thinly, using a vegetable peeler or small paring knife. If you wish, wear latex gloves to keep your hands from getting stained.

2 Place the beetroot on a clean chopping board and hold it steady. Use a chef's knife to trim the sides, doing this as evenly as possible to form a square shape.

3 Hold the trimmed block gently but firmly. Cut into equal slices – 3mm (⅛in) thick for julienne and 5mm (¼in) thick for batonettes.

4 Stack the slices a few at a time to prevent them from sliding. Cut each batch into square-edged strips as thick as the slices.

Making courgette batonettes
Young courgettes with glossy skins will not need peeling.

1 Place the courgette on a board and cut off both ends. Cut it in half lengthways, then hold it on its side and cut into slices 5mm (¼in) thick.

2 Put each slice on the board and cut across with a sharp chef's knife to make equal-sized batonettes, about 5mm (¼in) wide.

Making carrot batonettes
For the best flavour, scrape young carrots; older ones need peeling.

1 Set the mandolin blade to a thickness of 5mm (¼in) and hold the mandolin steady. Slide the carrot up and down to make uniform slices.

2 Stack the carrot slices and cut in half crossways. Trim off the rounded sides, then cut the slices lengthways into equal strips.

Preparing asparagus
Look for fresh, sprightly spears with tightly closed tips.

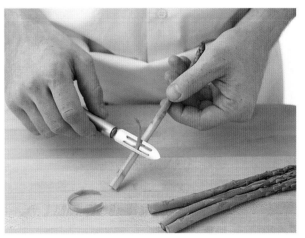

1 Lay the spears on a board with the ends in line. Cut off about 2.5–4cm (1–1¾in) of woody stem. If very fresh, the stems can be snapped off.

2 To ensure tender spears, hold the tip very carefully, then use a vegetable peeler to peel off a thin layer of skin from all sides of the stalk.

Preparing sweetcorn
Sweetcorn tastes best when used fresh rather than tinned or frozen.

1 Remove the husks and all the silk thread from the corn-on-the-cob. Rinse the husked corn under cold running water.

2 Place the blunt end on a chopping board. Using a sharp chef's knife, slice straight down the cob. Rotate the cob and repeat.

Preparing whole artichokes
Look for artichokes with tightly closed leaves and firm stalks.

1 Put the artichoke on a chopping board and hold firmly by the stalk. Then, with a pair of strong kitchen scissors, snip off the tough tips of the outer leaves.

2 Next, using a sharp chef's knife, cut through the stalk at the base of the artichoke head. Alternatively, if it is very fresh, twist off the stalk and the connective strings will come away, too.

3 Pull out any tough, darker green leaves and discard. Cut through the pointed tip. The artichoke is now ready to cook.

Eating whole artichokes

Steam in a vegetable steamer for 30 minutes. Dip the fleshy leaves in melted **butter** or **French dressing** and draw between your teeth to scrape off the flesh. When the outer leaves are eaten, pull away the cone of pale inner leaves, scoop out the choke underneath, and eat the succulent heart.

To **roast**, scoop out the cone and choke. Stuff with **breadcrumbs, Parmesan cheese**, and **olive oil**, and roast.

Preparing artichoke hearts
Make sure you remove the hairy choke as it is inedible.

1 Place the whole artichoke on a chopping board. Carefully cut or pull away all of the leaves from the artichoke first, then cut the stalk from the base and discard.

2 Hold the artichoke firmly on the board and, using a sharp knife, cut off the soft middle cone of leaves, which can be found just above the hairy choke.

3 Trim away the bottom leaves with a paring knife. Scoop out the hairy choke if you plan to cut the heart into pieces for cooking.

4 Using a spoon, scoop out the choke fibres. Rub the exposed flesh with lemon juice to stop it browning.

Preparing avocados

Once ripe enough to eat, avocados are easy to peel and stone.

1 Hold the avocado firmly in one hand then, with a chef's knife, slice straight into the flesh, making sure that you cut all the way around the stone.

2 Once the avocado has been cut all the way around, gently twist the two halves in opposite directions and carefully pull them apart to separate them.

3 Strike the cutting edge of your knife into the stone and lift the knife (wiggling it if need be) to remove the stone from the avocado.

4 To release the stone from the knife, use a wooden spoon to carefully prise it away, then discard it.

5 Use a spatula to remove the flesh from the skin, keeping it whole if possible. Then place the avocado on a chopping board and cut into slices or wedges.

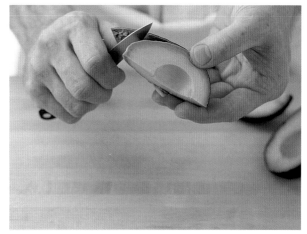

6 Alternatively, quarter the avocado and hold it very gently to avoid damaging the flesh. Then use a small paring knife to peel away the skin.

7 To dice the avocado, cut it into neat slices lengthways, then repeat the cuts crossways to the desired size.

Storing avocado

Store the fruits in a **cool, dark place**, but do not chill. Once cut and exposed to oxygen, an avocado will discolour quickly. The easiest way to slow this process is by rubbing the exposed flesh with the cut side of a **lemon or lime wedge**. Lay a sheet of **cling film** over the top, pressing down as close to the flesh as possible, and store in a refrigerator until needed.

les

g peppers

orange, and yellow peppers add colour to a dish.

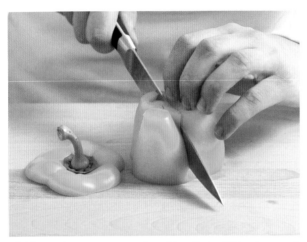

1 Place the pepper on its side. Cut off the top and bottom, then stand it on one of the cut ends and slice in half. Remove the core and seeds.

2 Lay each section flat. Remove the pale, fleshy ribs. Cut into smaller sections, following the divisions of the pepper, and chop as required.

Roasting and skinning peppers

Charring the skin makes peeling easier and lends a smoky flavour.

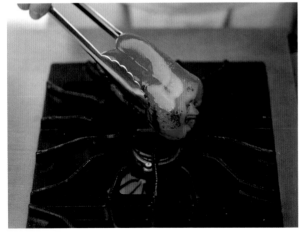

1 Use a pair of tongs to hold the pepper over a flame or place it under a hot grill to char the skin, turning occasionally. Cool in a plastic bag.

2 When it has cooled, peel away the skin. Pull off the stalk, with the core attached. Discard the seeds and dice the flesh or cut it into strips.

Preparing chillies

Removing the seeds and veins from chillies will reduce their heat.

1 Cut the chilli in half lengthways. Using the tip of your knife, scrape out the seeds and remove the membrane and stem.

2 Place the chilli half flesh-side down and flatten. Turn over and slice lengthways into strips. For dice, slice the strips crossways into equal pieces.

Roasting and grinding chillies

Remove the stems and seeds before dry-roasting the chillies.

1 To impart a smoky flavour to chillies, dry-roast in a heavy-based frying pan over a high heat. Remove when they begin to darken.

2 Use a mortar and pestle to grind dry-roasted chillies to a powder. Alternatively, they can be soaked, sieved, and ground to a paste.

Roasting potatoes

Scoring the potatoes before roasting gives them a good crust.

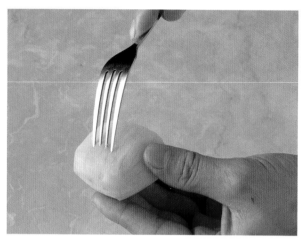

1 Peel and cut into equal-sized pieces. Boil in lightly salted water for 10 minutes. Drain and set aside until cool, then score with a fork.

2 Heat a pan with a layer of sunflower oil in the oven at 200°C (400°F/Gas 6). Coat the potatoes in the hot oil and roast for 1 hour, or until crisp.

Mashing potatoes

Use floury varieties, which have a soft, fluffy texture when cooked.

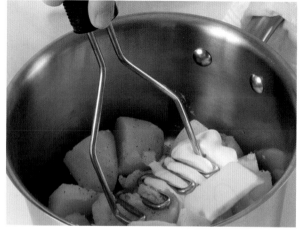

1 Boil until tender, drain, then return to the pan. Add butter, cream or milk, salt and freshly ground black pepper, and nutmeg to taste.

2 Cover and leave for 5 minutes. Mash with a potato masher until smooth and fluffy. Add extra butter and cream or milk if needed.

Pan-frying potatoes

Choose firm potatoes that have unbroken skins and no bruises.

1 Clean unpeeled potatoes by washing in water and scrubbing to remove any dirt. Heat a thin layer of sunflower oil in a frying pan until hot.

2 On a medium heat, fry a single layer of slices for 10 minutes. Turn over and fry until golden and tender. Drain on kitchen paper and season.

Making chips

Double-frying chips ensures that they will be really crisp.

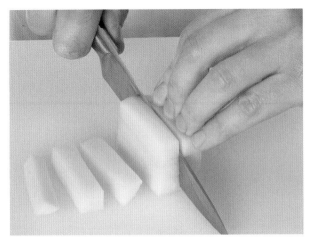

1 Cut large, floury potatoes into chip shapes. Heat oil for deep-frying to 160°C (325°F). Fry for 5–6 minutes until soft, but not brown. Drain.

2 Reheat the oil to 180°C (350°F) and fry all the chips again for 2–3 minutes until crisp and golden. Drain on kitchen paper.

Techniques
Boiling green vegetables
Texture and colour are best preserved if the cooking is brief.

1 Bring a pan of salted water to a boil. Add the prepared vegetables. Bring to a rapid boil and cook until they are tender.

2 Drain through a colander and serve, or, to set the green colour and stop the vegetables cooking, rinse under cold running water.

Stir-frying vegetables
Speed is the key to successful stir-frying; toss and stir continuously.

1 When the wok (or pan) is hot, add sunflower, rapeseed, or groundnut oil, tilting the pan to spread the oil. Then toss in garlic or ginger.

2 Add the desired vegetables and toss them continuously. Add a couple of tablespoons of water, cover, and cook briefly until tender.

Steaming vegetables

As the vegetables are not immersed, nutrients are better preserved.

1 Bring 2.5 cm (1in) of water to a boil in the bottom pan of a steamer. Place the prepared vegetables in the upper basket and position on top.

2 When the steam rises, cover the pan with a fitted lid and cook until the vegetables are just tender when pierced with a knife.

Sautéing firm vegetables

Use this quick method of cooking for batonettes or dice.

1 Set a sauté pan over a high heat. When hot, add a thin layer of oil. Once the oil is hot, add the vegetables and keep turning them to cook evenly.

2 Keep tossing the vegetables in the pan. Once they take on a light golden-brown colour and become tender, remove from the heat and serve.

Preparing herbs

Fresh herbs can be used whole, chopped, or pounded.

To strip the leaves off woody herbs, hold the top end and run the thumb and forefinger of the other hand along the stalk.

For a bouquet garni, tie a sprig of thyme and parsley with a bay leaf. Rosemary or sage could also be used. Discard before serving.

Chopping tender herbs

Herbs with easily bruised leaves should be chopped bunched together.

1 To chop herbs with tender leaves, such as basil, without bruising them, stack the leaves together and roll them into a tight bunch.

2 Holding the bunch steady and using the knife in a rocking motion, chop finely, turning the leaves 90 degrees halfway through.

Preparing spices
Bruising, cutting, and grinding help to release the aroma of spices.

To prepare whole fresh spices such as lemongrass, bruise them by pressing down with the flat side of a heavy knife. This will help to release their volatile oils.

To prepare spice roots such as ginger, turmeric, and horseradish, grate them or finely chop them by hand, using a knife. Peel off the skin beforehand.

When spices are fried until lightly coloured, the oil takes on their flavour. It can then be used along with the spices.

To dry-roast spices, place them in an oven preheated to 160°C (325°F/Gas 3), or toast them in a dry pan until lightly browned.

Techniques
Cooking rice by absorption
Always soak and rinse the rice before cooking; use stock for flavour.

1 Put the rice and 1½ times as much water in a saucepan. Bring to a boil, stir, simmer uncovered until the water is absorbed, then take off the heat.

2 Cover with a tea towel and lid, steam for 20 minutes, then remove the towel and replace the lid. Leave for 5 minutes. Fluff with a fork and serve.

Rehydrating instant couscous
Couscous is normally enriched with oil or butter before serving.

1 Pour twice its volume of boiling water or stock over the couscous. Cover with cling film and leave for 5 minutes. Fluff with a fork.

2 Add 1 tbsp olive oil, a knob of butter or other flavourings, and seasoning. Fluff up the grains again until they are separate, then serve.

Making risotto
Short to medium grains that swell but maintain their shape are ideal.

1 Heat 900ml (1½ pints) stock in a saucepan to a simmer. In another pan, heat 1 tbsp olive oil and 75g (2½oz) butter. Stir in 280g (10oz) risotto rice, coating the grains in the butter and oil.

2 Add 75ml (2½fl oz) white wine and boil, stirring until absorbed. Add a ladle of the hot stock and stir until absorbed. Continue adding the stock, one ladle at a time, and stirring constantly.

3 When all the stock is added and the rice is tender but with a bite (about 20 minutes), add some butter, season, and remove from the heat.

4 The risotto should have a creamy texture. It is best served straight away or it will continue to cook and become too soft.

Making shortcrust pastry by hand
Shortcrust pastry can be used for both sweet and savoury baking.

1 Sift 175g (6oz) plain white flour and a pinch of salt into a bowl (or use wholemeal flour without sifting). Add 85g (3oz) cold diced butter, margarine, or other fat. Lightly stir.

2 Using your fingertips, rub together the flour and butter until the mixture forms the consistency of coarse crumbs. Sprinkle 2 tbsp iced water over the mixture.

3 Use your fingers to gather the dough together and roll around to form a ball. Wrap in cling film and chill for 30 minutes before using.

The art of good pastry

Butter gives the best flavour, but half butter and half lard or white vegetable fat gives a shorter crust.

Keep the ingredients cold and handle them as little as possible.

Do not over-mix the dough or the pastry will be tough.

Leave to chill and rest before rolling. Always roll away from you and turn the dough, not the rolling pin.

Making shortcrust pastry in a food processor
Be careful not to over-process the pastry; pulse on a low speed.

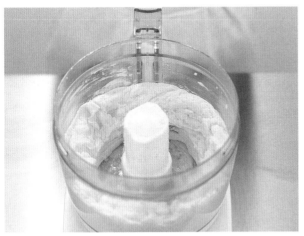

1 Fit the metal blade into a food processor. Tip in the butter, salt, egg yolk, sugar, and milk and whizz until smooth. Gradually add the sifted flour.

2 Pulse the mixture until it starts to come together to form a ball. Wrap in cling film and refrigerate for at least 2 hours.

Lining a flan tin with pastry
Remove excess pastry and decorate the edges for a finished look.

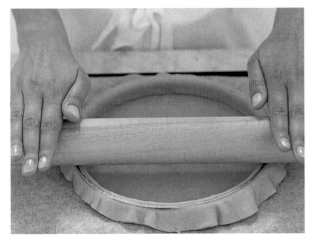

1 Roll the pastry out and press gently into the bottom of the tin and against the sides. Roll a rolling pin over the top to trim off excess pastry.

2 For a fluted edge, push an index finger against the outer rim and pinch the pastry with the other index finger and thumb to form a ruffle.

Techniques
Baking pastry blind
Pre-cook pastry if its filling will be baked only briefly, or not at all.

1 After lining a flan ring or dish with pastry, carefully prick the bottom all over with a fork. This will allow trapped air to escape during baking and prevent puffing.

2 Cut out a circle of baking parchment, slightly larger than the tin. Fold it in half 3 times to make a triangle. Snip the edges at regular intervals with scissors.

3 Place the parchment circle into the tin. Fill it with an even layer of ceramic baking beans. Bake at 180°C (350°F/Gas 4) for 15–20 minutes.

4 Leave to cool, then remove the beans and parchment. For fully baked pastry, bake the pastry for a further 5–8 minutes, or until golden.

Making a classic omelette

Always check eggs are free from any cracks; discard broken ones.

1 Beat and season the eggs. Melt a knob of butter in a non-stick frying pan over a medium heat. When frothy, add the eggs, tilting the pan so that they can spread across it.

2 Stir with a fork to distribute the eggs evenly. Stop stirring as soon as they are set. Fold the side of the omelette nearest to you halfway across the circle.

3 To form a neatly rolled omelette, sharply tap the handle to encourage the omelette to curl over and slide to the edge.

4 When the omelette is cooked to your taste, tilt the pan over a serving plate until the omelette slides onto it, seam-side down. Serve at once.

Index

Page numbers in *italics* indicate descriptions of ingredients. Page numbers in **bold** indicate illustrated preparation techniques. Variations on main recipes are indicated by (*V*).

About the author

Carolyn Humphries has been a food writer and editor for more than 30 years. She started her career as a chef, but soon realised she preferred to create food for people to cook at home. After training as a journalist, she became a food writer for *Woman* magazine in the mid 1970s. She has since written for numerous magazines, and is the author of more than 60 books. With a passion for good food, she cares deeply about what we eat and where it comes from. She is dedicated to promoting healthy eating, encouraging everyone to buy local produce where possible, and to creating sumptuous recipes celebrating the best ingredients.

Acknowledgments

The author would like to thank: Dorling Kindersley for giving me the opportunity to write this book. As the years have gone by I have become more and more vegetarian orientated and this book has been the perfect opportunity to encourage more people to eat more veg and to celebrate vegetables for what they are – nutritious and delicious. I would like to give special thanks to Diana Vowles, my editor, who has been a pleasure to work with (as always) and Bob Bridle who has managed things so efficiently at DK. I would also like to thank my family (and now my children's partners, too) who are used to eating a diverse range of foods at most meals when I am experimenting and testing new creations. They have always been incredibly encouraging and supportive – but are also my greatest critics!

Dorling Kindersley would like to thank: William Reavell for photography; Stuart West for additional recipe photography; Katherine Raj and Nicky Collings for photography art direction; Penny Stephens for food styling; Liz Hippisley for prop styling; Jade Wheaton for the illustrations; Chris Mooney for editorial assistance; Anna Burges-Lumsden, Jan Fullwood, Katy Greenwood, Anne Harnan, and Ann Reynolds for recipe testing; Claire Cross for proofreading; and Susan Bosanko for the index.

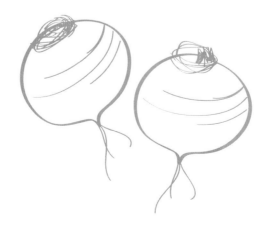